Corporate Environmental Management

Towards a Green Economy

SECOND EDITION

Bhabatosh Banerjee, Ph.D., FCMA
Former Professor of Commerce and
Dean, Faculty of Commerce,
Social Welfare and Business Management
University of Calcutta
Former Guest Faculty
Indian Institute of Management
Calcutta

PHI Learning Private Limited
Delhi-110092
2024

In fond memory of ***Shri Asoke K. Ghosh*** *(October 1942 – February 2024), Founder Chairman and Managing Director of PHI Learning, whose vision endlessly inspires.*

The Legacy Continues....

Published by Pushpita Ghosh, PHI Learning Private Limited, Rimjhim House, 111, Patparganj Industrial Estate, Delhi-110092 and Printed by Syndicate Binders, A-20, Hosiery Complex, Noida, Phase-II Extension, Noida-201305 (N.C.R. Delhi).

₹495.00

CORPORATE ENVIRONMENTAL MANAGEMENT—Towards a Green Economy
Second Edition
Bhabatosh Banerjee

ISBN-978-81-19364-41-1 (Print Book)
ISBN-978-81-19364-91-6 (e-Book)

Towards

Better Environmental Management

Contents

THE RAMAKRISHNA MISSION INSTITUTE OF CULTURE
(*A Branch Centre of Ramakrishna Mission, P. 0. Belur Math, Dist. Howrah, West Bengal 711202*)
GOL PARK, KOLKATA -700 029 , WEST BENGAL, INDIA
Phone: 033 - 4030 -1200, 2464 -1303, 4030 -1263; Fax: 033-2464·1307
E-mail : rmic.secretary@gmail.com, golpark.rmic@rkmm.org; Website: www.sriramakrishnqa.org; YouTube: rmicgolpark

May 18, 2023

Foreword

I am glad to write a Foreword to *Corporate Environmental Management* (publisher: PHI Learning Pvt. Ltd., Delhi) by Dr. Bhabatosh Banerjee, formerly of the University of Calcutta. An International Educator, Dr. Banerjee has been able to build up a reputation as an author of several text and reference books published by the same publisher.

Corporate Environmental Management is a crucial area particularly in the context of recent climate changes and its adverse impact. The subject-matter has been in hot debate since the United Nations' Climate Summit in 1992. Corporate organizations are the main polluters of climate through their several activities in spite of their contribution to the development of the economy. Dr. Banerjee has given more emphasis in identifying the environmental challenges due to their activities and talked about what should be the responses of these organizations keeping in view the Social Contract Argument and the Quality of Life Argument. He has also covered in brief all recent international developments concerning climate changes. He has also suggested course outlines of an environmental course both for undergraduate and postgraduate courses for introduction in educational institutions.

The present research volume, comprising seven well-written chapters, is the outcome of Dr. Banerjee's sustained efforts on the subject for several years. The approach is logical and the presentation is lucid yet penetrating. It is likely to motivate the readers to behave as a responsible citizen to achieve global climate goals.

I wish this research volume would have wider circulation and also promote further interactions and research on the subject.

Swami Suparnananda

(Swami Suparnananda)
Secretary

Preface

Sustainable development takes care of three essential aspects—economic growth, environmental aspects and social performance. Corporate enterprises are the vehicles of economic development of a country. Thus, the corporate sector has a very important role to play in economic development while, at the same time, taking care of the environmental and social issues.

The first edition of this research book was published in 2009 and was completely sold out. But because of Pandemic situation (2019–21), normal activities all around were heavily affected although I got the request for the Second Edition by early 2019. I was also in two minds as to how the second edition should be suitably modified to convert it into a text-cum-reference book in view of growing importance of the subject-matter and some emerging developments relating to climate change in the international arena.

Nevertheless, the basic structure of the book, Chapters 1–6, has been maintained though new developments in the subject have been incorporated in the relevant chapters. Short Exercise questions have been added to all the chapters. In some of them, multiple choice questions have also been added where necessary to facilitate learning of the subject-matter discussed. In my view, all these have enhanced the value of the book to the readers.

In updating the subject-matter, I have taken into consideration the available literature, newspaper reports, relevant websites and reports of various committees on climate change. Suitable acknowledgements at appropriate places have been made so that readers may further update their knowledge.

In view of expanding dimensions of the subject-matter, it is difficult to cover every aspect in a book. Chapter 7, dealing with some other topics of enormous importance, is an example to attempt to cover various other issues, which are now emerging, for the benefit of the readers. In the Appendix, two well thought out course outlines, one for undergraduate studies and the other for postgraduate studies, have been given. Needless to mention, educational institutions should introduce these courses for sensitizing the future generation of our citizens to equip them better for dealing with environmental issues.

My efforts would be amply rewarded if the thoroughly revised second edition of the book is found useful to those who are concerned with corporate environmental management. I believe, it will also promote interactions and further research on the subject.

Akshaya Tritiya (23rd April, 2023) **Bhabatosh Banerjee**

Acknowledgements

The first edition of this book was based on a UGC Major Research Project, *Accounting for Corporate Environmental Management: A Study of Selected Industries in India* [No.F.5-12/2002 (HRP) dated 07.03.2002]. I expressed my indebtedness to the authorities of University Grant Commission, New Delhi for providing me necessary financial assistance and infrastructural facilities for conducting the study.

The second edition is however a major revision of the subject matter based on available literature, websites and reports of various Committees on Climate Change. I express my gratefulness to all these sources which I have mentioned at appropriate places of the instant research publication. I have also taken help of various libraries in the City, namely, The University of Calcutta, British Council Library, Library of the Ramakrishna Mission Institute of Culture, Gol Park. Two of my former research scholars, Dr. Goutam Bhowmick and Dr. Ashish Kumar Dan, were very helpful in preparing my manuscripts for the Project.

Goutam, now a Professor of Commerce, Gour Banga University, continued his association with me during the revision of manuscripts for the second edition. In particular, for Chapter 6 in scanning the annual reports of a number of companies he put his serious efforts to help me in revamping the case study portion and other issues. I thank him profusely.

No words are adequate to express my deep gratitude to Swami Suparnananda Maharaj, Secretary, The Ramakrishna Mission Institute of Culture, Kolkata, for kindly writing Foreword to this book. Revered Swamiji has been a great source of inspiration to me to work for the benefit of the students' community at my age.

I am grateful to the authorities of Sri Sri Matri Mandir, Joyrambati, a Centre of the Ramakrishna Math and Mission, for acceptance of my proposal to utilize a lion's share of royalty of the book for improving the quality of life of the poor and needy people.

I am extremely grateful to Shri Ashoke K. Ghosh, Chairman and Managing Director, PHI Learning Pvt. Ltd., for publishing the second edition of this publication. Ms. Babita Misra, Editorial Coordinator, played a very positive role in persuading me to go for the second edition and also in checking the manuscripts. I am thankful to her.

My son, Arindam, daughter-in-law, Atrayee and grandson, Adwik, always kept me cheerful over regular telephonic conversation. I thank them all.

18th May, 2023 **Bhabatosh Banerjee**

1

Introduction

Be Environment-friendly
Enjoy Competitive Advantage

1.1 NATURE OF THE PROBLEM

Environment is affected by every human activity. Fortunately, today there is an increasing awareness about the close relationship between economic development and environmental management issues. Since corporate enterprises are important for economic development, they cannot ignore the significance of environmental management issues. Environmental management plays a crucial role in ensuring sustainable economic development. In other words, sustainable economic development has to be environment-friendly. In order to be a good corporate citizen, a firm should adopt policies and take actions that are environment-friendly. It cannot gain competitive advantage without adopting proper environmental management. While assessing last three decades of progress in the context of corporate enterprises—productivity, quality and environment—*The National Productivity Review* (1998) predicted that the first decade of the 21st century would focus on environmental management systems dealing with critical issues, challenges and opportunities.

In the long run, there is no conflict between environmental management and profitability of the firm, and hence it's competitive advantage. In order to enjoy competitive advantage based on effective environmental management, companies should develop strategies that translate actions into benefits, improving their environmental performance and meeting the environmental demands placed upon them by government and other stakeholders, and at the same time, provide them opportunities for financial benefits. "The long-term goal of environmental management is to move toward considering environmental aspects in an integrated fashion in product design, the entire manufacturing process, marketing, product delivery and use, consumer service, and post-consumer product disposition" (Klassen and McLaughlin, 1996). Given the internal and external demands to improve the environmental performance of a company, those companies that achieve higher standards of environmental performance will have *competitive* advantage over their rivals. Some of these *advantages* are:

1. better cost analysis, allocation, control and decision-making,
2. improved resource consumption efficiency,
3. improved product quality,
4. increased staff commitment,
5. reduced risk exposure,
6. cheaper finance,
7. lower insurance premium,
8. improved community relations,
9. improved media coverage, and
10. improved relations with the regulators.

Studies on environmental accounting and reporting issues (Sengupta, 1988; Eresi, 1996; Mishra, 1999; Ghosh, 2001; Paul and Pal, 2001) show that companies in India, particularly those belonging to the hazardous industries, are not properly fulfilling their responsibilities in environmental management. With the amendment of Companies Act, 2013, there is no concept of hazardous industries in the Act, though in reality there are many industries which need to take extra precaution while discharging their activities so that there is lesser and lesser pollution.

1.2 ISSUES

There are many unresolved issues regarding environmental management vis-à-vis corporate enterprises. Some such important issues are as follows:

1. What are the responsibilities of corporate entities in relation to sustainable economic development?
2. What environmental challenges do they face and how do they respond to such challenges?
3. What are the international developments that influence legislation of environmental laws across the world?

4. What is the overall corporate regulatory framework in India?
5. What environmental laws are in vogue in India?
6. What should be the administrative structure for monitoring corporate environmental performance and for ensuring compliance with environmental laws by the corporate entities?
7. Why should corporate citizens manage efficiently their business activities that affect the overall environment and quality of life?
8. What are the strategic issues concerning environmental management from the standpoint of corporate sector?
9. What is Strategic Environmental Management System (SEMS) and how do the companies implement SEMS to increase their competitive advantage?
10. How should a company manage the environmental aspects of its business activities innovatively, strategically, organizationally and technologically?
11. How do ISO 14000 family of standards promote better environmental performance?
12. What are the parameters of environmental accounting, reporting and auditing?
13. How can environmental performance of the corporate enterprises be measured?
14. How to recognize environmental effects on conventional accounting practice and framing accounting policies accordingly?
15. Are the environment related costs and revenues separately identified, measured and reported in the conventional system?
16. Is the capital expenditure decision-making process suitably adjusted for justifying 'green technology'?
17. Is there any scope for setting up a catastrophe reserve?
18. What accounting standards are needed for measuring and reporting economic activities that take care of environmental issues? Does the FASB[1] or IASB[1] issue any such standard? How can ICAI[1] co-operate with other notable international standard setting agencies that formulate suitable accounting standards for identification, measurement and disclosure of environmental costs and benefits of a firm in India?
19. What is the level of social responsibility reporting in the annual report of a firm? Does the reporting of environmental activities

1 Financial Accounting Standards Board (FASB), U.S.; International Accounting Standards Board (IASB); The Institute of Chartered Accountants of India (ICAI).

form part of social responsibility and shown separately? Or, is it shown only as a part of Director's Report?

20. Should the Indian industries have voluntary codes of conduct for 'Responsible Environment Care Programme'? If so, what would be the various aspects of such a programme?
21. Is it not the high time to introduce courses in environment in college and university education to sensitize the future citizens of India?
22. Do we need reorientation of the accounting education courses to make future corporate executives environment conscious?
23. What about other stakeholders? The public in general, the transport system, particularly, the motor transport system in the metropolitan and rural areas? Also the modern town planning agencies. Do they care for promoting better quality of life by planting trees?

The above and many such relevant issues are required to be properly addressed and resolved for evolving an effective environmental management system.

As the name suggests, the thrust of the book is on the corporate sector because they are the greatest polluters in spite of their contribution to the economic development of the country. But we have also discussed the desirable role of other stakeholders in different chapters of the book.

1.3 OBJECTIVES

We have identified many corporate environmental management issues in Section 1.2. With respect to these issues, the objectives of environmental management can now be stated briefly.

The *general objective* is to examine the strategic environmental management issues leading to the competitive advantage of a firm, and to analyse the environmental accounting and reporting issues and suggest appropriate measures for improving corporate environmental management. Some of the *specific objectives* relating to corporate environmental management may be stated as follows:

1. Taking active steps to incorporate the effects of business decisions on environmental management, and measure and disclose the financial impacts of such decisions.
2. Devising new forms of financial and non-financial accounting systems, information systems and control systems to encourage more environment-friendly management decisions.

3. Developing new forms of performance measurement, reporting and appraisal for both internal and external purposes taking environmental issues into account.
4. Developing suitable ways in which sustainability may be assessed and incorporated into organizational systems.
5. Recognizing environmental effects on conventional accounting practice and framing accounting policies accordingly.
6. Separately identifying environment related costs and revenues within the conventional accounting systems.
7. Ensuring proper allocation of hidden environmental costs for better decision-making. Since hidden costs form a significant part of the total costs of a firm, the impact of more accurate allocation of indirect costs to products or services would be significant.
8. Examining the present audit system (both internal and external) and suggesting improvements in it to take care of environmental management issues.

1.4 HYPOTHESES

The following hypotheses may be formulated in the context of environmental management:

1. In recent years, environmental awareness of the corporate sector has been increasing. This, in turn, is leading to the adoption of scientific management systems for managing business activities that affect the overall environment and quality of life.
2. The tendency to disclose environmental performance of the companies, both in qualitative and quantitative terms, is growing over time.

A number of supporting hypotheses may also be developed and tested by the interested readers. These may be put in the following categories:

- Environmental issues pertaining to the company and the industry.
- Financial and management accounting issues.

1.5 REDESIGNING THE SECOND EDITION OF THE BOOK

Based on the success of the first edition, the book has been redesigned to expand its coverage and make it a reference-cum textbook in view of growing importance of the subject-matter and some emerging developments relating to climate change the world over. Nevertheless, the basic structure of the book, Chapters 1–6, has been maintained though new developments in the subject have been incorporated in the relevant chapters. Short exercise questions have been added to all the chapters. In some of them multiple-choice-questions have also been added where necessary to facilitate learning of the subject-matter discussed.

In Chapter 6, the case studies under the Companies Act, 1956 have been edited to keep an abridged version of the study. Then we have new studies which include GRI Guidelines (2002) and (2021), Shell Reporting practices (previous and current) and Sustainability Reporting, both concepts and trends of reporting. Finally, two case studies, one on ITC Ltd. and the other on SAIL have been given in Chapter 6. One of the purposes is to help the readers to understand the developments that have taken place over the years in the matter of contents of corporate reports. To enrich the contents of the chapter, the international scenario has also been touched upon. The purpose is to help the readers to understand the reporting practices under the Companies Act, 1956 (old case studies) and those under the Companies Act, 2013 (new case studies) and to comprehend how over time reporting requirements and practices have changed. So far as Sustainability Reporting is concerned, the SEBI has made it mandatory for the listed companies with effect from the year 2022–23. The Public Enterprises under the Department of Public Enterprises are not also falling behind. The voluntary sustainability reports (2021–22) of both ITC Ltd. and SAIL incorporated new aspects of reporting and they are internationally competitive.

Chapter 7 is entirely new dealing with matters that could not be covered under the previous chapters but are subject matters of enormous importance. It is an attempt to cover various other issues relating to climate change for the benefit of readers to expand their horizon of knowledge. In the Appendix, two well thought-out course outlines, one for the undergraduate studies and the other for the postgraduate studies, have been given to make the book complete and also help the Educational Institutions to consider them for adoption.

REFERENCES

Eresi, K., "Environment–Information Disclosure in Annual Reports", *The Chartered Accountant,* January 1996, p. 48.

Ghosh, S., "Environmental Disclosure in Corporate Annual Reports in India: A case study", *The Indian Journal of Accounting,* June 2001, pp. 15–22.

Klassen, R.D. and McLaughlin, C.P., "The Impact of Environmental Management on Firm Performance", *Management Science,* August 1996, 42(8), pp. 1199–1214.

Mishra, K.K., "Environmental Reporting in Business", *The Management Accountant,* June 1999, p. 429.

Paul, K.C. and Pal, B., "Corporate Environmental Reporting in India", *Indian Accounting Review*, December 2001, pp. 27–45.

Porter, Michael E., *Competitive Advantage: Creating and sustaining superior performance,* The Free Press, New York, 1985.

Sengupta, P.R., "Pollution Disclosures in India", *The Chartered Accountant*, July 1988, pp. 20–22.

Welford, Richard and Gouldson, Andrew, *Environmental Management and Business Strategy,* Pitman Publishing, London, 1993.

Welford, Richard, *Corporate Environmental Management 3: Towards sustainable development,* Earthscan, London, 2000.

Wever, Grace, *Strategic Environmental Management: Using TPEM and ISO 14000 for competitive advantage,* Wiley, New York, 1996.

2

Environmental Challenges and Corporate Responses

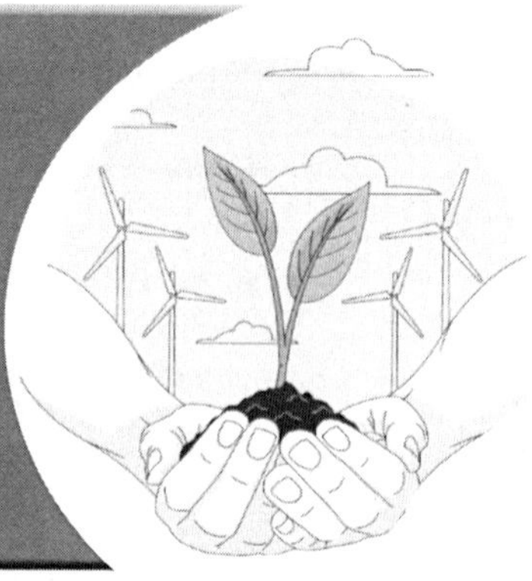

Plant a Tree and Get Oxygen Free
HUDA
(Hyderabad Urban Development Authority)

2.1 INTRODUCTION

The public debate about business and the environment had been going on since long. The 1970s saw an adversarial relationship between companies and environmental groups. During the 1980s, this relationship began to change as politicians, economists, executives and environmentalists began developing measures for the integration of economic and environmental objectives. Some companies began to view the environment as a business opportunity and proactively pursued a 'green market'. Others placed themselves at the forefront of 'a new form of capitalism' that considers environmental and social concerns while conducting business. This phenomenon came to be known as 'greening the corporations' (Robbins, 2001)[1].

Two important questions arise when we study the response of corporate sector to the environmental challenges. *First,* what are the environmental challenges faced by companies? *Second,* how do companies respond to such challenges?

2.2 ENVIRONMENTAL CHALLENGES

The environmental challenges faced by companies can be put under

1 'Greening' or 'going green' has its origin in C. Reich's book, *The Greening of America,* Random House, New York, 1970.

seven key categories: (i) Atmosphere, (ii) Toxic chemicals and waste, (iii) Freshwater, (iv) Land, (v) Oceans, (vi) Biotechnology and (vii) Biodiversity.

Atmosphere

Most companies should focus their attention on the atmosphere due to a number of factors. These factors are as follows:

1. There are wide-ranging environmental regulations in the world to regulate air quality and for atmospheric protection. The Clean Air Act, 1970 of the US is such an example. Under the Clean Air Act, the Environmental Protection Agency (EPA) is responsible for regulating airborne toxic emissions.
2. Public awareness of atmospheric issues is much higher now (Rowlands, 1995).
3. The international deliberations on ozone depletion and climatic change suggest that more regulatory changes are likely to come (Susskind, 1994). Again, of all the environmental regulations, regulation of air pollution has received the highest attention.
4. Companies should give priority to issues related to ozone depletion because of consumer pressure combined with competition from chlorofluorocarbon (CFC) alternatives (Porter and Brown, 1991).

Air Pollution

Pollution of air is one of the key issues which should be addressed to improve quality of life of citizens. Air quality index (AQI) gives us an idea about the quality of air. The range of AQI is generally given as follows:

AQI Range	*Nature of quality*
0–50	Good
50–100	Satisfactory
100–200	Moderate
200–300	Poor
300–400	Very Poor
400–500	Severe

The Times of India (ToI) Kolkata published the AQI of five metro cities in India, Bengaluru, Chennai, Delhi, Kolkata and Mumbai, on October 26, 2022 (popularly mentioned as 'Post-Diwali' AQI) which shows the following position (Table 2.1):

TABLE 2.1 Air Quality Index in Five Metro Cities in India[2]

City/Time	1 am	3 am	6 am	9 am	12 pm	3 pm	*Average*
Bengaluru	126	128	131	133	132	158	135
Chennai	189	169	244	261	256	261	230
Delhi	317	329	330	329	328	308	323.5
Kolkata	48	47	47	48	49	49	48
Mumbai	106	106	121	128	128	130	120

Source: ToI, Kolkata, October 26, 2022, p. 1.

On a post-Diwali day, Kolkata (the City of Joy) shows a remarkably high quality of air (good category) followed by Mumbai (Moderate), Bengaluru (Moderate), Chennai (Poor) and Delhi (very poor). Experts however said that the high wind speeds, due to the effects of cyclone *Sitrang*, along with intermittent rain played a big role in cleaning up Kolkata's air: not only were pollutants disbursed quickly, the rain also ensured suspended particulate matter (SPM) levels were low. Another huge factor was the significant drop in the use of polluting firecrackers, thanks to better awareness of the public and regulatory measures taken by the Government.

Air pollution issues have become important to companies ever since the debate on global environmental change started. This is because about half of all global greenhouse gases[3] are generally related to the activities of the corporate sector. Table 2.2 shows the corporations' involvement in the generation of greenhouse gases.

Around 50% of all greenhouse gases can be traced, in one way or the other, to the operations of various companies. This includes half of oil production, production of vehicles in developed countries, most of the CFC production, and a large proportion of electricity production and its use. Companies are also greatly involved in the production and

---

2 It does not necessarily mean that the air quality of five metropolitan cities in India as shown in Table 2.1 will continue to be same every day. It changes, sometimes rapidly, from day to day depending upon a host of contributing factors including human behaviour.

3 Concentration of greenhouse gases has increased greatly in the atmosphere because of human activities. These gases are believed to contribute to the greenhouse effect and, therefore, may cause global temperatures to rise (Robbins, Peter T., *Greening the Corporation–Management strategy and the environmental challenge*, Earthscan, London, 2001). The most important of these gases is carbon dioxide (CO_2) that contributes half of the effect of greenhouse gases.

use of toxic materials which include asbestos, dioxins, polychlorinated biphenyls (PCSs), and volatile organic compounds (VOCs) which, when discharged into the air, water and on land, can cause serious health problems (UNTC, 1992).

TABLE 2.2 Estimated Involvement of Corporations in the Generation of Human-generated Greenhouse Gases

Important sources	*Amount of gas generated (Per cent of total amount)*	*Measure*
Emissions from automobiles; use of coal, fossil fuel, etc.	50	CO_2
Oil and gas production and use; emissions from coal mines	10–20	CH_4
Use of aerosol sprays, air-conditioners, solvents, foam products and refrigerators	60–70	CFCs
Emissions from automobiles, use of coal, fossil fuel	50	NO_x and Q_3

(Adapted from UNTC, *Climate Change and Transnational Corporations: Analysis and trends*, UNO, New York, 1992, p. 15.)

At present, however, reduction of greenhouse gas emissions is not a priority for most of the companies. Many companies have policies that deal with air quality but not with greenhouse gases *per se*. This is because reduction of some of these emissions does not appear to be cost-effective (Hawken, 1994).

Toxic chemicals and hazardous waste

Chemicals are used to manufacture hundreds and thousands of end-products, many of which are toxic. These toxic chemicals are discharged into the environment, either directly or indirectly. The examples of the toxic chemicals that are discharged directly are fertilizers, pesticides and some solvents. Mining and fuel-burning industries indirectly discharge chemicals into various water bodies. Hazardous chemicals can be released in solid, liquid or gaseous form into the air, water and on land.

Every chemical is toxic to some extent and is harmful to living beings. It can create chronic health problems. Pesticides and herbicides kill between 10,000 and 40,000 people in developing countries every year (Robbins, 2001). Pesticides cause water pollution, soil degradation, insect resistance and their resurgence, and destruction of native flora and fauna. Some pesticides deplete the ozone layer as well.

Pesticides are big business for companies. Companies in developing countries market pesticides on the rationale that they will increase agricultural production, thereby increasing access to food and reducing hunger. Higher production will also boost exports and foreign exchange, thus increasing the country's gross national product (GNP). Fertilizers are marketed on similar grounds. The use of fertilizers is thus increasing rapidly in developing countries. However, the benefits of pesticides and fertilizers are declining due to the law of diminishing returns. Hazardous wastes, e.g., metallic compounds, acids, asbestos, organo-phosphorus compounds and many others, are also produced by industries. Thus, toxic and hazardous chemicals are the most important environmental issues that should concern the corporate sector. There are many instances of unscrupulous dumping of wastes by some companies (Allen, 1992). For example, in 1992 alone, Pepsi Cola Bottling Corporation exported over 7,000 tonnes of plastic waste from California to Chennai and Mumbai (Leonard, 1993).

There have, of late, been some important international agreements on trans-boundary movements of toxic chemicals and hazardous wastes. An example of such a treaty is the Rome IV Convention between the European Union (EU) and the African, Pacific and Caribbean (APC) countries, which bans toxic waste exports from the EU to the APC countries (DESD/TCMD, 1993). Nevertheless, the export of toxic waste to developing countries is continuing and is unlikely to stop in the near future because companies need to dispose of their wastes, and governments in developing countries need 'the business' (Slaughter, 1996).

Corporate responses to toxic chemicals and hazardous wastes have mostly been brought about as a result of highly publicized accidents in chemical factories. These responses include formulation of policies and programmes, taking measures to assure the public of the safety of the operations, and so on.

Freshwater

A number of countries today are facing water scarcity. If the population of the world reaches 10 billion by 2050 as predicted, the current patterns of freshwater use will become unsustainable (IUCN/UNEP/WWF, 1991).

In developed countries, industry is the largest consumer of freshwater accounting for 50%–80% of the total demand, while in developing countries, it accounts for about 10%–30%. However, in majority of the countries, especially in the developing part of the world, agriculture is the major consumer of freshwater. Globally, it accounts for about 70% of freshwater use (UN Survey, 1993).

Industries use water mainly for cooling, processing, cleaning and removing industrial wastes. Water thus becomes heavily polluted with chemicals and heavy metals. It is termed as *polluted water* which accounts for 87% of industry's total freshwater use (Robbins, 2001, p. 8). Among various industries, pulp and paper, chemicals, petrochemicals and refining, electricity generation (thermal plant), iron and steel, food processing, textiles, etc., are the major sectors that pollute freshwater. For example, production of one kilogram of paper and that of one tonne of steel may consume up to 700 kg and 280 tonnes of water, respectively (Postel, 1993).

In developed countries, industrial waste discharges are rigorously controlled. In contrast, in developing countries, the discharges of industrial wastes into the water bodies are mostly uncontrolled; this adversely affects the water quality. In these countries, contamination of water is a common and severe problem, especially in those areas where industrial plants are concentrated. The jute mills located along the banks of the Hooghly river in West Bengal are a prime example of how the 'Ganga Water' gets polluted by discharges of wastewater from industries.

Many developed countries now require industries to meet specific water quality standards before discharging wastewater to the water bodies. The most effective and economic way to comply with these requirements is to treat and recycle water, thereby discharging less polluted water (Postel, 1993). Thus, pollution control laws in many countries have helped in the conservation and efficient use of water by companies.

Land

Land is an important and scarce natural resource. Environmental problems on land are generally created by desertification, soil loss, deforestation and degradation. Hazardous wastes and toxic materials are also dumped on land, which pollute the environment. The loss of forests or deforestation has become an important environmental issue because forests support a variety of plant and animal species and provide a carbon sink that could help counteract global warming. It also affects biodiversity.

There are many international pacts that deal with some of the above problems. These include Tropical Forestry Action Plan (TFAP) developed by the World Bank to promote sustainable use of tropical forests; the Food and Agriculture Organization (FAO) Code of Conduct on the Distribution and Use of Pesticides to promote preservation of agricultural resources, human health, etc. Companies must support and implement such plans for ensuring sustainable use of land resources. This will benefit the long-term interests of business (UN Survey, 1993). Corporate environmental policies and programmes should focus on desertification, deforestation, and soil degradation. Companies should build *safety zones* around their manufacturing plants[4].

Oceans

Human activities on land and at sea are degrading marine resources in many parts of the world. Most ocean pollution originates on land and ends up in the sea—40% of this pollution enters the sea from rivers, 30% from the atmosphere, and the remaining 30% is the result of shipping, dumping, offshore mining and oil production (Robbins, 2001, p. 11). According to the Group of Experts on the Scientific Aspects of Marine Pollution, the main contaminants of the oceans (UNDP, 1990, p. 184), arranged in descending order, are:

1. nutrients from urban sewage and runoff,
2. microbial contamination from sewage,
3. plastics from land and sea dumping,
4. synthetic organic compounds (e.g., pesticides and industrial chemicals), and
5. oil from transportation and spills.

The corporate sector is the major producer of arsenic, mercury, chlorinated hydrocarbons and other toxic substances. Companies that are active in mining and metal and chemical processing and oil production are responsible for polluting seas and oceans by dumping industrial wastes. Oil exploration and transportation are another important source of sea pollution. Many big petroleum companies have lobbied against tougher international agreements on ocean resources since the 1950s (Porter, Brown, 1991). Compared to other regions, there is little regulation on the use of marine resources. Although there are some corporate efforts to minimize oil and chemical spillage, environmental issues concerning the oceans are not high on the corporate agenda as yet.

4 A safety zone is a cordoned off area of land surrounding a plant. It can minimize human death and injury in the event of an accident. For example, in Union Carbide's Bhopal accident in which thousands of people died, safety zones were minimal or non-existent (Srivastava, P., *Greening Business: Profiting the corporation and the environment*, Thompson Executive Press, Ohio, 1996).

Biotechnology and biodiversity

Biotechnology is a relatively new area of scientific research. The application of biological organisms, systems and processes to industrial processes is known as biotechnology. Living organisms have been exploited over centuries for producing food, drugs and other products. Micro-organisms have been used to make bread, convert milk to cheese and brew alcoholic beverages. Vinegar and many types of antibiotics and vitamins are manufactured by using microbial organisms. Of late, genetic engineering has allowed an unprecedented degree of flexibility and control in industrial processes (Crump, 1991).

Biodiversity or diversity of biological species is very important for sustaining life on earth. But industrial activities may result in the loss of species due to deforestation, oil and gas drilling, mining and road building, etc. Species are being lost at a faster rate than in any other recent geological time period (Goldsmith, Hildyard, 1988). Twenty-five per cent of the species are expected to be extinct or in serious danger of extinction by 2050 (IUCN/UNEP/WWF, 1991).

Biotechnologies may have devastating environmental effects also. The attempt to develop pesticide tolerant plants by pesticides and seed companies has often led to greater chemical dispersal into the environment leading to its degradation. This is a cause for serious concern, especially for developing countries. Most biotechnology firms are US-based corporations and have successfully lobbied against agreements that may result in restriction in the production of pesticides. Therefore, the first step towards better environment management in this context would be for every company to honestly assess its environmental impact on plants and animals, and try to formulate appropriate environmental management policies.

2.3 CORPORATE RESPONSES TO ENVIRONMENTAL CHALLENGES

Companies generally respond to issues which are concrete and easily quantifiable, and where there is pressure on them to change from governments and other regulatory or voluntary groups (UN Survey, 1993). Issues that have a history of regulation are well addressed by the companies. For example, the US led corporations focus their attention on land issues because of Superfund legislation in the US. Issues in developing countries, on the other hand, are normally ignored by many companies based in these countries due to lack of proper legislation. Thus, we need to address the following three questions:

1. Why should corporate management respond to the environmental challenges that affect their operations?
2. Do various users of accounts need environmental information for evaluating corporate environmental performance?
3. Why should management be obliged to provide environmental information in their annual reports?

Corporate environmental responsibility, as a part of broad Corporate Social Responsibility (CSR), has been discussed extensively in various economics and management literature. However, all economists are not fully convinced about the need for CSR. For example, Prof. Milton Friedman (1970) believes that corporate goal is to maximize profits and firms should thus focus on their business activities only. Accordingly, the social and environmental activities do not fall within the purview of the corporate sector. Rather, the government at different levels should deal with such problems. This is, however, a minority viewpoint. The concept of corporate social and environmental responsibility has been widely supported in the literature under social contract argument, and quality of life argument. We deal with them briefly.

2.3.1 Social Contract Argument

The discussion on social contract argument in favour of corporate social responsibility became prominent in the early 1970s (Dahl, 1972; Votaw, 1973; Shocker and Sethi, 1973). Later, Ramanathan (1976) formalized a general accounting framework. Expanding the ideas of external diseconomies, Ramanathan developed a comprehensive theoretical work on Social Accounting by using the concept of Social Contract (Jaggi, 1997).

The social contract argument is based on the notion that business firms do not exist in a vacuum—they are a part of society that creates and supports them. Also, companies owe their existence to laws which have been developed by the society. Thus, society's support for the existence of the companies depends on their socially desirable performance. In other words, it is the natural expectation of the society that business firms would not engage in socially undesirable activities including pollution of the environment. If they are engaged in such activities, society may be forced to take steps such as boycotting the firm's products and services, taxing the offending activities, shutting down plants, modification of existing laws, development of new laws, etc., to penalize the offenders with a view to bringing them back on the desirable track.

But the validity of the social contract argument has also been challenged by many (Lindblom, 1984; Puxty, 1986). It has been argued (Tipgos, 1977) that the social contract argument is based on ambitious corporate legal rights and obligations which are not enforceable by law. The argument is considered to be too narrow to capture the true nature of the relationship between society and firms. The opponents of social contract notion argue that the firm as a social institution exists as a *matter of privilege* and not as a matter of right. It is, therefore, difficult to explain this relationship by the social contract approach. Since this concept is not capable of explaining the true nature of the relationship between society and firms, the concept appears to be inadequate and unrealistic for the development of objectives and reporting format for social and environmental accounting.

In spite of the above, the social contract concept has been found useful in projecting the social and environmental concerns of the society and in emphasizing the need for socially and environmentally desirable behaviour from firms. Nevertheless, to make the social contract argument more desirable and acceptable, it is important that questions with regard to the form it takes and the social accountabilities that might be attached to it need to be properly answered (Gray, *et al.*, 1987).

2.3.2 Quality of Life Argument

According to Dierkes (1979), the 'quality of life' argument changed both the society's expectations from and attitude towards the corporate sector. Unrestrained economic development increased the social costs to staggering proportions, as is evident from environmental pollution and social ills, and triggered a shift in the society's attitude towards industrialization. Industrialization began to be perceived as maximizing its profits by exploiting environmental and social systems. In order to stop this exploitation, society revalued its attitude towards the corporate sector, and revised its expectation from it. Accordingly, only the type of economic development that does not adversely affect the quality of life was considered desirable. This shift in society's expectations and attitude was moulded by a number of developments which took place during the last few decades. Some of them are as follows:

1. The power of labour unions resulted in inclusion of the quality of life issues in labour negotiations during the 1970s. Consequently, safety in work environment, among others, is now considered an important factor.

2. The emergence of the consumer movement in many countries led to a greater awareness of corporate social responsibility with regard to the safety of products. This awareness resulted in several legislative actions designed to protect consumers from corporate abuses.
3. Damage to the physical environment in the form of air and water pollution alarmed society and resulted in a movement towards protecting the environment. Consequently, several environment protection laws were passed in many countries.
4. Society recognized that natural resources were limited and their unrestricted use would result in their depletion. Accordingly, conservation of resources and efficiency in the use of resources assumed new importance.

This shift in the attitude of the society led to its expectation that corporate enterprises should behave in a socially and environmentally responsible way. With the passage of time, companies also realized their social and environmental responsibility and recognized the need for greater cooperation with society.

Regarding the question as to why management should be obliged to provide environmental information in the annual reports, first we have to identify the *users* of environmental information and the *purposes* for which they need such information.

Investors are generally considered to be the major users of financial information. It can, therefore, be argued that they would also be the primary users of environmental information. Another group of users would be the public, especially the environmentalists, who represent the society's interest in protecting the environment. Regulating agencies, involved in setting standards for emission of pollutants, would require environmental information to evaluate whether or not the standards are complied with. The concerns for environmental pollution and the need for proper information on the firm's environmental performance has now assumed greater importance at the international level also. We will now elaborate these points.

Environmental information to meet investors' needs

Many studies have analysed the relationship between social information disclosed in financial statements and movement of stock prices (Belkaoui, 1976; Anderson and Frankle, 1980; Jaggi and Freedman, 1982; Shane and Spicer, 1983). The major assumption of these studies was that the movements in stock prices at the time of disclosure of social information would indicate that investors' decisions were influenced by the social information contained in financial statements. Jaggi and Freedman (1982), in particular, examined the relationship between pollution disclosures and stock price movements. Their results provided evidence that supported the relationship between stock price movements and disclosure of social information in general, and pollution information, in particular, in the financial statements, thereby implying that the investors used social information including environmental information for their investment decisions. Accordingly, investors needed environmental information for their investment decisions. However, the results of the empirical studies need to be interpreted with caution because movement in stock prices could be caused by several factors other than disclosure of social and environmental information. Nevertheless, it is now being increasingly realized that pollution information plays an important role in the investment decisions, especially for investments in firms belonging to polluting industries. Investors would be at a greater risk if the firms were found to be in violation of certain environmental laws and would likely to incur heavy clean up costs to comply with the standards. Accordingly, availability of environmental information would enable the investors to properly evaluate their risks before making their investment decisions.

Society's need for environmental information

There is no doubt that the society is more concerned with a firm's economic health. Information on financial performance of the firm meets the needs of the society. But over time, due to increasing awareness of environmental pollution, the society is increasingly showing its concern on the firm's activities on environmental issues. It is now being recognized that for achieving sustainable growth, economic, social and environmental concerns should be properly balanced. If a firm, especially from polluting industries, achieves economic growth by polluting the environment, the society is ultimately likely to bear the cost of this pollution in terms of medical costs and lower quality of life. Therefore, society needs environmental information for evaluating a firm's environmental performance.

Environmental activists observe the environmental performance of the firms in many countries. There are many non-government organizations (NGOs) also which take active interest in watching economic, social and environmental performance of firms. In India, High Courts of different states and the Supreme Court of India are giving priority to environmental litigations, and with a view to protecting quality of life and environment, 'Green Benches' have been constituted to deal with environmental issues on a priority basis. Consequently, firms can no longer ignore environmental issues and their environmental responsibility. The various environmental groups would, accordingly, need relevant and timely information on the firm's environment related activities for proper evaluation of its environmental performance. Thus, society becomes an important user of environmental information.

Environmental information for regulation

Regulatory bodies watch a firm's environmental performance to ensure that the norms are complied with. In Chapter 3, we have dealt with various regulatory bodies created in India to protect the quality of environment and life. One of the requirements is that firms, especially those belonging to polluting industries, should disclose all environment related and social information, either in financial statement and/or in special reports to be filed with the regulating agencies. The details of the Indian scenario in this context have been given in this chapter. Thus, regulating agencies need pollution information in order to monitor the firm's environmental performance and ensure compliance with the standards.

Environmental information needs: the international dimension

Many developments have taken place at the international level to deal effectively with concerns for environmental pollution in both developed and developing countries. They have been discussed in Chapter 3. The World Environmental Congress held in 1992 at Rio de Janeiro had a great impact not only on creating awareness about protecting environment among the member countries of the UN but also in translating this awareness into legislative actions in many countries, including India, to regulate the activities of the corporate sector for better environmental management. In the new globalized economy, the corporate sector needs to be even more environment-conscious and manage their activities properly to enhance their competitive advantages. Firms, especially multinational ones, have to meet the demand of the international community to show that they are controlling the harmful effects of industrialization. To ensure that the corporate enterprises meet these demands, national and international regulating bodies require their environmental information. So, the concern for environment and need for pollution information are now crossing the national boundaries and is assuming greater international importance.

The foregoing discussion emphasizes the need for information on environmental performance to satisfy the needs of various interested parties—the investors, environment activists, regulatory bodies and society at large. How can such information be made available to all of them? Would these information be available in the financial statements of corporate enterprises to comply with legislative requirements? In the absence of legislative requirements, would the management of companies be obliged to publish such information voluntarily?

At present, there is no disclosure format for publishing environmental information even in the developed economies. So long as the regulatory disclosure requirements are not streamlined, users of environmental and pollution information would have to depend on the voluntary efforts of the management to publish such information. So, the key question is—why should the management publish environmental information voluntarily?

Research studies have shown that a variety of considerations motivate management of a company to disclose information voluntarily and not wait for mandatory requirements. Although cost-benefit analysis plays an important role in such a decision, some of the important considerations for *voluntary disclosure of information* are (Banerjee, 2002) discussed below.

Stock market consideration

The most important reason for voluntary disclosure is the stock market consideration. Gray *et al.* (1990) have argued that companies may be motivated to provide additional information to influence the stock prices. Several studies (Belkaoui, 1976; Andersen and Frankle, 1980; Shane and Spicer, 1983; Jaggi and Freedman, 1982) have been conducted to test the association between stock price movements and environmental disclosures. These studies have shown that management of a company may be motivated to provide environmental disclosures to influence the stock prices.

Political costs consideration

The political cost motive was originally developed by Watts and Zimmerman (1986). Fines, penalties, potential public hostility towards the company are some examples of political costs. It is now recognized that political costs may play an important role in decisions relating to additional disclosure in the form of social and environmental information (Belkaoui and Karpik, 1989). Disclosure of environmental information can be considered to reassure the public, or the regulating agencies, that companies are concerned about the environment and are doing everything possible to reduce the negative impact of their activities on the environment.

Users' needs consideration

Guthrie and Parker (1990) have argued that companies may disclose social and environmental information to meet the stakeholders' demand for such information. The argument is based on Users' Utility Model. This is based on the premise that users need additional information to meet their utilities and companies may respond to such needs based on their perception of utilities of the users. Thus, disclosure of additional information on a voluntary basis depends on the users' needs, and how these needs are perceived by the management of companies.

Ideological goal consideration

It has been argued that companies would be motivated to disclose voluntarily additional information to serve their own political and ideological goals (Guthrie and Parker, 1990). Such disclosure would be guided by companies' agenda, ideologies and goals which are likely to be different for different companies even within the same industry. Consequently, disclosure of such information will vary from one company to another.

So, disclosure of additional information on a voluntary basis by the management of companies cannot be looked upon as something made by management without any purpose.

SUMMARY

The available studies on sustainable development underpin the responsibilities of corporate enterprises to manage effectively activities that affect, directly or indirectly, the wholesome environment and hence quality of life. Here, we have examined briefly the nature of environmental challenges faced by companies and how they should respond favourably to the challenges. We have also analysed the concept of corporate social and environmental responsibility on the basis of social contract argument and quality of life argument. Then the need for environmental information for evaluation of corporate environmental performance has been argued from the standpoint of investors, society, and international community. The supply of environmental information in the corporate annual reports for use by stockholders has then been stressed. Although in the absence of any legal compulsion, the willingness of management of a company to disclose environmental information is heavily influenced by a cost-benefit analysis, research studies have shown that a variety of considerations (e.g., stock market consideration, political costs consideration, user needs consideration and ideological goal consideration) motivate management of a company to disclose environmental information voluntarily without waiting for mandatory requirements.

EXERCISES

1. What are environmental challenges to the corporate enterprises? Give a brief account of *any one* of them.
2. Why should companies focus their attention on the atmosphere?
3. What do you understand by "air pollution"? How this pollution can be measured?
4. What is 'greenhouse gas'? How does greenhouse gas increase? Name one contributing factor.
5. How do toxic chemicals and hazardous waste pollute environment? What should be the corporate response to this problem?
6. What are the main contaminants of ocean?
7. "Biodiversity or diversity of biological aspects is very important for sustaining life on earth." What should be the corporate response in this context?
8. Why should corporate management respond to the environmental challenges that affect their operations?
9. What is 'social contract argument' in favour of corporate social responsibility for protecting environment? Explain briefly.
10. What is 'quality of life argument' in the context of better environment management?
11. How does 'stock market consideration' promote better environmental management?

REFERENCES

Allen, R., *Waste Not, Want Not: The production and dumping of toxic waste,* Earthscan WWF, London, 1992.

Anderson, J.C. and Frankle, A.W., "Voluntary Social Reporting: An ISO beta portfolio analysis", *Accounting Review,* 1980, pp. 468–479.

Ashford, N., "Understanding the Technical Responses of Industrial Firms to Environmental Problems: Implications of government policy", in Fischer, K. and Schot, J. (Eds.), *Environmental Strategies for Industry: Inter-national perspectives in research needs and policy implications,* Island Press, Washington D.C., 1993.

Banerjee, B., "Corporate Responses to Environmental Challenges", *Indian Accounting Review,* December, 2022, pp. 1–15.

Banerjee, B., "Accounting for Corporate Environmental Management in India", *The Management Accountant,* December 2002.

Belkaoui, A., "The Impact of the Disclosure of the Environmental Effects of Organizational Behaviour on the Market", *Financial Management,* April 1976, pp. 26–31.

Belkaoui, A., and I.G. Karpik, "Determinants of the Corporate Decision to Disclose Social Information" *Accounting, Auditing and Accountability Journal*, Vol. 2, No. 1, 1989, pp. 36–51.

Crump, A., *Dictionary of Environment and Development: People, places, ideas, and organizations*, Earthscan, London, 1991.

Dahl, R., "A Prelude to Corporate Reform", *Business and Society Review*, Vol. 12, No. 1, 1972, pp. 17–23.

DESD/TCMD, *International Environment Law: Emerging trends and implications for transnational corporations*, United Nations, New York, 1993.

Dierkes, M., "Corporate Social Reporting in Germany: Conceptual developments and practical experience", *Accounting, Organizations and Society*, Vol. 4, 1979, pp. 87–109.

Friedman, M., "The Social Responsibility of Business is to Increase Its Profits", *New York Times Sunday Magazine, September 13*, 1970, pp. 32–33, 124–126.

Goldsmith, E. and Hildyard, N., *The Earth Report: The essential guide to global ecological issues*, Price Stern Sloan, New York, 1988.

Gouldson, A. and Murphy, J., *Regulatory Realities: The implementation and impact of industrial environmental regulation*, Earthscan, London, 1998.

Gray, R., Owen, D. and Maunders, K., *Corporate Social Reporting: Accounting and accountability*, Prentice-Hall Inc., London, 1987.

Hawken, P., *The Ecology of Commerce: A declaration of sustainability*, Harper Business, New York, 1994.

IUCN/UNEP/WWF, *Caring for the Earth: A strategy for sustainable living*, Earthscan, London, 1991.

Jaggi, B. and Freedman, M., "An Analysis of the Information Content of Pollution Disclosures", *Financial Review*, 1982, pp. 142–152.

Jaggi, Bikki, "Environmental Responsibility and Disclosures in Global Business Environment", *Proceedings of the 5th International Accounting Conference*, IAA Research Foundation, January, 1997.

Krishnamoorthy, Bala, *Environmental Management: Text and Cases*, PHI Learning, 2022.

Leonard, A., "South Asia: The new target of international waste traders", *Multinational Monitor*, Vol. XI, No. 2, 1993.

Lindblom, C.E., "The Accountability of Private Enterprise: Private—No. Enterprise—Yes!" in A.M. Tinker (Ed.) *Social Accounting for Corporations*, Manchester University Press, 1984.

Petry, E.S. (Ed.), *Business, Ethics and the Environment: The public policy debate*, Quorum Books, New York, 1990.

Porter, G. and Brown, J. (Eds.), *Global Environmental Politics*, Westview Press, Boulder, Colorado 1991.

Porter, M.E., *Competitive Advantage: Creating and sustaining superior performance*, The Free Press, New York, 1985.

Postel, S., "Facing Water Scarcity", in L. Brown, *et al.* (Eds.), *State of the World 1993: A Worldwatch Institute Report on Progress Towards Sustainable Society*, Earthscan, London, 1993.

Puxty, A.G., "Social Accounting in Immanent Legitimation: A critique of a technicist ideology", in Neimark, M. (Ed.), *Advances in Public Interest Accounting*, Vol. 1, JAI Press, Greenwich, Connecticut, 1986, pp. 95–112.

Ramanathan, K.V., "Toward A Theory of Corporate Social Accounting", *Accounting Review*, 1976, pp. 704–11.

Reich, C., *The Greening of America*, Random House, New York, 1970.

Robbins, Peter T., *Greening the Corporation: Management strategy and the environmental challenge*, Earthscan, London, 2001.

Rowlands, I., *The Politics of Global Atmospheric Change*, MIT Press, Cambridge, 1995.

Shane, P. and Spicer, B., "Market Response to Environmental Information Produced Outside the Firm", *Accounting Review*, 1983, pp. 521–538.

Sharp, M. and Pavitt, K., "Technology Policy in the 1990s: Old trends and new realities", *Journal of Common Market Studies*, Vol. 31, 1993, pp. 129–151.

Shocker, A.D. and Sethi, S.P., "An Approach to Incorporating Societal Preferences in Developing Corporate Social Action", *California Management Review*, Summer 1973, pp. 97–105.

Shrivastava, P., "*Greening Business: Profiting the corporation and the environment*", Thompson Executive Press, Cincinnati, Ohio, 1996.

Slaughter, T., "The Improbability of Third World Government Consent in the Coming North-South International Toxic Waste Trade", in W.M. Hoffmen, R. Frederik and Shrivastava, P., *Greening Business: Profiting the corpora-tion and the environment*, Thompson Executive Press, Cincinnati, Ohio, 1996.

Susskind, L., *Environmental Diplomacy: Negotiating more effective global agreements*, Oxford University Press, New York, 1994.

Tipgos, M.A., "Toward A Theory of Corporate Social Accounting: A comment", *The Accounting Review*, 1977, pp. 977–983.

United Nations Organization, *Global Reporting Initiative–Sustainability Guidelines*, New York, 2002.

UN Survey, 1993.

UNDP, 1990, p. 184.

UNTC, *Climate Change and Transnational Corporations: Analysis and trends*, UNO, New York, 1992.

Votaw, D., "The Nature of Social Responsibility", *Journal of Contemporary Business*, Winter, 1973, pp. 1–20.

Watts, R. and Zimmerman, J.L., *Positive Accounting Theory*, Prentice Hall, Englewood Cliffs, New Jersey, 1986.

Welford, R. and Gouldson, A., *Corporate Environmental Management Systems and Business Strategies*, Pitman Publishing, London, 1993.

3

Environmental Regulations

Respond to Environmental Challenges and Flourish
Or, Ignore Environmental Challenges and Perish

3.1 INTRODUCTION

In India, corporate accounting and reporting system have changed over time in response to the changing societal requirements (Dasgupta, 1977; Chakravorty, 1985; Banerjee, 2002). The process can best be described as evolutionary. Every democratic government with an aim of maximizing social welfare has to act as an independent and impartial regulator. But the approach may differ among various countries due to differences in the state of development in the economy, culture, availability of professional accountants, state of accounting education and the stock market, to mention a few. In India, regulation of accounting by government, directly or through any of its agents, changed considerably during the 1960s when the financial accounting system became the subject of much criticism on many grounds. These grounds (Banerjee, 2002) are:

- multiplicity of accounting practices,
- lack of uniformity,
- increase in international trade, and
- emergence of social accounting.

The reported corporate results are now treated as 'social goods' and they are used by different 'segments of society'. Naturally, the society has a right to receive quality reported results. Emergence of the concept of Social Responsibility Reporting (SRR) is, therefore, a step in the right direction. For SRR by a corporate citizen, one needs to derive data from their financial and non-financial statements.

Thus, to make those corporate data reliable and uniform, regulation by government along with its agencies is a *sine qua non*. The overall corporate regulatory framework in India may be shown as in Figure 3.1 (Banerjee, 2017, p. 614). Accordingly, the basic question is—why do we need environmental regulations? Porter and Linde (2000) argued in its favour because of the following:

1. To create pressure that motivates companies to innovate
2. To improve environmental quality in cases in which innovation and the resulting improvements in resource productivity do not completely offset the cost of compliance
3. To alert and educate companies about likely resource-inefficiencies and potential areas for technological improvement
4. To raise the likelihood that product and process innovations in general will be environment-friendly
5. To create demand for environmental improvement until companies and customers are able to perceive and measure the resource-inefficiencies better, and
6. To level the playing field during the transition period to innovation-based environmental solutions.

Regulation at the national level is greatly influenced by the international scenario, among others. Cross-border listing, emergence of MNCs, foreign direct investment, foreign institutional investment, etc., have their own impact on national regulation. Thus, we need to address the issue from two angles:

- International conferences and agreements
- National governance.

Since we are concerned with corporate environmental performance and their disclosures in annual accounts, we will discuss only those developments and regulations that have direct bearing on environmental management. Section 3.2 gives a general view on the major international developments. Section 3.3 gives a brief account of legislations enacted in some advanced economies, while Section 3.4 gives an overview of the national panorama.

3.2 INTERNATIONAL DEVELOPMENTS

3.2.1 The Stockholm Conference (1972)

The Stockholm Conference was the first global environment conference organized by the United Nations. It discussed the relationship between

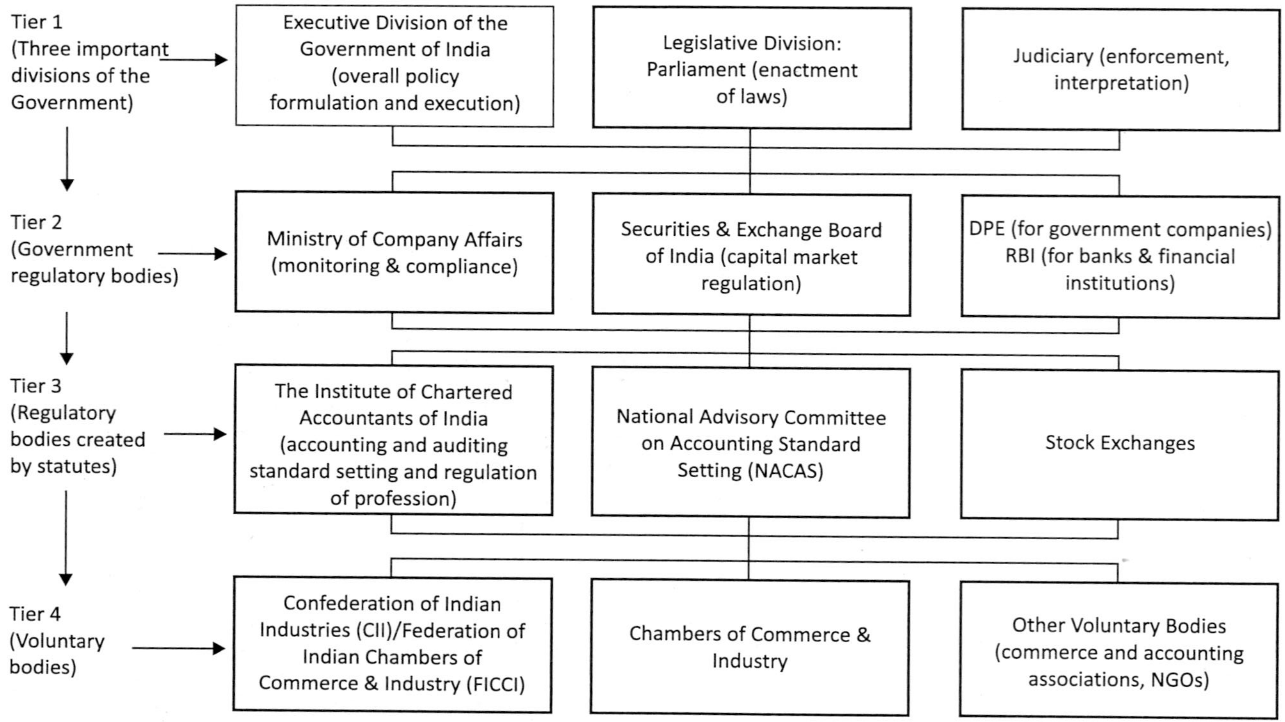

Figure 3.1 Regulatory framework influencing supply of financial statement information in india.

economic development and environmental degradation for the first time to find out ways and means to provide to the world citizens a healthy and productive life in harmony with nature. On June 16, 1972, the United Nations Conference on Human Environment adopted a 'declaration' consisting of a 'preamble' and 26 'principles'. According to the preamble, defence and improvement of both natural and man-made environment have become an imperative goal for mankind, to be pursued together with the fundamental goal of peace and worldwide economic and social development (Krishnamoorthy, 2005). It is the responsibility of all citizens, communities, enterprises and institutions, at every level, to achieve this goal.

Among the 26 principles, two principles, namely, Principle 17 and Principle 25, relate to environmental concerns and deserve special mention.

> ***Principle 17***: Appropriate national institutions were to be entrusted with the task to plan, manage and control the environmental resources of states with a view to enhancing environmental quality.
>
> ***Principle 25***: States were to ensure that international organizations played a coordinated, efficient and dynamic role for the protection and improvement of the environment.

Thus, for the first time, the UN stressed on the proper planning and management of environmental resources for enhancement of environmental quality. International organizations were expected to play a coordinated, efficient and dynamic role for the protection and improvement of environment.

The Stockholm Conference led to the establishment of United Nations Environment Programme (UNEP) which acts as a global catalyst for action to protect the environment. The Conference was instrumental in awakening the consciousness on environmental issues across the world. It also strengthened and accelerated international action against dumping wastes in the sea and trading in endangered species.

3.2.2 World Commission on Environment and Development (1983)

In spite of the setting up of the UNEP (as a result of the United Nations Conference on the Human Environment, Stockholm, 1972), little progress was achieved in the ensuing years to integrate environmental concerns into national economic planning and decision-making. Consequently, environmental concerns continued to be ignored and problems like ozone depletion, global warming, and water and air pollution grew more serious and destruction of natural resources continued to accelerate at an alarming rate. Around 1983, the UN set up the World Commission on Environment and Development (WCED). The Commission considered environmental degradation as an offshoot of industrialization and recognized the need for survival of developing countries from the menace of environmental degradation due to economic development. Accordingly, in its report submitted in 1987, the Commission put forward the concept of 'sustainable development' as an alternative approach to one simply based on economic growth and defined it as follows:

> Sustainable development meets the needs of the present without compromising the ability of the future generations to meet their own needs.

The concept of sustainable development was broad and environment-friendly, and it underscored the efficient management of environmental resources so that not only the present generation but also the future generations would be able to meet their needs. This was indeed a very dynamic concept brought into the arena of economic development of a nation.

After considering the 1987 Brundtland Report (named after the Chairman, Gro Harlem Brundtland of Norway), the UN General Assembly called the UN Conference on Environment and Development (UNCED) in 1992 at Rio de Janeiro, Brazil.

3.2.3 The Earth Summit (1992)

Twenty years after the first Global Conference on Environment, the UN General Assembly organized the Earth Summit in 1992 at Rio de Janeiro. The thrust of the Conference was to:

- provide an understanding of development that would support socio-economic development;
- prevent continued deterioration of environment, and
- build a foundation for a global partnership between the developing and more industrialized countries for serving mutual needs and interests towards a healthy future for our planet.

Representatives of the 108 member countries of the UN General Assembly recognized the need to redirect international and national plans and policies to ensure that all economic decisions fully took into account any environmental impact. Thus, the traditional goal of achieving economic development was replaced by **sustainable development** and the member countries adopted Agenda 21 for a wide-ranging blueprint for action to achieve sustainable development. Thus, three major agreements aimed at changing the traditional approach to development were adopted in the Summit (Ramamoorthy, p. 28):

1. A series of principles defining the rights and responsibilities of the states (popularly known as **the Rio Declaration on Environment and Development**).
2. A comprehensive programme in all areas of sustainable development for adoption at the global level **(Agenda 21)**.
3. A set of principles to stress the sustainable management of forests worldwide (known as **the Statement of Forest Principles**).

The summit made eco-efficiency a guiding principles for industrial operations both by business firms and governments alike. It covered patterns of production, alternative sources of energy, new reliance on public transportation systems, greater awareness of and control over the growing scarcity of water. Among the **rights and responsibilities** of the member states, defined in Agenda 21, the following are worth mentioning (Ramamoorthy, pp. 28–29):

1. That human beings are at the centre of concerns for sustainable development. They are entitled to a healthy and productive life in harmony with nature.
2. That scientific uncertainty should not delay measures to prevent environmental degradation where there are threats of serious or irreversible damage.
3. That States have a sovereign right to exploit their own resources but not to cause damage to the environment of other States.
4. That eradicating poverty and reducing disparities in worldwide standards of living are 'indispensable' for sustainable development.
5. That full participation of women is essential for achieving sustainable development.
6. That developed countries acknowledge the responsibility that they bear in the international pursuit of sustainable development in view of the pressures their societies place on the global environment and of the technologies and financial resources they command.

Similarly, the statement of Forest Principles was the first global consensus reached on forest management. Its provisions include the following (Ramamoorthy, p. 29):

1. That all countries, notably developed countries, should make an effort to 'green the world' through reforestation and forest conservation.
2. That States have a right to develop forests according to their socio-economic needs, in keeping with national sustainable development policies.
3. That specific financial resources should be provided to develop programmes that encourage economic and social substitution policies.

The Environmental and Development Comprehensive Programme, or **Agenda 21,*** recommends the following action areas:

1. International cooperation to accelerate sustainable development in developing countries and related domestic policies
2. Combating poverty
3. Changing consumption patterns
4. Demographic dynamics and sustainability
5. Protecting and promoting human health conditions
6. Promoting sustainable human settlement development
7. Integrating environment and development in decision-making
8. Protecting the atmosphere
9. Integrated approach to the planning and management of land resources
10. Combating deforestation
11. Managing fragile ecosystems: combating desertification and drought
12. Managing fragile ecosystems: sustainable mountain development
13. Promoting sustainable agriculture and rural development
14. Conservation of biological diversity
15. Environmentally sound management of biotechnology
16. Protection of the oceans, all kinds of seas, including enclosed and semi-enclosed seas, and coastal areas and the protection, rational use and development of their living resources
17. Protection of the quality and supply of freshwater resources: application of integrated approaches to the development, management and use of water resources
18. Environmentally sound management of toxic chemicals, including prevention of illegal international traffic in toxic and dangerous products

---

* www.un.org

19. Environmentally sound management of hazardous wastes including prevention of illegal international traffic in hazardous wastes.
20. Environmentally sound management of solid wastes and sewage related issues.
21. Safe and environmentally sound management of radioactive wastes
22. Global action for women towards sustainable and equitable development
23. Children and youth in sustainable development
24. Recognizing and strengthening the role of indigenous people and their communities
25. Strengthening the role of non-government organizations: partners for sustainable development
26. Local authorities' initiatives in support of Agenda 21
27. Strengthening the role of workers and their trade unions
28. Strengthening the role of business and industry, scientific and technological community
29. Strengthening the role of farmers
30. Financial resources and mechanisms
31. Transfer of environmentally sound technology, cooperation and capacity building
32. Science for sustainable development
33. Promoting education, public awareness and training
34. National mechanisms and international cooperation for capacity building in developing countries
35. International institutional arrangements
36. International legal instruments and mechanisms
37. Information for decision-making.

The Earth Summit succeeded in presenting new perspectives on economic progress. It was considered as the beginning of a new era that was expected to address all relevant issues relating to environment management and integrate environment management issues with economic development for its sustenance.

Since the Rio Summit, the UN has taken many steps to integrate the concepts of sustainable development into relevant policies and programmes. Project evaluation increasingly takes into account environmental consequences to ensure that environment-friendly projects are given preference. Women's role as mothers and caretakers of families is now no longer neglected in selecting appropriate development assistance programmes. Forest management in a sustainable manner is now given more consideration for finding alternatives to meet the needs of the people and stop them from over-exploiting the forests and other natural resources. The moral and social imperatives for alleviating poverty are also given additional urgency by recognizing that poor people can cause extensive damage to the environment. Finally, foreign investment decisions increasingly take into account the fact that using natural resources for short-term profits is not good for business in the long run and that, in the long run, there is no conflict between profitability of a firm and its strategic environment management.

In accordance with the views of the Earth Summit, the UN has established three bodies to ensure the full implementation of Agenda 21 across the world:

1. Inter-agency Committee on Sustainable Development (1992) to ensure effective system-wise cooperation and coordination;
2. UN Commission on Sustainable Development (1993);
3. A high level Advisory Board on Sustainable Development to advise the Secretary General and the Commission on issues concerning the implementation of Agenda 21.

The programmes suggested and the actions taken thereon by various bodies of the UN General Assembly have not only created environmental awareness among national and international bodies, MNCs and others, but also contributed significantly towards the overall guiding goal that *people are entitled to a healthy and productive life in harmony with nature.* The progress made and problems faced by various countries are now monitored on the basis of the annual reports submitted by governments. By 1996, governments of about 100 countries established national sustainable development councils and other such coordinating bodies. More than 2,000 municipal and town governments have formulated local Agenda 21 of their own. Many countries sought legislative approval for sustainable development plans and non-government organizations (NGOs) to get them involved in the process.

3.2.4 The Paris Agreement (COP26[1])

It is a legally binding treaty on Climate Change[2] and is also known as Paris Climate Accords (2016). It was adopted by 196 member-countries of UNO on 12th December, 2015 and signed on 22nd April, 2016 (Google.com). The Agreement was opened for signature on 22nd April, 2016 at a

1 COP stands for Conference of Parties.

2 See Section 3.2.6 (p. 38)

ceremony at New York at the headquarters of UNO. The Agreement came into force on 4th November, 2016. The United States withdrew from the Agreement in 2020 but re-joined in 2021.

The United Nations Framework Convention on Climate Change (UNFCCC) is a long-term agreement, the goal of which is to limit global temperature to well below 2°C (or 35.6° F) above pre-industrial (1860) levels. To achieve this long-term temperature goal, countries aim to reduce global peaking of greenhouse gas emissions as soon as possible to achieve a climate neutral world by 2050.

The Paris Agreement is a landmark in the multilateral climate change process as, for the first time, a binding agreement brings all countries into a common cause to undertake very ambitious efforts to combat climate change and adapt to its effects.

How does the Agreement work?

It requires economic and social transformation on the part of the participating countries. The transformation can be achieved based on the best available science. It works on a five-year-cycle of increasingly ambitious climate action carried out by the participating countries. Countries submit their plans for climate action known as **nationally determined contributions (NDCs).** In their NDCs, countries will communicate actions they will take to reduce their **Greenhouse Gas Emissions** with a view to reaching the goals of the Paris Agreement. Secondly, countries will also communicate in the NDCs actions taken by them to build resilient to adapt to the impact of rising temperatures. Long-term low greenhouse gas emissions development **strategies providing a vision and direction for future development** are to be adopted by the countries. The submission of long-term horizon to the NDCs is however voluntary.

The Agreement also provides a framework for technical, capacity building and financial support to those countries who need them. These may be called the three important arms of the Agreement. A brief outline of each of them is given below:

(i) **Technology:** Technology development and transfer are necessary for both improving resilience to climate change and reducing Greenhouse Gas (GHG) emissions. The Agreement also provides a framework to provide overarching guidance to the well-functioning Technology Mechanism. The mechanism is to accelerate technology development and transfer through its policy implementation arms.

(ii) **Capacity Building:** There must be sufficient capacities to deal with many of the challenges brought by climate change. A large number of the developing countries do not have that kind of capacity. The Agreement, therefore, places great emphasis on climate-related capacity building for developing countries and urges upon the developed countries to increase support for capacity building actions in developing countries.

(iii) **Finance:** Finance is the building block particularly to the developing countries. Without adequate financial support, the implementation of the Agreement will be a far cry because it is required both for technology development and for mitigation of the negative impact of climate. For example, large-scale investments are required to reduce emissions. So, **climate finance** is required for both adaptation and mitigation. Developed countries should contribute *voluntarily* for achieving the goals of the Agreement for those countries who need it badly. So, the Agreement reaffirms that developed countries should take the lead in providing financial assistance to countries that are "less-endowed and more vulnerable".

How to track the progress

Countries have to establish an **Enhanced Transparency Framework (ETF)** with effect from 2024. The *modus operandi* will be as follows:

- Countries will **report transparently** on actions taken and progress in climate change mitigation, adaptation measures and support provided and received.
- It also provides for international procedures for the **review** of the submitted reports.
- The information gathered through ETF will feed into **Global Stocktake** which will assess the collective progress towards the long-term climate goals.
- Based on the above, recommendations will be made for less-active countries to **set more ambitious plans in the next round.**

What are the achievements, so far?

There is no doubt that climate change actions need to be massively increased to achieve the goals of the Paris Agreement. It is satisfying to note that the years since its entry into force have witnessed some progresses, namely:

- Low carbon solutions and new markets;
- More and more countries, cities, regions and also companies are establishing carbon neutrality targets;
- Zero carbon solutions are becoming competitive across economic sectors representing 25% of emissions. This trend is most noticeable in power and transport sectors;
- Many business opportunities have been created for early movers;
- It is estimated that by 2030, zero-carbon solutions could be competitive in sectors representing over 70% of global emissions.

3.2.5 The Climate Summit Held in 2022 (known as COP27)

The climate talks among 195 countries and the EU concluded on Sunday, the 20th November 2022 at Sharm El-Sheik, Egypt. Originally it was planned for a two-day Summit but for reaching consensus on certain key issues, it was extended by one day. At the opening plenary session of the Climate Implementation Summit at COP27, Mr. Antonio Guterres, the Secretary-General of the UNO, called for a historic pact between developed and developing countries to combine capacities, and pivot the world towards reducing carbon emissions, transforming energy systems and avoiding climate catastrophe. He said: "Humanity has a choice: co-operate or perish. It is either a Climate Solidarity Pact or a Collective Suicide Pact".

Some of the key decisions are:

- Countries agree to set up a "loss and damage" fund mainly from contributions of developed countries (the U.S., the EU, Japan, etc.). The purpose is to support developing countries that are vulnerable to extreme weather and are worsened by cumulative emissions of developed nations. The issue of "loss and damage" found place in the Agenda for the first time. The task of setting up a new fund looked difficult but the rich nations (including the US and the EU) showed flexibility to make it happen.
- Institutional arrangements are put in place for averting, minimising and addressing "loss and damage". The Agreement calls for multinational development banks (MDBs) and international financial institutions (IFIs) to reform practices and provisions to ensure simplified access to climate finance. Some of the Asian countries like Bangladesh, India, Indonesia, Nepal and Pakistan are likely to be benefitted out of this "loss and damage" clause.
- Countries to further integrate water into adaptation efforts to increase in protecting, conserving and restoring food security,

agriculture and water-related eco-systems including river basins aquifers and lakes.

- There has been an inclusion of "sustainable life style" in the final COP27 document. As the maintenance of "quality of life" is an important argument for mitigating the negative impact of sustainable environment management, this clause will help giving more attention to the maintenance of sustainable life style.
- Paris Agreement will remain intact, that is, commitments have been reaffirmed.

However, **certain key aspects were not included** in the final decision. They are:

- The countries could not agree to "phase down" all fossil fuels to keep the 1.5°C goal alive to limit global warming. This was one of the very important clauses of Paris Agreement. Both India and the EU nations wanted it to be included in COP27 decision but there was no consensus on this key issue.
- There was no pledge from the participating countries, particularly the developed ones, for new emission reduction targets. This is one of the important measures to keep the global warming within 1.5°C (34.7° F) by 2050.
- There was little additional money that was put on the table. Global climate finance (2019–20) was estimated to be only 32% of annual investment required (ToI, Kolkata, p. 1).

3.2.6 Climate Change and its Impact

(a) **Climate change and its meaning:** In ordinary parlance, the phrase "climate change" means natural shift of weather from one season to the other. Generally, changes take place in four seasons[3] of the year—summer, autumn, winter and spring.

But for the last two centuries, it has wider connotation embracing all nations and all areas of the world. According to United Nations, climate change refers to long-term shifts in temperatures and weather patterns. These shifts may be natural but since 1860s human activities have been the main

3 In Bengali, there are six seasons: *Grisha, Barsa, Sarat, Hemanta, Shit and Basanta*, each comprising a duration of two months. Because of change of climate, there is however wide variation of weather among these seasons even though they work in a cycle of four or six, as the case may be.

drivers of climate change primarily due to burning of fossil fuels like coal, oil and gas which produces heat trapping gases (UNO, 1992). It has now become a matter of great concern to the living beings—people, animals and others. The United Nations has been organising conferences of the nations of the world from time to time to discuss about negative impact of the climate change and suggesting measures, which if implemented by its member nations, will mitigate the impact of adverse impact of climate change.

(b) **Global warming and climate change:** The Scientists and the UNO now prefer to use "climate change" to "global warming". Is there any difference between these two terms? Global warming refers to the long-term warming of the planet. Climate change encompasses global warming but refers to broader range of changes that are happening to our planet including rising sea levels, shrinking mountain glaciers, accelerating ice-melt in Greenland, Antarctica and the Arctic and shifts in flower/plant blooming times.

(c) **Impact of climate change:** What are the adverse or negative impacts of possible climate change? The problem is created because of use of fossil fuels which increase global warming. It does not require to stress that the adverse impact of climate change is multi-dimensional. They include:

- Devastating cyclones, floods, earthquakes and draughts
- A fair proportion of global land being affected due to draught
- Heat-linked deaths particularly among 65+ age-group people
- Loss of labour hours due to heat exposure
- Rise in diseases like malaria, dengue, etc.

The 2022 Global Report of the Lancet Countdown[4] states in its opening paragraph that people around the world are increasingly feeling the negative impact of climate change on their health and wellbeing and these compounding crises are amplifying those harms. Yet governments and companies in both high and low income countries continue to prioritise fossil fuel interests. According to the report:

1. Only 27% of urban centres are classified as moderately green or above.
2. People rely on air conditioning for cooling, which in 2020 was

4 https://lancet countdown report 2022.

responsible for 900 billion tonnes of carbon dioxide emissions, and for 24,000 deaths from $PM_{2.5}$[5] exposure.

3. Human exposure to days of very-high or extremely high fire danger increased in 61% of countries from 2001–2004 to 2018–2021.
4. Heat exposure led to 470 billion potential labour hours lost globally in 2021 with income losses equivalent to substantial proportion of countries GDP.
5. Influence of the climate on the risk of dengue transmission rose by 12% globally in 2012–2021, compared to 1951–1960. Recently many people have been affected by dengue in Asian countries like Bangladesh, India and Malaysia. Similarly, length of time suitable for malaria transmission rose by 32.1% in highland areas of the Americas, and 14.9% in Africa in the same period.
6. Heat-related deaths increased by 68% between 2017 and 2021, compared to 2000–2004.
7. On an average, 29% or more of the global land area was affected by extreme draught annually, from 2012–2021, than from 1951–1960.
8. Children under one year old experienced collectively 600 million more days of heat waves (44 more days per child) in 2012–2021, compared to 1986–2005.

In another International Study on Climate Change in India[6] the damage caused to ecologically crucial but fragile Sunderbans, spread across West Bengal (India) and Bangladesh, has been given. The Sunderbans is home of 7.2 million of some of the world's most vulnerable population. It says:

- Temperature increased 1°C in past century and may increase by up to 3.7°C by 2100.
- From 2000 to 2020, 110 sq. km of mangroves disappeared. The loss of mangroves has made embankments weaker.

According to an analysis by an International Climate Research Agency[7], Sunderbans have suffered losses of more than 2 lakh crore ($25 billion in current exchange rate) in life, property and livelihood in the last four decades because of climate change.

5 $PM_{2.5}$ are tiny particles in the air that reduce visibility and cause the air to appear hazy when levels are elevated (https://health.ny.gov).

6 www.google.com

7 International Panel on Climate Change (IPCC). The IPCC is the United Nations body to assess the science related to climate change.

A staggering 1.6 lakh crore ($20 billion) of the damage occurred in the last three years alone, from four major cyclones. The loss and damage is dominated by damage to the eco-system (₹32,549 crore) and loss in agricultural production, caused by salinity of land and water. It caused extensive loss of land. This has caused 62% of the zone's workforce to lose their original livelihood in the last 25 years and forced 1.5 million of them to move to safer places. Researchers from International Climate Research Agency, Zero Carbon Analytics[8], estimated a loss of ₹27,000 crore in "eco-system services" of the Sunderbans Biosphere Reserve in the last 30 years, over 80% of which is mangroves.

Source: Wikipedia and https://lakshmisharath.com/sundarbans-mangrove-forest-west-bengal/

In the last 23 years, the area has witnessed 13 super-cyclones. In the Bay of Bengal along the Sunderbans, the occurrence of cyclones increased by 26% between 1881 and 2001. Additionally, research has shown that there has been a significant rise in the frequency of very severe cyclones in the post-monsoon season from 2000 to 2018. Scientists project an increase of about 50% in the frequency of post-monsoon cyclones in the period between 2041 and 2060. Interestingly, the Sunderbans bear little responsibility for global emissions. The entire State of Bengal and the whole of Bangladesh together account for only 0.56% of global emissions.

There are many other broader range of changes due to Climate Change that are happening to our planet viz.:

- Rising sea levels

8 Zero Carbon Analytics research and analysis is a valuable resource for writing and reporting on climate change action and impacts, for journalists (www.google.com).

- Shrinking mountain glaciers
- Accelerating ice-melt in Greenland, Antarctica and the Arctic Sea, and
- Shifts in flower/plant blooming times.

As per Third and Fourth National Climate Assessment Reports, future effects of global climate change in the U.S. will be as follows:

- Sea level will rise by 1–8 feet by 2100
- Hurricanes will become stronger and intense
- More draughts and heat waves
- Longer wildfire season
- Changes in precipitation (rain and snow) patterns
- Frost-free season (and growing season) will lengthen affecting eco-system and agriculture
- Arctic is very likely to become ice-free.

The Reports say that, taken as a whole, the range of public evidence indicates that the net damage costs of climate change are likely to be significant and to increase over time.

According to World Meteorological Organisation (WMO)[9], the rise in sea level is very alarming. It has been 4.5 mm per year during 2013–2022. It could continue through this century, recording a total rise of 0.6 metre by 2100, as compared to 1995–22 level, even under the low greenhouse gas (GHG) emissions scenario.

This will affect not only small island nations but also big coastal cities like Shanghai, Dhaka, Bangkok, Jakarta, Mumbai, Mapulo, Lagos, Cairo, London, Copenhagen, New York, Los Angeles, Boeness Aires and Santiago. It is therefore a major economic, social and humanitarian challenge. The WMO in its fact-sheet on the global sea-level rise said that the human influence (activities) was the main driver of the rise in the sea-level ever since 1971 compared to the rise of 1.3 mm per year between 1901–1971. According to WMO, global mean sea-level has risen faster since 1900 than over any preceding century in at least the last 300 years.

The above statistics and estimates should cause sleepless nights to a rational citizen of the world. Accordingly, the leaders and organisations around the globe have meeting periodically under the umbrella of UNO to take both short-term and long-term measures to mitigate the adverse impact of climate change and to reduce greenhouse gas emissions to make the planet worth living. We have already discussed many of them

9 *Times of India*, Kolkata, 15th February 2023, p. 2.

earlier. Now one good example of world-wide growing actions for green technology is given in Section 3.2.7.

3.2.7 Green Hydrogen

Keeping an eye on Climate goals, The Government of India approved on January 4, 2023, the National Green Hydrogen Mission. It is part of India's climate action pledge under the Paris Agreement. The details of the project are given below under separate headings.

(a) **Objectives:** The mission aims to make India a global hub for production, utilisation and export of green hydrogen and its derivatives. This will help the country to become energy independent while taking a big leap towards decarbonisation of major sectors of the economy as part of its long-term goal of carbon neutrality by 2070. Green hydrogen is one of the cleanest sources of energy with close to zero emission.

(b) **Estimated costs[10] of the project:** As announced by the Prime Minister[11] the project cost would be ₹19,774 crore comprising:

Particulars	₹/Crore
Pilot Projects	1,466
Strategic Interventions for Green Hydrogen Transition Programme (SIGHT)	17,490
Research and Development	400
Other related initiatives	388
Total	**19,774**

(c) **Expected outcomes by 2030:** There will be wide ranging benefits out of the successful implementation of the project. As projected, they are:

1. Development of green gas production capacity of at least 5 million metric tonne (MMT) per annum;

10 *Times of India*, Kolkata, January 5, 2023, p. 12.

11 Mr. Narendra Modi, the Prime Minister of India, as President of the Science Congress, in his virtual talk to the 108th Science Congress, held at Nagpur, mentioned various aspects of the Green Hydrogen on 4th January 2023.

2. An associated renewable energy capacity addition of 125 GW
3. Over ₹8 lakh crore in total investments with ancillary benefits
4. Creation of over 6 lakh jobs
5. Cumulative reduction of fossil fuel imports by over ₹1 lakh crore
6. Abatement of nearly 50 MMT of annual greenhouse gas emissions.

In general, the benefits to the economy will be wide ranging. The following sectors of the economy will be benefited:

- Energy intensive industries, such as, steel, chemicals and cement
- Transport sector, such as, automobiles, heavy duty vehicles, rail[12] and maritime
- Power sector.

The use of green hydrogen will facilitate decarbonising energy-intensive sectors. Consequently, it will improve air quality and mitigate carbon emissions.

(d) **The process and costs:** The grey hydrogen uses natural gas for production. But the green hydrogen is produced by the electrolysis of water using renewable energy. It does not therefore emit carbon dioxide into the atmosphere.

Electrolysis is the process of using electricity to split water into hydrogen and oxygen. This reaction takes place in a unit called an electrolyser.

The costs of green hydrogen production currently in India ranges from \$320 to \$330 per kg. It is likely to fall by half to as low as \$160–170 per kg by 2030 as per a KPMG study[13].

(e) **International position:** The production of green hydrogen is surging ahead worldwide because it is the fuel of the future. It is a good sign that many countries are taking efforts to contribute to their pledge to reduce greenhouse gas emissions and improve quality of life. Australia, China and Gulf countries can become regions of green hydrogen export.

12 By the end of 2023, pollution-free hydrogen-run trains would be ready. West Bengal to get India's first hydrogen train on the Darjeeling heritage route (*Times of India*, Kolkata, February 4, 2023, p. 5).

13 https//www.fortuneIndia.com.macro.>green-hydrogen>

Number of green hydrogen production as of 2022 by many countries[14] are given in the table below:

Country	*Number of plants*
Australia	96
Germany	50
Spain	50
Netherlands	48
United Kingdom	46
United States	37
Russia	36
Portugal	28
China	26
Chile	22

Source: N. Sonnichsen, June 2, 2022.

In India, state-owned Oil India Ltd. commissioned India's first 99.9 per cent pure green hydrogen plant in Jorhat, Assam. Reliance India (Adani Group) started in 2022. Tata Engineering Company is stepping up its focus on the green hydrogen market, as the need for non-fossil-fuel gathers pace in the country. In some companies, research and development efforts are going on for a reduction in the cost of production, storage and transportation of hydrogen.

3.2.8 Stepping up Green Energy Towards Net-zero Emission[15]

There are certain proposals in the Union Budget that are expected to push the green energy resulting in net-zero emission by 2030, as per claim of the Finance Minister, Ms. Nirmala Sitaraman, in her budget speech. A few important aspects of the proposals are given below:

---

14 https://www.hydrogeninsight.com/production/exclusive

15 In the Union Budget (2023–2024), *Times of India,* Kolkata, February 2, 2023, p. 10. Readers may compare the actual numbers from government and other sources to ascertain as to what extent budget proposals have been implemented.

1. The aim of achieving 5 million tonne annual green hydrogen production capacity by 2030 has been set.
2. GST-paid bio-gas used for blending in CNG (compressed natural gas) has been exempted from excise duty to promote bio-gas projects that have a positive bearing on waste management in cities and potential to create rural earning avenues.
3. Viability Gap Funding (VGF) of ₹8,000 crore for the proposed ₹20,700 crore transmission line for evacuating power from the proposed 13 GW solar-wind battery storage project in Ladakh. The support will reduce the transmission tariff and breathe life into the expected showstopper renewable project that has the potential to change the socio-economic scenario in the region.
4. The Budget also focussed on bio-fuels by reducing customs duty on denatured ethyl alcohol to improve availability by blending 20% ethanol—petrol blended with ethyl alcohol—and flex engines with the aim of reducing automotive emission.
5. The 'green credit programme' under the Environment (Protection) Act will incentivise environmentally sustainable and responsive actions by companies, individuals and local bodies and help mobilise additional resources for such activities in tune with India's pitch for LiFE (lifestyle for environment) both domestically and globally. The programme granting credit for cleaner actions seeks to encourage behavioural change in the country as India has been strongly advocating for an "environmentally conscious lifestyle".
6. The PM Programme for Restoration, Awareness, Nourishment and Amelioration of Mother Earth (PM-PRANAM) will be launched to incentivise States and Union Territories to promote alternative fertilisers and balanced use of chemical fertilisers. Besides, the Government will facilitate 1 crore farmers to adopt natural (chemical pesticide/fertilisers-free) farming over the next three years. PM-Pranam can be a major step towards saving soil nutrients which are adversely affected by excessive use of fertilisers and pesticides. For this, 10,000 bio-input resource centres will be set up, creating a national-level distributed micro-fertiliser and pesticide manufacturing network.

3.2.9 Climate Change: Effects to be Part of Medical School Syllabus and in Others

It is reported[16] that the National Centre for Disease Control (NCDC) is working with various medical councils to introduce concepts, such as rising heat and damaging air quality and their effects, in medical education and the training of medical personnel in India. The NCDC has roped in the National Medical Council, the Dental Council, Ayush, the Nursing Council and the Pharmacy Council, among others, for this purpose.

Medical Schools will also have to teach students about environmental health—a decades-old plea that has unfortunately been ignored so far. The "goal is to address the reality that our altering climate conditions are affecting people's health and our medical professionals need to recognise this".

We should also be equally concerned with syllabus of undergraduate levels and graduate levels of arts, science and business education in India. It is time now, better late than never, to sensitize young generation about not only climate change and its adverse impacts but also how as a responsible citizen they can make their positive contributions towards maintenance and improvement of quality of life.

At the undergraduate level, there should be at least one paper on climate change covering conceptual, factual and preventive aspects to make the young generation aware about the nature of the problem and their adverse impacts and also measures to combat them to the extent possible. At the graduation levels, an advanced course should be developed and implemented. This course should include, among others, climate finance and its management, accounting for climate change, impact of measures suggested by the United Nations, measures adopted by the member-countries, setting up of climate fund at the national level and its management, to mention a few. The course curricula should also have a module on Project Work. In the Appendix (pp. 225–228), two possible course curricula have been suggested.

3.3 INTERNATIONAL ENVIRONMENTAL LAWS

Some advanced economies have enacted legislations to prevent environmental degradation and uphold the quality of life. In this section, we will briefly discuss some relevant legislations in the US, Norway, Germany, Japan and the European Union.

16 *Times of India*, Kolkata, February 15, 2023, p. 2.

The **US Congress** passed the Comprehensive Environmental Response, Compensation and Liability Act, better known as the **Superfund**, in 1980. Under this Act, the Environmental Protection Agency (EPA) is an independent environmental body with significant power. The Act requires the corporations to report potentially toxic spills and releases exceeding a clearly defined minimum. There are stringent penalties (both fines and imprisonment) for violation. The Act also deals with uncontrolled hazardous waste sites where previous or present owners and operators of the sites must take any remedial action deemed necessary. If the previous operator has gone out of business, the EPA can obtain funds from corporations that sent the waste there for treatment or disposal in the first instance.

The US Government has formulated some of the most extensive regulations relating to disclosure of environmental management information. The accounting regulations in the USA are enforced through the Securities and Exchange Commission (SEC) formed under the federal securities legislation. The SEC has issued a large number of statements having regulations and opinions on accounting matters, especially in its 'Accounting Series Releases'. Regulation S-K governs the form and content of financial statements filed with the SEC by the registered companies. Form 10-K must be filed annually by each registered company to the SEC. Regulation S-K specifies the contents of the items required by Form 10-K (Most, K.S., 1986). Regulation S-K includes three requirements that may involve environmental disclosures. These are:

Item 101: Description of Business: It requires the disclosure of any material effects of compliance with environmental laws, the amount of required environmentally related capital expenditures and the effect upon profitability and competitive position.

Item 103: Legal Proceedings: Disclosure of relevant litigation of potential sanctions that exceed $100,000 or 10% of current assets and capital expenditure likewise that exceeds 10% of current assets (Price Waterhouse, 1992).

Item 303: Management's Discussion and Analysis (MD&A): Any known trends, demands, commitments, events or uncertainties that are likely to affect liquidity should be mentioned.

The main accounting rules that apply in the above context are contained in SFAS-5, Accounting for Contingencies, and FIN-14, Reasonable Estimate of the Amount of a Loss. Along with the above, the provisions of the Comprehensive Environmental Response, Compensation and Liability (CERCLA) or Superfund Act of 1980 require companies to clean up both existing and previous sites which are on the national priority list as posing serious environmental risks declared by the Environmental Protection Agency. The potential responsible parties for the damage of sites, such as waste generator, transporter, manager or operator of the site, are held severally and jointly liable for all the costs of investigation, remediation, and monitoring of the site. Thus, the above requirements will have far-reaching impact on the disclosure of information of environmentally related capital expenditures, their effect on profitability, the competitive position of the business, contingent liability relating to litigation of potential sanctions that exceed certain specified amount, demand, uncertainties and commitments that are likely to affect liquidity of the company.

In **Norway**, there is a requirement for disclosure of certain non-financial information in the Directors' Report.

> If the company has more than 10 employees, the annual report shall describe the working conditions, and review the measures that have been implemented in this field. The annual report shall also state whether the business pollutes the external environment, and review any measures that have been implemented or are being planned to counteract such pollution (Choi, 2003).

In some countries, there are a number of voluntary industry specific guidelines (e.g., for chemical industry in **Germany**) on environmental accounting and reporting. In **Japan**, 10-point Environmental Guidelines have been issued for companies that are operating outside Japan. These guidelines focus largely on environmentally related activities. Two of the 10 points on information disclosure are as follows:

(i) Provide the local community with information on environmental measures on a regular basis.

(ii) Actively publicize, both at home and abroad, the activities of overseas businesses that reflect our activities showing an environmental consideration.

A wide range of supranational bodies have issued guidelines on reporting. Some examples are:

- United Nations Environmental Programme, 1972
- European Union's 5th Action Programme in March, 1992
- Environmental Management and Audit Scheme, 1993

- International Chamber of Commerce (Business Charter for Sustainable Development), 1991
- World Industry Council, 1993
- World Business Council for Sustainable Development, 1995
- Public Environmental Reporting Initiative formed by some of the big North American Companies in 1993.

By and large, these guidelines call for quantified information on global activities and they clearly recognize that environmental impacts are the concern, not only of shareholders but of other users of corporate accounts as well.

3.4 ENVIRONMENTAL LAWS IN INDIA

In India, many acts have been enacted to implement the decisions reached at the UN Conference on Human Environment held in 1972 at Stockholm. Article 253 of the Constitution of India gives Parliament the power to enact laws on virtually on any matter arising out of international treaty, agreement, convention or conference. It states:

> ... The Parliament has power to make any law for the whole or any part of the territory of India for implementing any treaty, agreement or convention with any other country or countries or any decision made at any international conference, association or other body (Basu, 2001, p. 1174).

The following laws have been enacted in conformity with the above provisions:

- Article 48A and Article 51A(g) of the Constitution (through 42nd Amendment, 1976)
- The Water (Prevention and Control of Pollution) Laws Act, 1977
- The Forest (Conservation) Act, 1980
- The Air (Prevention and Control of Pollution) Act, 1981
- The Environment Protection Act, 1986.

Nevertheless, India had enacted a number of legislations even prior to the Stockholm Conference. Also, in some other legislations, there were certain provisions relating to the management of environment. The following are some examples:

- The Indian Forests Act, 1927
- The Factories Act, 1948
- The Atomic Energy Act, 1962

- The Insecticides Act, 1958
- The Wildlife (Protection) Act, 1972
- The Water (Prevention and Control of Pollution) Act, 1974.

Therefore, it cannot be said that all environmental legislations in India took place only after the Stockholm Conference. But, certainly, the agreements arrived at the Stockholm Conference paved the way for increasing the environmental awareness and emboldened the process of environment management among many member countries of the UN General Assembly. India is a glaring example of this.

In view of the above developments, we will now discuss the issues of environmental laws in India under three heads: (i) Administrative structure, (ii) Constitutional laws, and (iii) Other laws.

3.4.1 Administrative Structure

In November 1980, the Government of India set up a Department of Environment to recognize that environmental conservation contributes to sustainable development. Since January 1985, the Department has become part of the Ministry of Environment and Forests. In September 1985, the said Department was renamed as Department of Environment, Forests and Wildlife. The Department is playing the role of a watchdog and serves as a *nodal agency* in the administrative structure of the government for integrating environmental concerns in the planning process (Ramamoorthy, p. 38). It facilitates planning, promotion and co-ordination of environmental and forestry programmes.

The Ministry at the Centre created, in turn, the Departments of Environment at the State level to control pollution caused by industrial activities in various States. The statutory responsibilities for pollution control are implemented through the Central Board for the Prevention and Control of Water Pollution. Similarly, many State Governments have created their own Pollution Control Boards which control industrial pollution in the respective States.

The Central Board for Prevention and Control of Water Pollution and the State Pollution Control Boards look after the implementation of the government policy in respect of improvement of water and air quality in the country. Minimal National Standards (MNS) for pollution discharges in respect of different industry groups have been formulated for compliance. Manufacturing industries are classified into three groups—red, yellow and green. The *red category* pollutes the environment to the maximum extent, while *green category* is environment-friendly and the *yellow category* occupies a place between the two. For red category industries, more frequent monitoring, more strict compliance schedule, etc., are observed.

To prevent water pollution, the Government of India adopted the Ganga Action Plan under the Central Ganga Authority (CGA), under the chairmanship of the Prime Minister, and approved ₹304.26 crore during the Seventh Five Year Plan for numerous schemes in 27 cities of UP, Bihar and West Bengal. Many schemes in different cities of the three states have already been implemented and many more are in the process of execution.

3.4.2 Constitutional Laws

Earlier, we have referred to Article 253 of the Constitution that gives Parliament power to enact laws for giving effects to international agreements. Articles 48A and 51A(g) are also important environmental laws. Environmental protection and improvement were explicitly incorporated into the Constitution by the 42nd Constitution Amendment Act, 1976.

Article 48A was added to the Directive Principles[17] of State Policy. It states:

> The state shall endeavour to protect and improve the environment and to safeguard the forests and wildlife of the country.

Article 51A(g) in a new chapter entitled 'Fundamental Duties' stipulates responsibility on every citizen. It states:

> It shall be the duty of every citizen of India:
>
> ...to protect and improve the natural environment including the forests, lakes, rivers and wildlife, and to have compassion for living creatures.

It may be observed that the provisions made in the above-mentioned two articles underscore the national consensus on the importance of environmental protection and improvement.

The 42nd Constitution Amendment Act also expanded the Concurrent List by introducing a new entry 'Population Control and Family Planning' and bringing in 'Forests' and 'Preservation of Wild Animals and Birds' from the State List. The latter subjects, namely, 'Forests', etc., relate to natural resources. Therefore, the expansion of the concurrent powers by the

---

17 The Directive Principles are policy prescriptions that guide the Government. Although not enforceable in a court of law, these Principles are increasingly being cited by the judiciary as being complementary to the fundamental rights.

42nd Amendment only made the powers that Parliament already possessed explicit under Article 253.

There are also some important judicial pronouncements which have a direct impact on environmental management and compliance.

Protection of environment and fundamental rights

Article 21 of the Constitution enshrines fundamental right to life and personal liberty of the citizens. It states:

> No person shall be deprived of his life or personal liberty except according to procedure established by law.

The Supreme Court of India expanded Article 21 of the Constitution to include environmental protection. It interpreted the right to life and personal liberty to include 'the right to wholesome environment'. This view was upheld by the Court in a number of writ petitions filed under Article 32 of the Constitution. Some such petitions are mentioned below:

1. **In July 1983,** representatives of the Rural Litigation and Enlistment Kendra, Dehradun, wrote to the Supreme Court alleging that illegal mining of limestone in the Mussoorie-Dehradun Region was destroying the fragile 'ecosystems' of the area. The Court accepted the letter as a writ petition and ordered the closure of polluting units [known as the Ganga Pollution (Tanneries) Case] on the ground of violation of Article 21 due to the limestone mining activities and observed that "closure of tanneries may bring unemployment, loss of revenue, but *life, health and ecology* have greater importance to the people". (AIR, 1988, SC 1048).
2. In *R.L. & E. Kendra* v. *State of UP*, the Supreme Court entertained environmental complaints alleging that the operations of limestone quarries in the Himalayan range of Mussoorie resulted in the degradation of environment affecting ecological balance and ordered the closure of some of these quarries (AIR, 1985, SC 652). Although Article 21 was not referred to in this judgement, there was no doubt that the Supreme Court entertained the complaints under Article 32 as involving violation of right to life as enshrined in Article 21 (Ramamoorthy, p. 36).
3. Several High Courts, e.g., the High Courts of Rajasthan, Kerala and Himachal Pradesh, decided similar cases in favour of the petitioners on the ground that environmental degradation violates the fundamental right to life (AIR, 1988 RAJ 2, 4; KER LT 730, 731, 1988; AIR 1988 HP 4,9).

The above and many other similar case laws on degradation of environment have given additional arms in the hands of the Pollution Control Boards in the exercise of their administrative authority in protecting environment and introducing stiffer penalties for the violating industrial enterprises. Now, the Pollution Control Boards may close down a defaulting industrial plant or may stop supply of electricity or water to such unit for violation of environmental norms. The Boards may also seek court's intervention to restrain emissions that exceed the prescribed limits.

3.4.3 Other Laws

In this category, we will discuss a few important environmental laws relating to forest management, conditions of work in manufacturing units, nuclear energy and radioactive substances, use of pesticides, protection of wildlife, enforcing effluent standards on factories discharging pollutants into water bodies and management of air pollution, etc.

1. *The Indian Forests Act, 1927*

The Act deals with four categories of forests:

(i) Reserved forests
(ii) Village forests
(iii) Protected forests
(iv) Non-government (or private) forests.

A state may declare forest lands or wastelands as **reserved forests** and may sell the produce from these forests. A reserved forest assigned to a village community is called a **village forest**. Any unauthorized cutting of trees, quarrying, grazing and hunting in reserved forests carries punishment with a fine or imprisonment or both. The Act has empowered the state governments to designate protected forests and to prohibit the cutting of trees, quarrying and the removal of forest produce from these forests. **Protected forests** are preserved through enforcement of rules and licences. Any violation of the rules is a criminal offence.

For administration of the Forests Act, 1927, there are forest officers under the forest department/ministry. These officers have administrative and quasi-judicial powers for protecting forests for maintaining ecological balance. Being concerned with deforestation and the resulting degradation of environment in the country, the Government of India enacted Forest (Conservation) Act, 1980. The Act was amended in 1988. According to the Act, a state has to seek approval of the Central Government before it 'dereserves' a reserved forest, uses forest land for non-forest purposes, assigns forest land to a private person or corporation, or clears forest land for the purpose of reforestation. An Advisory Committee constituted under the Act advises the Central Government in the matter of approval as mentioned above.

2. *The Factories Act, 1948*

The object of the Factories Act is to regulate the conditions of work in manufacturing enterprises coming within the definition of the term 'factory' as per the Act (Sen and Mitra, 2000, p. 5). There are provisions relating to health of workers (Sections 11–20), safety of workers (Sections 21 to 41) and welfare of workers (Sections 42–50). The Act empowers the state governments to appoint inspectors who enjoy powers under Section 9 to examine the premises, plant and machinery or exercise such other power for administration of health, safety and welfare of the workers. Every District Magistrate is an inspector of the district.

Based on the judgement of the Supreme Court in the *Shriram Gas Leak Case* (AIR 1987, SC 965), the Amendment Act, 1987, introduced in the Factories Act special provisions on hazardous industrial activities. The 1987 Amendment Act empowers the state governments to appoint Site Appraisal Committees to advise on the initial location of factories using hazardous processes. The factory inspector and the local authority keep a close watch on all the particulars regarding health hazards at the factory and the preventive measures taken thereof. The Amendment Act defines 'occupier' as a senior level manager who is responsible for compliance with the new provisions for hazardous processes. Section 7A prescribes the general duties of the occupier in regard to the health, safety and welfare of the workers in the factory. Section 7–4(1) requires that every occupier shall ensure, as far as reasonably possible, the health, safety and welfare of all workers while they are at work in the factory. There are stiffer penalties for non-compliance.

The permissible limits of exposure to toxic substances are prescribed in the Second Schedule of the Act. Safety Committees, comprising managers and workers, have to monitor and review periodically the factory's safety measures.

3. *The Atomic Energy Act, 1962*

The regulation of nuclear energy and radioactive substances is governed by the Atomic Energy Act, 1962 and the Radiation Protection Rules, 1971, respectively. The Central Government is responsible for preventing radiation hazards, guaranteeing public safety and the safety of workers handling radioactive substances and the disposal of radioactive wastes. The Government also has the authority on nuclear research, manufacture and transport of radioactive substances, and the production and supply of atomic energy and nuclear-generated electricity. In order to maintain secrecy of nuclear activities in the country, the Government is empowered to withhold 'restricted information' from the public. Such 'restricted information' may include information relating to nuclear research, the theory, design, construction and operation of nuclear reactors and of industrial plants that produce radioactive substances and information regarding the location, quality, quantity, processing, acquisition and disposal of radioactive substances.

4. *The Insecticides Act, 1968*

The use of insecticides has detrimental effects on the natural resources of the environment. The Act, accordingly, regulates the manufacture and distribution of insecticides, and violation of the provisions of the Act carries prosecution and penalties. The Insecticides Rules, 1971, prescribe the procedure for licensing, packaging, labelling and transporting insecticides. Workers' safety during the manufacture and handling of insecticides through protective clothing, respiratory devices, and medical facilities is also taken care of.

5. *The Wildlife (Protection) Act, 1972*

Based on the enabling resolutions of 11 states under Article 252(1)[18], the Government of India enacted in 1972 the Wildlife (Protection) Act which regulates

- hunting wild animals and birds,
- establishment of sanctuaries and national parks, and
- trading in wild animals, animal products and trophies.

The Act provides for wildlife advisory boards at the state level, and is administered through wardens and their staff. The Act prohibits causing harm to endangered species (listed in Schedule I) throughout India. The Act also regulates, through licensing, hunting other species that require special protection (Schedule II), big game (Schedule III) and small game (Schedule IV). There is no restriction on hunting of a few species classified as vermin (Schedule V).

---

18 It empowers the Government of India to enact laws for two or more States on State subjects where the state legislatures have consented to such legislation.

The 1982 Amendment Act introduced provisions that permit the capture and transportation of wild animals for scientific management of animal populations.

6. *The Water (Prevention and Control of Pollution) Act, 1974*

The object of the Act is to establish and enforce effluent standards for factories discharging pollutants into water bodies. Both the State Boards and the Central Board are empowered to fulfil the objectives. The Central Board discharges its functions in the union territories and coordinates activities of different states. The State Boards function within the respective states to control sewage and industrial effluent discharges by approving, rejecting or conditioning applications for consent to discharge. The State Boards have to advise the respective state governments on appropriate sites for new industries with a view to minimizing water pollution. The Act also authorized the State Boards to initiate criminal proceedings against the polluters. The Amendment Act, 1988 further strengthened its implementation provisions by giving administrative power to the State Boards to close a defaulting industrial plant or withdraw supply of power or water for violation of the provisions. Provision for filing of suit by citizens and stringent penalties for polluters have further bolstered the enforcement machinery.

In order to meet the expenses of the Central and State Water Boards, the Water (Prevention and Control of Pollution) Cess Act, 1977, was passed to enforce payment of tax for water consumption by local authorities and certain designated industries. The revenues collected through the Cess Act are used for enforcement of the Water Act. The Central Government distributes the revenues (net of expenses for collection) to the Central and State Water Boards. The Cess Act also makes a provision for a 70% rebate on the applicable cess to an industrial unit for making investment in effluent treatment equipment.

7. *The Air (Prevention and Control of Pollution) Act, 1981*

To reduce the detrimental effect of air pollution on the health of the people and animal life, the Government of India enacted the Air (Prevention and Control of Pollution) Act, 1981. The legislation of the Air Act empowers the Central and State Boards to have an integrated approach to the management of environmental problems. According to this Act, all industries operating within the designated air pollution control areas must obtain a 'consent' (permit) from the respective State Boards. The emission standards of industry and automobiles are required to be prescribed by the States in consultation with the Central

Board after taking into account its ambient air quality standards. The Act was amended in 1987 to further bolster the enforcement machinery.

8. *The Environmental Protection Act, 1986*

The Bhopal Gas Tragedy might have motivated the Central Government to enact a comprehensive piece of legislation, viz., The Environment Protection Act, 1986, for protection and improvement of the human environment and the prevention of hazards to human beings, wildlife, plants and property. The Act also facilitates the coordination of the activities of various Central and State authorities established under the Wildlife Act, the Water Act, and the Air Act. The Environment Protection Act empowers the Central Government to take all such measures as it deems necessary or expedient for:

- protecting and improving the quality of the environment, and
- preventing, controlling and abating environmental pollution.

'Environment', as defined in the Act, includes "water, air, land and the interrelationships which exist among these, and human beings, and other living creatures, plants, microorganisms and property" [Section 2(a)]. 'Environment Pollution' is the presence of any environmental pollutant defined as any solid, liquid, gaseous substance present in such concentration as may be, or may tend to be, injurious to environment [Sections 2(b) and (c)]. According to Section 2(e), 'hazardous substances' include any substance or preparation, which may cause harm to human beings, other living creatures, plants, microorganisms, property or the environment.

The Central Government is empowered to set new national standards for the quality of the environment as well as standards for air emissions and effluent discharges. The Department of Environment, Forests and Wildlife under the Ministry of Environment and Forests is empowered to make rules to implement the Environment (Protection) Act. Actions taken by the Department for implementation of the Act include the following:

(i) Adoption of industry-specific standards for effluent discharge and emissions for 21 designated industries.

(ii) Prescription of general effluent standards for other water polluters.

(iii) Identification of specific laboratories for testing samples of air, water and soil.

(iv) Designating central and state officials to carry out specified duties.

The Act also empowers the Department to make *Rules* from time to time for better administration of the Act. Accordingly, the Department has issued the following Rules:

(i) The Hazardous Wastes (Management and Handling) Rules (July, 1989) to regulate the handling and disposal of hazardous wastes through 'permit'.

(ii) The Manufacture, Storage and Import of Hazardous Chemical Rules (November, 1989) to fix up responsibilities, i.e., identification of major accident hazards, taking adequate preventive measures, submitting a safety report to the designated authority, etc., of those handling hazardous substances (other than hazardous wastes).

(iii) The Environment (Protection) Rules, 1986 (amended in December, 1989) to prescribe ambient air quality standards in respect of noise.

Thus, the scope of the Environment (Protection) Act is very broad and it empowers the Central Government to establish standards for the quality of the environment in its various aspects—air, water, noise—to protect public health and welfare. Under the Rule, the Central Government may prohibit or restrict the location of any industry and the operation of certain activities in the notified areas. The Act prohibits the discharge of environmental pollutants in excess of prescribed regulatory limits and makes provisions for stringent punishment for the violators. The provision that authorizes 'any person' to file a complaint with a court alleging an offence, has strengthened its enforcement.

9. *The Companies Act, 2013*

In India, regulations on disclosure of environmental information in annual accounts are minimal. Section 134(3)(m) of the Companies Act, 2013, states that the Directors' Report shall include particulars as to "The conservation of energy, technology absorption, foreign exchange earnings and outgo" in the prescribed manner. The Government of India accordingly prescribed Rules as follows:

> Rule 8(3). The Report of the Board shall contain the following information and details, namely:
>
> **(A) Conservation of energy:**
>
> (i) the steps taken or impact on conservation of energy;
>
> (ii) the steps taken by the company for utilising alternate sources of energy;
>
> (iii) the capital investment on energy conservation equipments.

The Government also specified 21 industry groups which should furnish information in Form A. Thus, to comply with the provisions of Section 134(3)(m) a company, falling within the 21 industry groups, has to disclose information in Form A, as part of Directors' Report, with respect mainly to conservation of energy (see Appendix). These requirements are no longer in the Companies Act, 2013. There is no provision for disclosure, in the annual reports, of the value of assets acquired for prevention of pollution, if any, and depreciation thereof, contingent liabilities arising out of actions of the Pollution Control Board or those of the government or the judicial forum.

SUMMARY

In this Chapter, we have analysed the need for environmental regulation, and also briefly discussed some of the important international developments leading to environmental treaties/agreements and legislations in different parts of the globe in general, and in India in particular. In the Indian context, a brief account of the present administrative structure for monitoring and ensuring compliance, provisions of the Constitution, protection of environment and fundamental rights, salient features of some important environmental laws including the provisions of the Companies Act, 2013 with respect to disclosure of environmental information in the Director's Report has also been given.

MULTIPLE CHOICE QUESTIONS

1. Financial Accounting System became the subject of much criticism during a period prior of regulation by Government and professional institute on may grounds such as:
   (a) Lack of uniformity
   (b) Multiplicity of accounting practices
   (c) Emergence of social accounting
   (d) All of the above
2. Why do we need environmental regulations? Which of the following is not the correct answer in this context?
   (a) To create pressure that motivates companies to innovate
   (b) To win prizes from different bodies
   (c) To mitigate the impact of pollution
   (d) To improve environmental quality in order to improve quality of life
3. The Stockholm Conference was the first global environmental conference organised by the United Nations. Select the correct answer from the following:

(a) It was held in 1972
(b) It was held in 1982
(c) It was held in 1992
(d) It was held in 2002

4. Many international environmental conferences were organised by the United Nations over several decades. Find the correct match from the following pairs:

Name of the conference	*City in which it was organised*
(a) First Global Conference (1972)	Paris
(b) The Earth Summit (1992)	Stockholm
(c) COP26	London
(d) Climate Summit (2022)	Egypt

5. The Paris Agreement on Climate Change provides a framework that includes:
   (a) Technology
   (b) Capacity building
   (c) Finance
   (d) All of the above
6. The Secretary-General of UNO said during the Opening Convention of COP27 (2022) that:
   (a) Member countries will have adequate freedom to go ahead as they like
   (b) They have to co-operate to flourish
   (c) They are not required to reduce the carbon emissions
   (d) Developing countries need to set-up "loss and damage fund"
7. Whic of the following is not happening to the planet due to climate change?
   (a) Rising sea levels
   (b) Shrinking mountain glaciers
   (c) Shorter wildfire season
   (d) Shifts in flower/plant blooming times
8. According to the 2022 Global Report of the Lancet Countdown, the impact of climate change includes the following *except:*
   (a) Only 27% of urban centres are classified as moderately green or above
   (b) Increase in risk of dengue transmission
   (c) Increase in heat-related deaths
   (d) Increase in agricultural production
9. In Sunderbans, the home of millions of world's most vulnerable population, people are facing many problems due to Climate Change. Which of the following is not true?
   (a) Afforestation of mangroves
   (b) Rise in temperature
   (c) Huge losses in life, property and livelihood
   (d) Forced movement of millions of people to safer places due to four cyclones in last three years

10. Green Hydrogen Gas will be beneficial for the following sectors *except:*
    (a) Steel, chemical and cement
    (b) Power sector
    (c) Transport sector
    (d) Dairy sector
11. Which of the following is not a correct match in respect of production of Green Hydrogen gas as of 2022?

Name of the country	*No. of plants*
(a) USA	37
(b) Russia	46
(c) Australia	56
(d) China	26

12. Rule 8(3) framed under Section 134(3)(m) of the Companies Act, 2013 provides that an enlisted company must furnish in its annual report the following *except:*
    (a) Promotion of exports
    (b) Conservation of energy
    (c) Technology absorption
    (d) New capital outlay for production

EXERCISES

1. Why do we need environmental regulations?
2. Give a regulatory framework influencing supply of financial statement information in India.
3. The Stockholm Conference (1972) on environmental issues adopted a "declaration" consisting of, among others, 26 'principles'. Among them, Principle 17 and Principle 25 relate to environmental concerns. Briefly state them.
4. What is sustainable development? What are the 'rights and responsibilities' of the member countries, as defined in Agenda 21 of Earth Summit?
5. What are included in the Environmental and Developmental Comprehensive Programmes (Agenda 21) of Earth Summit? Enumerate ten of them.
6. "The Earth Summit succeeded in presenting new perspectives on economic development". Elaborate the statement.
7. Why would you consider Paris Agreement as a landmark in the multilateral climate change process? How does the Agreement work?
8. "Technology development and transfer are necessary for both improving resilience to climate change and reducing Greenhouse Gas emissions". Elucidate the statement.
9. How would you track the progress of Paris Agreement? Are there any achievements?
10. "Humanity has a choice: co-operate or perish. It is either a Climate Solidarity Pact or a Collective Suicide Pact". Examine the statement and give your views.

11. State some key aspects that were not included in the final decision of COP27. Enumerate them.
12. What do you understand by "Climate Change"? How would you distinguish between "Global Warming" and "Climate Change"?
13. What are the negative impacts of climate change? As per the 2022 Global Report of the Lancet Countdown, enumerate five negative impacts of climate change.
14. Sunderbans, spread across West Bengal (India) and Bangladesh, have been facing problems of sever nature due to climate change. Mention any five of them.
15. What are the future effects of climate change in the U.S. as per Third and Fourth National Climate Assessment Reports?
16. What do you understand by green hydrogen? State the estimated costs in detail of Green Hydrogen Project approved by the Government of India.
17. What are the expected outcomes of Green Hydrogen Project approved by Government of India in 2023.
18. State the present international position of production of green hydrogen gas.
19. Which are the companies in India that are going for production of green hydrogen gas? Give a brief account of them.
20. For environmental disclosure in the annual accounts of a registered company in the U.S., Regulation S-K includes three requirements. State them in detail.
21. In Japan, 10-point Environmental Guidelines have been issued for companies that are operating outside the country. Mention two of them that relate to environmental information disclosure.
22. State the provisions of Article 253 of the Constitution of India that gives Parliament power to enact laws virtually on any matter arising out of international treaty, agreement, convention or conference.
23. India has enacted a number of legislations prior to and after the Stockholm Conference where there are some provisions relating to management of environment. Enumerate them. Do you think the Stockholm Conference paved the way for increasing the environmental awareness? Explain.
24. State the provisions of Article 21 of the Constitution of India. How did the Supreme Court of India expand Article 21 to include environmental protection?
25. Why was the Air (Prevention and Control of Pollution) Act, 1981 enacted? State its principal objects and modus operandi.
26. "The Environment Protection Act, 1986 is a comprehensive piece of legislation in India". Elaborate the statement and state the main actions taken by the Ministry of Environment and Forests for implementation of the Act.
27. What are the main provisions of the Companies Act, 2013 regarding environmental information to be included in the annual accounts of a company enlisted to a Stock Exchange?

28. Examine the provisions of Rule 8(3) framed under Section 134(m) of the Companies Act, 2013 regarding technology absorption and foreign exchange earnings and outgo.
29. Schedule under Rule 8(3), framed under Section 134(3)(m) of the Companies Act, gives a list of 21 industries which should furnish information in Form A. Enumerate them.
30. Write short notes on the following:
    (a) COP27
    (b) Paris Agreement
    (c) Greenhouse Gas
    (d) Green Hydrogen Gas
31. In the Union Budget (2023–24) several proposals have been made for improvement of environment in India. State them in brief.

REFERENCES

Case Laws

AIR, 1985, SC 652

AIR, 1987, SC 965

AIR, 1988, RAJ 2, 4

KER LT 730, 731, 1988

AIR, 1988 HP 4, 9

Banerjee, Bhabatosh, *Regulation of Corporate Accounting and Reporting in India*, The World Press, Kolkata, 2002, p. 11.

Banerjee, Bhabatosh, *Financial Policy and Management Accounting*, 9th ed., PHI Learning, New Delhi, 2017, p. 614.

Chakravorty, D.K., *Development of Corporate Reporting in India*, Venus Publishing House, New Delhi, 1994.

Dasgupta, N., *Financial Reporting in India*, Sultan Chand & Sons, New Delhi, 1977.

Krishnamoorthy, Bala, *Environmental Management: Text and cases*, 3rd ed., PHI Learning, New Delhi, 2022.

Most, K.S., *Accounting Theory,* Holt, Rinehart and Winston of Canada Ltd., 1986.

Porter, M.E. and Linde, C.V.D., "Green and Competitive", *Business and the Environment, Harvard Business Review*, 2000, pp. 146–7.

Sen, A.K. and Mitra, J.K., *Commercial Law and Industrial Law*, The World Press, Kolkata, 2000.

Appendix

COMPANIES (ACCOUNTS) RULES, 2014 (Related to Chapter IX of the Companies Act, 2013)

Rule 8(3). The Report of the Board shall contain the following information and details, namely:

(A) Conservation of energy

(i) the steps taken or impact on conservation of energy;

(ii) the steps taken by the company for utilising alternate sources of energy;

(iii) the capital investment on energy conservation equipments.

(B) Technology absorption

(i) the efforts made towards technology absorption,

(ii) the benefits derived like product improvement, cost reduction, product development or import substitution,

(iii) in case of imported technology (imported during the last three years reckoned from the beginning of the financial years):

- (a) the details of technology imported;
- (b) the year of import;
- (c) whether the technology has been fully absorbed;
- (d) if not fully absorbed, areas where absorption has not taken place and the reasons thereof; and

(iv) the expenditure incurred on Research and Development.

(C) Foreign exchange earning and Ontgo

The Foreign Exchange earned in terms of actual inflows during the year and the Foreign Exchange Ontgo during the year in terms of actual outflows.

Provided that the requirement of furnishing information and details under this sub-rule shall not apply to a Government company engaged in producing defence equipment.

FORM A

(See rule 2)

Form for Disclosure of Particulars with Respect to Conservation of Energy

A. Power and Fuel Consumption

	Current Year	Previous Year
1. Electricity		
(a) ***Purchased***		
Units		
Total amount		
Rate/unit		
(b) ***Own generation***		
(i) *Through diesel generator*		
Units		
Unit per litre of diesel oil		
Cost/unit		
(ii) *Through steam turbine/generator*		
Units		
Unit per litre of fuel oil/gas		
Cost/unit		
2. Coal (Specify Quality and Where Used)		
Quantity (tonnes)		
Total cost		
Average rate		
3. Furnace Oil		
Quantity (kilolitres)		
Total amount		
Average rate		
4. Others/Internal Generation (Please Give Details)		
Quantity		
Total cost		
Rate/unit		

B. Consumption Per Unit of Production

	Standards (if any)	Current Year	Previous Year
		1	2
Products (with details) unit			
Electricity			
Furnace oil			
Coal (specify quality)			
Others (specify)			

NOTES:

(1) Please give separate details for different products/items produced by the company and covered under these rules.

(2) Please give reasons for variation in the consumption of power and fuel from standards of previous year.

(3) In case of production of different varieties/specifications, consumption details may be given for equivalent production.

SCHEDULE

(*See rule 2*)

List of Industries which should Furnish Information in Form A[19]

1. Textile
2. Fertilizer
3. Aluminium
4. Steel
5. Refineries
6. Petrochemicals and chemicals
7. Cement
8. Dairy and food processing
9. Cold storage plant
10. Electric arc furnaces
11. Chlor alkali
12. Edible oil
13. Engineering (Steel forging and re-rolling)
14. Glass
15. Jute
16. Paper
17. Refractory and pottery
18. Tea
19. Tyre
20. Sugar
21. Drugs and pharmaceuticals

19 The Companies Act 2013 does not provide any such provision.

FORM B

(*See rule 2*)

Form for Disclosure of Particulars with Respect to Absorption

Research and Development (R&D)

1. Specific areas in which R&D carried out by the company
2. Benefits derived as a result of the above R&D
3. Future plan of action
4. Expenditure on R&D
   (a) Capital
   (b) Recurring
   (c) Total
   (d) Total R&D expenditure as a percentage of total turnover.

Technology Absorption, Adaptation and Innovation

1. Efforts, in brief, made towards technology absorption, adaptation and innovation.
2. Benefits derived as a result of the above efforts, e.g., product improvement, cost reduction, product development, import substitution, etc.
3. In case of imported technology (imported during the last 5 years reckoned from the beginning of the financial year), following information may be furnished:
   (a) Technology imported
   (b) Year of import
   (c) Has technology been fully absorbed?
   (d) If not fully absorbed, areas where this has not taken place, reasons therefor, and future plans of action.

4

Corporate Environmental Management for Sustainable Development

Sky is like a Father
Earth is like a Mother
Space as their Children
The Rig Veda

4.1 INTRODUCTION

The corporate sector is an important medium of economic development of a country. There is a close relationship between economic development issues and environmental management issues. Therefore, sustainable economic development should be environment-friendly. In Chapter 2, we have discussed in detail the two arguments, viz., the social contract argument and the quality of life argument, that underpin a company's duty for managing its environmental activities in a responsible way. It has to be emphasized that, in the long run, there is no conflict between environmental management and the profitability of a firm.

But a company may be guided by short-term considerations where environmental issues, in the absence of legal compulsions, may be ignored. But companies must not forget that, with economic development, the environmental awareness has also been on the increase. Therefore, there is likely to be pressure from the stakeholders on the corporate sector for better environmental performance. This is illustrated in Figure 4.1.

Studies on cost-benefit analysis suggest that companies tend to be more competitive if they respond to environmental challenges that affect their operations (Gouldson, Murphy, 1998). This aspect is discussed in Section 4.2. Section 4.3 gives an overview of how a firm can manage the environmental aspects of corporate activity innovatively, technologically, organizationally and strategically. In Section 4.4, we discuss the need for environmental management system, and the limitations of traditional management system. Section 4.5 briefly addresses issues relating to sustainable economic development and the strategic environment management system. Section 4.6 deals with the standardization of environmental management systems to show the concern of the International Organization for Standardization (ISO) to help the corporate citizens improve their environmental performance, while Section 4.7 briefly examines the impact of standardization on the firm and the criteria for its assessment.

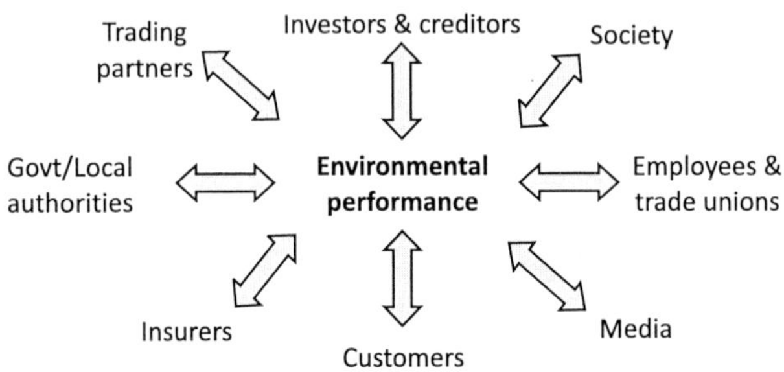

Figure 4.1 Stakeholder pressure and environmental performance (Adapted from Welford and Gouldson, 1993.)

4.2 COST-BENEFIT ANALYSIS OF ENVIRONMENTAL MANAGEMENT SYSTEM

Any proposal to introduce an environment management system must satisfy the test of cost-benefit analysis. This is more so when there is no legal compulsion to adopt a management system that contributes to the quality of life. In this context, some relevant questions are as follows:

1. What are the costs of environmental management?
2. What are its benefits in terms of (a) processes, (b) products and (c) company in general?
3. Does better environmental performance of the firm add to its profitability in the long run?

The various costs and benefits of environmental management system are now enumerated.

Environmental costs

The direct, hidden and potential future costs are as follows:

(i) *Direct costs*
- Capital expenditure
- Depreciation
- Maintenance.

(ii) *Hidden costs*
- Waste treatment
- Compliance management
- Training
- Legal support.

(iii) *Potential future costs*
- Remediation (contingent liability costs)
- Public relation and goodwill
- Higher insurance and lending costs.

Both hidden and potential future costs are of indirect nature.

The issues relating to environmental cost management are discussed in Chapter 5.

Environmental benefits

The benefits of environmental management system are listed in terms of (i) process benefits, (ii) product benefits, (iii) fiscal benefits, and (iv) other benefits.

(i) *Process benefits*
- Materials savings resulting from more complete processing, substitution, reuse, or recycling of production inputs
- Increases in process yields
- Less downtime through more careful monitoring and maintenance
- Better utilization of by-products
- Conversion of wastes into valuable forms
- Lower energy consumption
- Improved energy efficiency
- Reduced waste management costs
- Reduced material storage and handling costs
- Savings from safer workplace conditions
- Elimination or reduction of cost of activities involved in discharges or waste handling, transportation, and disposal
- Better quality of product due to process changes.

(ii) *Product benefits*
- Higher quality of products
- Lower product costs (e.g., product substitution)

- Lower packing costs
- More efficient resource use by by-products
- Safer products
- Lower net costs of product disposal to customers
- Higher product resale and scrap value.

(iii) *Fiscal benefits*

- Tax concessions (Section 35CCB of the Income Tax Act)
- Long-term capital gains are exempt from tax for shifting of industrial unit from an urban area to any other area by sale of assets (Section 54G of Income Tax Act)
- For installing pollution control equipment—100% depreciation allowance
- Production of building material using fly ash and phospho-gypsum in 25% or more quantities as raw material is exempt from excise duty
- Customs duty concessions for installation of appropriate pollution abatement equipment.

(iv) *Other benefits*

- Improved safety performance
- Reduced risk exposure
- Lower insurance premiums
- Lower cost of capital
- Increased staff commitment and productivity
- Improved public relations due to assured present and future compliance.

Thus, a cost-benefit analysis will put the management of the company on a solid footing to take a decision in favour of introducing an environment management system.

4.3 MANAGING ENVIRONMENTAL ASPECTS OF CORPORATE ACTIVITY

Whether companies will choose to exploit these advantages is determined by their own cost-benefit analysis including, an estimation of the great uncertainty and risk that are associated with environmental improvements and investments for companies (Robbins, 2001). There are, however, a few organizational barriers (Ashford, 1993) that exist. They are lack of:

- information on the costs and benefits of environmental management because many environmental issues are not easily convertible into monetary values;

- awareness of the long-term benefits of environmental management;
- confidence in the performance of new technologies and techniques; and
- managerial capacity and financial capital to deal with transition costs associated with reorganizing the production process.

How should a firm manage the environmental aspects of corporate activity innovatively, strategically, organizationally and technologically? In other words, the ways in which corporations can take actions can be delineated into four major groups (Gouldson and Murphy, 1998)—(i) environmental innovation, (ii) environmental strategy, (iii) environmental management, and (iv) environmental technology. These are briefly discussed now.

Environmental innovation

Innovation refers to engaging in new economic activity and may comprise all stages of this process, i.e., from initial invention to product development and introduction to the market. In response to environmental challenges due to corporate activities, innovation can be thought of as corporate change or the process of making environmental improvements. It can take place rapidly involving new technologies or techniques, or it can take place slowly with small incremental steps to new technologies or techniques. Whatever policy of environmental innovation a company may decide to adopt, the management needs to evaluate the role of existing and potential technologies used.

Environmental strategy

A strategy is an integrated set of actions aimed at securing sustainable competitive advantage. A good management system must adopt suitable strategies. According to Porter (1985), the ultimate objective of a firm is to achieve a long-term sustainable advantage over its key competitors in all of its business. Environmental strategy concerns focusing the attention towards environmental challenges and adopting suitable set of actions for better environmental performance of the firm. To put it in simple terms, how does a firm organize its thinking for better environmental management?

According to Sharp and Pavitt[1] (1993), senior management of organizations can approach strategic decisions in myopic or dynamic

---

1 Sharp, M. and Pavitt, K., "Technology Policy in the 1990s: Old trends and new realities", *Journal of Common Market Studies*, Vol. 31, 1993, pp. 129–151.

ways, which have direct relevance to understanding how they view environmental strategy. The former approach deals with traditional cost-benefit analysis focusing on the direct and tangible economic impacts of an investment. On the other hand, the dynamic approach considers indirect and intangible economic impacts of an investment. Consequently, a myopic approach is less likely to advocate radical changes where high risks and uncertainty are evident, as in many environmental investments.

Many Japanese firms have been following strategic environmental management (SEM). SEM takes into account the overall economic strategy of the firm and seeks to use the growing green market. It goes beyond environmental management and audit and moves towards 'cradle to grave' analysis, environmental research and development. It responds to environmental challenges for strategic reasons by anticipating or pursuing potential green markets. In many cases, this can be part of a total quality management (TQM) strategy which most of the companies are practising. For example, Xerox and Volvo have been following life cycle or 'cradle to grave' policies (Shrivastava, 1996).

Environmental management

Management systems are designed to promote corporate objectives. They help planning, coordination, control and decision-making. They define authorities, fix up responsibilities and facilitate flow of information throughout the organization. A good environmental management is, therefore, a *sine qua non* for improvement of environmental performance.

Many national and international organizations, viz., the Confederation of British Industry (CBI), International Chamber of Commerce (ICC), the European Industry Association (EUIA), the Global Reporting Initiative (GRI), and others have issued guidelines and principles for environmental management to improve corporate environmental performance. There are many common elements in their guidelines. These are as follows:

1. Guidelines have a policy statement indicating the firm's commitment to improve the environmental performance.
2. The policy statement is translated into plans and programmes and implemented. Such plans and programmes are designed to cover all value-creating functions of the firm. The two important segments of the chain—suppliers and customers—are also covered by the organization's plans and programmes.
3. Environmental plans are integrated into day-to-day operations of the organization. Innovative technologies and techniques are developed and applied to reduce the impact of organizational activities on the environment.

4. There is provision for education and training of the employees within the organization to increase their awareness and commitment in order to improve environmental performance.
5. The environmental performances are measured, compared against targets, audited and reviewed vis-à-vis adopted policies.

Determining environmental performance is not an easy task. A good environmental management system also defines it in measurable units to provide a suitable 'index'. The index gives the overall impact of the corporate activities in the environment. Since sustainable development comprises three important components, namely, economic performance, environmental performance and social performance, any effective management system must identify and adopt suitable criteria to measure them (e.g., GRI Sustainability Guidelines, 2002). The measurement system should then be an element of a strategic management system.

The objective of having a good environmental management is to help companies to make decisions and channel the available resources into those areas where benefits to the environment will be the greatest. The system identifies the ecological weaknesses of the firm and focuses attention of the management to problem areas. It covers the entire product range, product techniques, and processes, marketing and post-consumption disposition of the product.

Environmental technology

All technologies have some impact on environment. Environmental technologies reduce unfavourable impacts on the environment. Gouldson and Murphy (1998, p. 29) define them as those that "reduce the absolute or relative impact of a process or product on the environment". Environmental technologies may be of two types—**end of pipe** or **control technologies** and **green** or **clean technologies**. Control technologies are easy and less-expensive to incorporate into existing systems in order to comply with environmental regulations. Green technologies are 'general process or products' which integrate environmental considerations into their design and/or application in order to reduce their impacts on the environment. Accordingly, green technologies tend to be more expensive and need to be properly planned and installed after proper cost-benefit (direct and indirect) analysis. They may have higher initial costs compared to control technologies but will have greater economic and environmental efficiency in the long run. So, a company may adopt control technologies in the short run and, in the long run, it might gradually switch over to green technologies. The implementation of these short- and long-term policies concerning environmental technologies cannot, however, take place without an organizational structure that can effectively incorporate responses to environmental challenges (Robbins, 2001).

4.4 NEED FOR AND THE DESIGN OF AN ENVIRONMENTAL MANAGEMENT SYSTEM

There is a growing interest among the companies in improving their environmental performance. Once a company has decided to embark upon a concerted effort to improve its environmental performance, it must build a comprehensive environmental management system within the organization in as much as a lack of a comprehensive and effective management system may often lead to failure. Inadequate management systems may cause environmental damage and may cost firms and organizations heavily in terms of clean up costs and damaged reputations. Exxon Valdez oil spill and Union Carbide explosion in Bhopal are two such examples where the environment became irreparably damaged due, at least in part, to inadequacies in systems which were supposed to prevent such disasters.

An effective management system is crucial for avoiding environmental degradation. Such a system will pull together all the tools and strategies for avoiding risks. It will provide a framework for a clear and focused approach to environmental improvement. The management system should be developed and implemented for the purpose of accomplishing the objectives set out in a company's policies to improve environmental performance and prevent degradation of environment.

What attributes are then essential for an environment management system to be successful? The *first* and foremost is the comprehensiveness of the system. Every part of the organization must be involved in the implementation of the system and every individual in the organization must be clear about his/her responsibility for effective implementation of the system. *Second*, the system and procedures within the management system need to be understandable to everyone involved. Roles, duties and responsibilities must be clearly defined and communicated to the individuals. This helps fixing up responsibilities and promotes reviewing and auditing function. Workers' participation and their decision-making are part of the system. The commitment of senior management to systems-based approach is crucial. *Third*, the system must be open to review and there must be a commitment to a continuous improvement in the operation of the system. *Fourth*, companies must recognize their wider responsibility and manage the entire life cycle of their products. This means that companies must insist on maintaining high environmental standards from suppliers, ensure that raw materials are extracted or produced in an environment-friendly way to provide a good start. The processing operations need to be suitably designed to be environment-friendly. Damage to the environment during use and disposal of the product must also be kept at the minimum.

In view of the above, we have to design a suitable environmental management system. The *traditional approach* to environmental management emphasizes control of various types of pollutions at the process and output levels such as emission to air, discharges to water, solid and other wastes, contamination of land, noise, heat, etc. Figure 4.2 sketches such an environment management system.

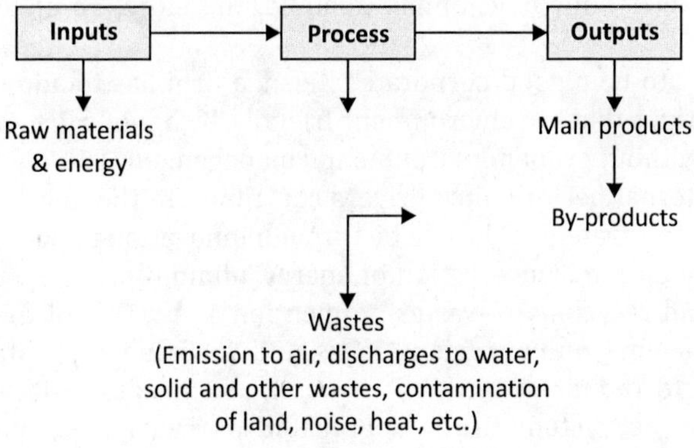

Figure 4.2 Environment management: Traditional approach

As shown in Figure 4.2, the system places emphasis on processing operations in reducing wastes, etc. But if the technology used for production purposes is not environment-friendly, the management system cannot be effective in preventing environmental degradation. Recycling of waste materials, consumption of products by the consumers, disposal of packing materials after consumption, are some such important issues in an environment management system that need to be properly addressed in any effective management system.

An effective management system should not only take care of the present needs of the society but also promote sustainable economic development.

4.5 SUSTAINABLE ECONOMIC DEVELOPMENT AND THE STRATEGIC ENVIRONMENTAL MANAGEMENT SYSTEM

Sustainable development is defined as the development that meets the needs of the present generation without compromising the ability of future generations to meet their own needs (World Commission on Environmental Development, 1987). It refers to preserving the ecosystem as well as maintaining long-term profitability of the firms (Stead and Stead, 1996). At the macro-level, any sustainable development has to take care of three aspects, namely, economic growth, environment-friendliness and social justice (Welford and Gouldson, 1993). Ethical investing, popularly known as **Socially Responsible Investing (SRI),** is one of the key tools for building a sustainable future (Chakraborty, 2005). Sustainable economic development should, therefore, be environment-friendly.

In order to be a good corporate citizen, a firm has to adopt policies and take actions that are environment-friendly. It cannot gain competitive advantage without proper environmental management. The key issue is—how can internal performance drivers contribute to the development of environmental strategies? It may be through innovation of new products, control of pollution, conservation of energy, minimization of wastes and effluents, and recycling of wastes, to mention a few. One of the popular examples of environment-friendliness and increasing profitability of the firm is to reduce generation of waste and maximise its recycling. Wastes may be systematically segregated as hazardous, biomedical, nuclear, non-hazardous, biodegradable and non-biodegradable, to be appropriately treated, recycled or disposed. In many industries, recycling of wastes not only becomes environment-friendly, but it also reduces cost and increases profitability and competitive advantage of the firm. So, in order to be environment-friendly, companies must adopt suitable policies and formulate action plans to implement them. Demonstrating the firm's concern for the environment helps build up good corporate image that may increase its market share. This may be called **strategic environmental management**.

Strategic environmental management issues embrace formulation of suitable business strategies for decision-making. In order to realize competitive advantage based on environmental management, companies must seek to develop strategies which translate actions into benefits, improving their environmental performance and addressing the environmental demands placed upon them by government and other regulators and stakeholders. By incorporating the increasingly important environmental dimension into the decision-making processes and strategies of the firm, managers can seek to exploit the opportunities offered by increased public environmental concern within a dynamic marketplace. The process can be shown in Figure 4.3 (Welford and Gouldson, 1993).

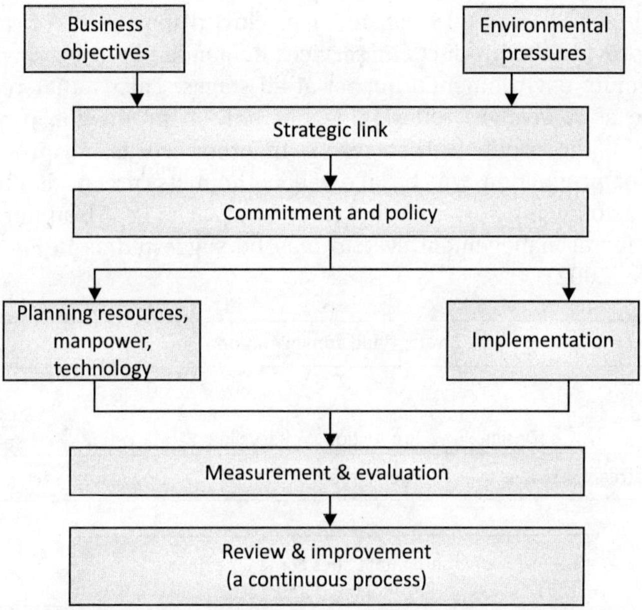

Figure 4.3 Strategic environmental management system

The **Strategic Environmental Management System (SEMS)** makes an altogether different approach. The environmental issues are incorporated in the corporate objectives that lead to commitment and policy formulation. Resources are accordingly planned, mobilized and put to use. Finally, performances are measured, evaluated and monitored for continuous improvement. This approach is followed by many successful Japanese firms which adopt the **Kaizen process**. Literally translated from Japanese, '*Kaizen*' means "improvement"—it implies continuing and incremental improvement across a firm. Accordingly, planning, implementing, evaluating, monitoring and action-taking are all significant parts of the process. Now the question arises—how can we do it better tomorrow than we did today? It has to be recognized that for a highly visionary company, there is no ultimate finish line; there is no point at which they feel they 'have made it'. The journey for attaining excellence goes on—it is never ending.

According to Klassen and McLaughlin (1996), "The long-term goal of environmental management is to move towards ... considering environmental aspects in an integrated fashion in product design, the entire manufacturing process, marketing, product delivery and use, consumer service, and post-consumer product disposition." A firm must seek to provide the products or services demanded by consumers with the minimum environmental impact at all stages. This is a far-reaching challenge as it involves redesigning not only of production processes but also of the products themselves. In other words, no product or method of production will be allowed without its 'green justification'. Therefore, following Porter's value chain approach (1985), an integrated environmental management system may be suggested as in Figure 4.4 (Banerjee, 2002).

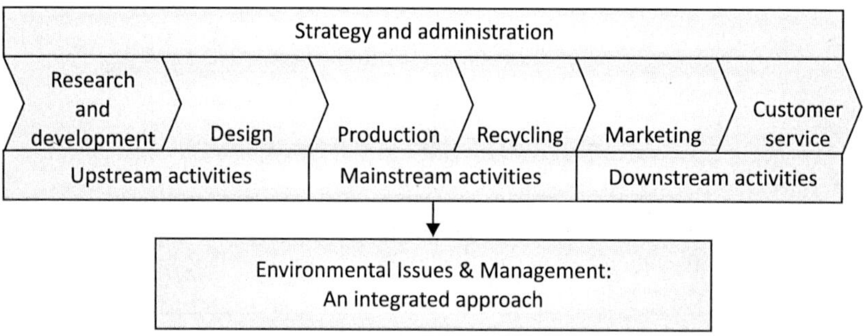

Figure 4.4 An integrated environmental management approach

The value-chain approach suggests that a company's main functions be segregated into value-creating activities and examined in terms of their value-creating capabilities. If an activity does not create any value, it is discontinued. Therefore, depending on such analysis, activities may be merged, discontinued or outsourced to optimize value. The environmental issues should also be integrated with the value-chain analysis so as to make the strategic environmental management system an integrated one.

4.6 STANDARDIZATION OF ENVIRONMENTAL MANAGEMENT SYSTEMS

In Sections 4.4 and 4.5, we discussed some of the important issues concerning environmental management system (EMS). In this section, we deal with standardization of environmental management.

The lack of guidance on the development of the EMS within the organizations and proliferation of environmental 'credentials' stress the need for having some quality standards in environmental management. In the early 1990s, a number of voluntary environmental management schemes had been developed to try and ensure a certain quality of the EMS to help organizations to improve their environmental performance. They included the British Standard Specification for Environmental Management Systems (BS 7750) in 1994, the European Union Eco-Management and Audit Scheme in 1993, and the standards issued by the International Organization for Standardization (ISO 14000).

All these standards are voluntary and are designed to be externally verified by nationally accredited bodies. Of these, we discuss here only ISO 14000 series because of its impact on the member countries or bodies of ISO. It is argued that organizations which get ISO accreditation will gain market advantages and build better relationship with regulatory authorities, investors and insurance companies in addition to experiencing financial benefits through a greater efficiency in its management structure and areas such as energy, waste and water management (Welford, 1996, p. 47).

4.6.1 ISO 14000 Series

With the success of ISO 9000 series [relating to quality management (process) standards] and environmental issues gaining prominence throughout the world, the ISO[2] began to consider whether international standards in environmental management could serve to:

2 The International Organization for Standardization (ISO) is a private sector organization, formed just after the World War II, based in Geneva, Switzerland, and has a membership of over 100 countries. It is not affiliated with the United Nations or with any European organization. The ISO 9000 series were completed in 1987. In 1991, ISO formed an advisory group named the Strategic Advisory Group on the Environment (SAGE). By mid-1992, SAGE decided that it was appropriate for ISO to develop standards on environmental management.

- promote a common approach to environmental management similar to that for quality management,
- enhance the organization's abilities to attain and measure improvements in environmental performance, and
- facilitate trade and remove trade barriers.

By late 1995, ISO 14000 and ISO 14001 standards were issued. They cover a wide range of subjects that relate to environmental management system (EMS), environmental auditing (EA), and environmental performance evaluation (EPE). ISO 14000 series help in developing and implementing EMS. ISO 14001 standards deal with EMS documents. These standards are voluntary as stated earlier. To become registered under ISO 14000, an organization needs only to show its conformance to EMS documents - ISO 14001. The ISO 14000 standards are not intended to replace or duplicate a country's regulatory system—they are only complimentary to national regulatory systems.

ISO 14000

ISO 14000 is a guiding document. It is based on a set of principles as stated below.

Principle 1: An organization should focus on what needs to be done—it should ensure commitment to the EMS and define its policy.

Principle 2: An organization should formulate a plan to fulfil its environment policy.

Principle 3: For effective implementation, an organization should develop the capabilities and support mechanisms necessary to achieve its environmental policy, objectives and targets.

Principle 4: An organization should measure, monitor and evaluate its environmental performance.

Principle 5: An organization should review and continually improve its environmental management system, with the objective of improving its overall environmental performance.

ISO 14001

ISO 14001 covers subjects under two areas, viz.,

1. Organization's management and evaluation system, and
2. Environmental tools for product evaluation.

These standards are shown in Figure 4.5.

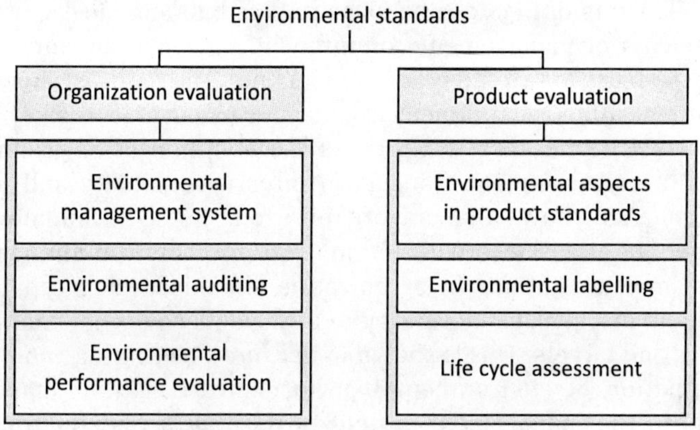

Figure 4.5 ISO 14001 standards
(Adapted from Cascio *et al.*, 1996, p. 32.)

The different aspects of organization evaluation and product evaluation are now briefly explained.

4.6.2 Environmental Management System (EMS)

Environmental Management System includes the organizational structure, planning, activities, responsibilities, practices, procedures, processes and resources for developing, implementing, achieving, reviewing and maintaining the environmental policy (Section 3.5). The elements of the EMS, as described in the definitions and other places in the Standard, are given in Figure 4.6.

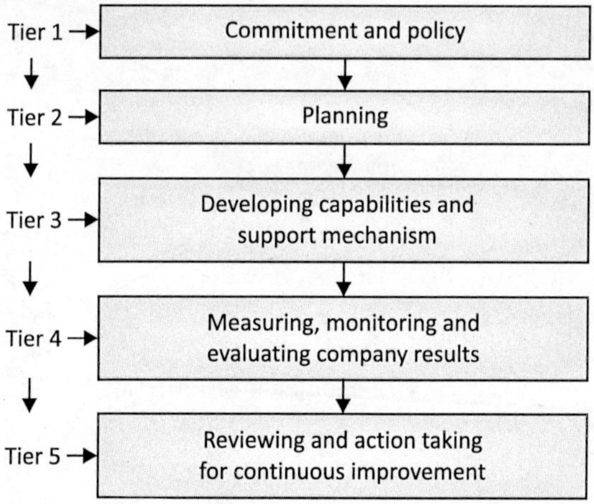

Figure 4.6 Environmental management system

The elements of EMS can be visualized as building blocks, with the core elements of management commitment and environmental policy forming the basis for all the other components. The *first tier* shows that in any organization, commitment from senior management is key to the adoption of EMS because it facilitates the adoption of environmental policy and its subsequent translation into responsibility and action. The *second tier* shows that an organization should formulate plans and targets in accordance with its policy to meet its commitment. For effective implementation, an organization should develop capabilities and support mechanisms necessary to achieve its environmental policy, objectives and targets. This is shown in *tier three*. Measuring, monitoring and evaluation of environmental performance constitute important elements in the management system in the *fourth tier*. Auditing and corrective action taking is also a part and parcel of the system at this stage. In the *fifth tier*, it is shown that an organization should review the system, take corrective and preventive actions, wherever necessary, to improve continually its EMS with the objective of improving its overall environmental performance. It highlights the overall goal to ensure continual improvement of the EMS in order to ensure that the organization is consistently meeting its environmental obligations and protecting the environment. Thus, the EMS is designed to provide a structure and systematic approach to overall environmental management.

The five major elements of the EMS, as given in an Annexure to 14001, are shown in Figure 4.7.

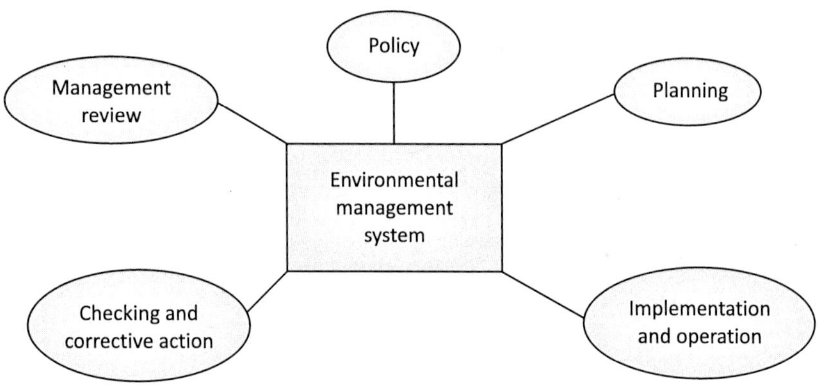

Figure 4.7 Elements of an EMS

Regarding the overall structure of the document, it may be stated that ISO 14001 has been constructed around the Deming Cycle[3], a process management tool devised by W. Edwards Deming, a pioneer in the field of quality management (Welford, p. 77). For example, the ISO 14001 elements may be shown corresponding with the four stages of Deming Cycle (Figure 4.8).

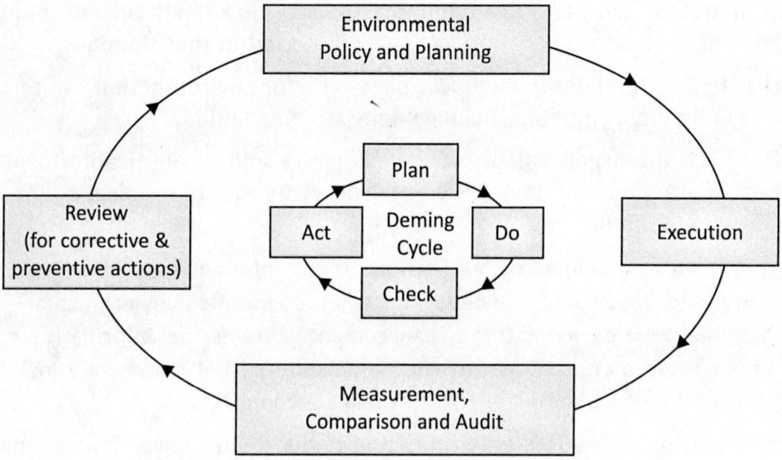

Figure 4.8 ISO 14001 and the Deming cycle
(Adapted from Welford, 1996, p. 80.)

The ISO has not only prepared EMS specification document (ISO 14001), it has also prepared a series of environmental auditing standards (ISO1 4010-12).

4.6.3 Environmental Auditing (EA)

Environmental auditing guidelines are contained in ISO 14010 to 14012. These are briefly outlined below.

---

3 In the Deming Cycle:

- 'Plan' refers to planning what is to be done
- 'Do' denotes to doing that has been planned
- 'Check' indicates checking that what was planned has actually been done
- 'Act' refers to acting on the results on the checking procedure to revise/ modify the initial plans.

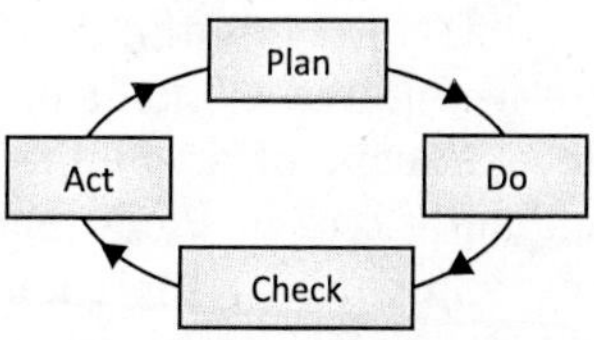

Deming cycle

ISO 14010: These guidelines give *general principles* on environmental auditing. They contain scope, definitions, objectives, objectivity, independence, competence, audit criteria, evidence, reliability of findings and the like.

ISO 14011: It specifies *audit procedures*—auditing of environmental management systems. Matters like audit objectives, roles, responsibilities and activities, auditor, audit team, preliminary document review, audit plan, audit report preparation, etc., are discussed in this standard.

ISO 14012: It relates to *qualification criteria* for environmental auditors performing environmental management systems audits.

ISO 14010 gives general principles of an EA and is applicable to all types of EA and not just EMS auditing. This standard also defines environmental audit as:

> a systematic, documented verification process of objectively obtaining and evaluating evidence to determine whether specified environmental activities, events, conditions, management systems, or information about these matters conform with audit criteria, and communicating the results of this process to the client (Section 39).

According to ISO 14010, environmental audit should have its focus on a clearly defined and documented subject matter. The auditors do not enjoy freedom to select the subject of audit. Rather, they must audit those aspects that are predetermined. It is the responsibility of the client (but not the auditor) to formulate the audit objectives. The document also asserts objectivity and independence of the audit process. Environmental audit may be done by an external or an internal auditor, according to the discretion of the client. The audit report should include many items including audit conclusions. **Audit conclusion** is referred to as professional judgment or opinion expressed by an auditor about the subject matter of the audit, based on and limited to reassuming that the auditor has applied to audit the evaluation of the collected audit evidence and compared it against the agreed audit criteria.

ISO 14011 is the guidance document used for EMS audits which are a required element of ISO 14001. The key to an ISO 14011 is the development of an audit plan which includes audit objectives, scope and audit criteria. Audit plan should be flexible, and should be reviewed and approved by the client. ISO 14011 requires the auditor to assess the internal management review process to ensure that it accomplishes continuing suitability and effectiveness of the EMS. The standard also makes it optional to include audit conclusions in the audit report. In the audit findings, all significant non-conformances must be documented.

The *qualification criteria* for internal and external environmental auditors to perform EMS audit are given in ISO 14012. It specifies that auditors should have at least a secondary education, or equivalent, and must have five years of appropriate work experience. In case of an auditor having a graduation degree, four years experience is prescribed. In addition, the auditor should have formal training in environmental science and technology, technical/environmental aspects of facility operations, requirements of environmental laws, environmental management systems and standards, and audit procedures, processes and techniques. Formal training can be waived if other accepted methods of competence can be proved, such as through accredited examinations or relevant professional qualifications. ISO 14012 further specifies that the auditor should have completed on-the-job training for a total of 20 equivalent workdays of auditing encompassing a minimum of four audits. Such on-the-job training must occur in a period of not more than three consecutive years. For lead auditors, however, additional requirements are specified.

Auditors are expected to possess numerous attributes and skills. These include good verbal and writing skills; good interpersonal skills such as diplomacy, tact and the ability to listen; objectivity and independence; good organizational skills, and the ability to reach sound judgments on the basis of objective evidence. Finally, auditors are also expected to maintain their competence by updating their knowledge through refresher courses, as and when needed. He or she has to maintain his/her level of experience in the execution of audits to a satisfactory level.

4.6.4 Environmental Performance Evaluation (EPE)

In ISO 14001, there is a requirement (Clause 4.4.1) to record information to track performance known as **monitoring and measurement**. Thus, Environmental Performance Evaluation (EPE) is essentially a subsystem of the EMS. ISO 14031 specifies guidelines on EPE.

ISO 14031 defines environmental performance as the result of an organization's management of the environmental aspects of its activities, products and services. The EPE guidelines also provide a 'toolbox' of environmental performance indicators. For example, an indicator of performance might be reduction in emissions over time taking product variability into consideration. In the guidelines, numerous indicators, that can be used by organizations of all types, are defined. Although these indicators are not comprehensive in nature, they provide ample examples of the types of performance indicators that can either be used by themselves or serve as a basis for developing additional and applicable guidelines. For those organizations which have not previously done EPE, it may serve as a primer on how to approach the subject matter in a reasonable way (Cascio, 1996).

Relationship between the EMS and its subsystems

What is the relationship between environmental audit and environmental performance evaluation in the Environmental Management System (EMS)? It can be stated that EMS is the key element in organization evaluation where environmental audit and environmental performance evaluation act as the subsystem to support the EMS. This relationship is shown in Figure 4.9. It shows key elements of the EMS. The dotted line in the figure shows dependence on corporate management for multifacility enterprises.

Figure 4.9 EMS and its subsystems
(Adapted from Cascio, 1996, p. 54.)

Product evaluation

The ISO 14000 series include a number of tools for specialized uses. Environmental aspects in product standards, environmental labelling and life cycle assessment are such tools that may be used by practitioners and others in those fields. They are not necessarily part of an EMS and not required under ISO 14001, although labelling and life cycle assessment guidelines are certainly useful to EMS managers.

ISO 14064, entitled **Environmental Aspects in Product Standards**, is to be used by all ISO standard writers. It becomes beneficial to the standard writers to have an environment guide when writing product standards in that the standard writers can (i) incorporate characteristics into standards that would improve the environmental profile of product, and (ii) avoid inserting specifications in product standards that could turn out to be environmentally detrimental.

Environmental Labelling (EL) Programmes have been in use in many developed countries over the last 25 years. These countries include Germany, the US, the Netherlands and Canada. ISO accordingly included EL standards in its series of environmental management standards. An international labelling standard can have a significant positive impact on environmental management. Apart from providing a consistent approach and uniform rigour in the development of criteria for labelling, it provides a better opportunity to obtain needed respectability worldwide. EL may also be used for the purpose of competing in the market. The objective of an EL standard is to ensure that the information on the label is accurate, verifiable, and non-deceptive. There are *five EL standards* under ISO 14000 series:

1. **ISO 14020,** which deals with principles of all environmental labelling.
2. **ISO 14021,** entitled Environmental Labelling–Self-declaration on Environmental Claims: Terms and definitions, applies to manufacturers who declare that their product has an environmental attribute (e.g., it is recyclable, energy-efficient or made without ozone-depleting chemicals).
3. **ISO 14022,** is on 'Environmental Labelling—Symbols'.
4. **ISO 14023,** deals with 'Testing and Verification Methodologies'.
5. **ISO 14024,** is on 'Environmental Labelling—Practitioner Programmes: Guiding principles, practices and certification procedures for multiple criteria (Type I) programmes'. It

applies to traditional third-party labelling programmes or 'seal' programmes. These programmes use criteria based on many product characteristics and attributes to assess which products have overall environmental superiority. Products that meet the specified environmental criteria are awarded seal so that consumers know which products are environmentally favourable.

Life cycle assessment implies a scientific process that is used to evaluate the environmental impact of all aspects of a product—its raw materials, method of manufacture, use, disposal, and other applicable elements. There are several life cycle assessment standards. These standards include the following:

- *ISO 14041*, entitled 'Life Cycle Assessment—Goals and definition/ scope and inventory analysis', describes special requirements and guidelines for the preparation, conduct, and critical review of the life cycle inventory analysis. It is involved in the compilation and quantification of environmentally relevant inputs and outputs of a product system.
- *ISO 14042*, 'Life Cycle Assessment—Impact assessment,' is aimed at evaluating the significance of potential environmental impacts using the results of the life cycle inventory analysis. Because of the inherent subjectivity in impact assessments the most critical requirement for their conduct will be transparency, so that decisions and assumptions can be clearly described and reported.
- *ISO 14043* on 'Life Cycle Assessment—Improvement assessment' addresses interpretations of LCA results in relation to the goal definition phase of the study. It may involve reviewing the scope of the LCA as well as the nature and quality of the data collected. It is a useful supporting tool for EMS.

4.7 IMPACT OF STANDARDIZATION ON ENVIRONMENTAL PERFORMANCE OF THE FIRMS

What purpose can ISO 14000 family of standards serve to a company? As already mentioned, in general, such standards would help:

- promoting a common approach to environmental management across companies,

- enhancing a company's ability to attain improvements in environmental performance, and
- measuring environmental performance more rationally so as to promote continuous improvement in the system.

What are the criteria by which we can explore the impact of ISO 14001 adoption on management goals and their subsequent effect on environmental performance (Hillary, 2000)? If the changes that have taken place before and after implementation of ISO 14000 standards are examined, the impact is easily discernible. For example:

1. We can look at changes in the content of the goals themselves to ascertain if they move in ways that might be environmentally beneficial—placing regulatory compliance at a minimum or reducing emissions (stringency).
2. What changes have taken place in the process by which goals were established to see if it has become more open to outside stakeholders (participatory), more externally verifiable (transparent) and more comprehensive?

CASE STUDY

Nine ISO 14001-registered companies and one non-registered small business (Table 4.1) were contacted to interview their corporate and facility-level environmental managers. The identity of the firms and the interviewers was kept confidential.

TABLE 4.1 Type of Corporations whose Managers were Interviewed

Sl. no.	*Company name*	*Description*	*Corporate manager*	*Facility manager*
1.	Akoshi	Asian auto-maker	A_1	
2.	Beta	European chemical manufacturing	B_1	B_2
3.	Chips	American aviation company	C_1	
4.	Data	Asian microelectronics manufacturing		D_2
5.	Epsilon	European microelectronics manufacturing		E_2, E_3
6.	Fido	Asian microelectronics manufacturing		F_2
7.	Giant	US microelectronics manufacturing	G_1	G_2, G_3, G_4
8.	High	Small US power generator		H_2
9.	Impact	Small US parts manufacturing	I_1	

(Adapted from Hillary, 2000, p. 265.)

Notes:

(i) The first seven companies are multinationals and the last two are small businesses.

(ii) Sl. no. 9 considered obtaining registration to ISO 14001, but chose not to pursue it.

Even though the study is limited by its methodology and small size of sample, it examined the impact of ISO 14001 registration on the content of environmental management goals, the process by which these goals were established and the likely link between those goals and resulting environmental performance. The major findings were as follows:

1. Although the firms did not substantially modify the stringency of their environmental goals, they increased their commitment to goal attainment as evidenced by increased senior management commitment, more measurable goals and more specific designation of roles and responsibilities.
2. The firms established compliance assurance-related goals and set environmental management goals that went beyond regulated substances and included aspects such as water use and energy efficiency. The firms also indicated enhanced sensitivity to local variations in environmental constraints and community interests.
3. In terms of process, firms broadened internal participation drawing on cross-functional teams in contrast to leaving environmental management goal-setting to the environmental manager alone. However, they did not increase outside stakeholder involvement in their goal-setting processes nor were they more likely to disclose their environmental performance goals.

In short, it can be concluded that ISO 14000 family of standards help a firm manage systematically those areas of operation that are regulated by environmental reasons, identify the areas in which it is using resources inefficiently and adjust its focus to be sensitive to societal concerns. Therefore, it may be argued that companies which obtain ISO accreditation and follow ISO 14000 standards enjoy a competitive advantage, both nationally and internationally.

SUMMARY

In the long run, there is no conflict between environmental management and profitability of a company. If a company becomes environmentally conscious and adopts scientific environmental management system to improve its environmental performance, the company's competitive advantage is enhanced as a responsible corporate citizen. So, the main issue for the corporate sector is how to manage the environmental aspects of corporate activity innovatively, strategically, organizationally and technologically. These issues have been examined at length to stress upon the need for an integrated strategic environmental management system. The issue of standardization of environmental management systems has been discussed to show the concern of the ISO to help the corporate citizens to improve their environmental performance. The ISO 14000 family of standards have then been summarized and, finally, examined the impact of such standardization on the company and the criteria for assessment of such impact.

MULTIPLE CHOICE QUESTIONS

1. Direct costs of environment management include the following *except*:
   (a) Waste treatment
   (b) Maintenance
   (c) Capital expenditure
   (d) Depreciation
2. Hidden cost of environment management does not include the following:
   (a) Waste treatment
   (b) Lending costs
   (c) Legal expenses
   (d) Compliance management
3. Potential future costs of environment management include the following:
   (a) Contingent liability costs
   (b) Public relation and goodwill
   (c) Higher insurance cost
   (d) All of the above
4. Benefits of environment management include the following:
   (a) Process benefits
   (b) Product benefits
   (c) Fiscal benefits
   (d) All of the above
5. Which of the following are not product benefits arising out of environment management?
   (a) Lower energy consumption
   (b) Lower packing costs
   (c) Lower product costs
   (d) Additional contribution

6. Which of the following is not a benefit arising out of improved process of environmental management?
   (a) Better quality of product
   (b) Safer products
   (c) Reduced waste management costs
   (d) Lower downtime
7. Management of corporate activities from environmental aspects involves the following:
   (a) Environmental innovation
   (b) Environmental strategy
   (c) Environmental technology
   (d) All of the above
8. The traditional approach to management in a corporate organisation follows the following activity in the sequence of:
   (a) Inputs → Processing → Outputs → Marketing
   (b) Marketing → Outputs → Inputs → Processing
   (c) Inputs → Marketing → Outputs → Processing
   (d) Processing → Inputs → Outputs → Marketing
9. The strategic environmental management can be shown in the following sequence:
   (a) Strategic link → Implementation → Measurement and Evaluation → Review
   (b) Strategic link → Commitment & Policy → Implementation → Review
   (c) Strategic link → Commitment, Policy & Planning → Implementation & Evaluation → Review
   (d) Strategic link → Planning, Commitment & Policy → Implementation and Evaluation → Review
10. Following Michael Porter's Value Chain theory, an integrated approach to Environment Management can be sequentially shown as:
    (a) Strategy and administration → For Main Stream Activities → For Upstream Activities → For Downstream activities
    (b) Strategy and administration → For Upstream Activities → For Mainstream Activities → For Downstream Activities
    (c) Strategy and administration → For Downstream Activities → For Upstream Activities → For Mainstream Activities
    (d) None of the above
11. ISO 14000 and ISO 14001 Standards cover a wide range of subjects that relate to the following except:
    (a) Environment Management System (EMS)
    (b) Environmental Auditing (EA)
    (c) Environmental Performance Evaluation (EPE)
    (d) Environmental Accounting (EA)
12. The elements of Environmental Management System (EMS), as described in the definitions and other places of the Standard, can be given in a sequential manner as follows:

(a) Commitment, Policy & Planning → Developing capabilities and support mechanism → Measuring, monitoring and evaluating results → Review and action taking
(b) Developing capabilities and support mechanism → Commitment, Policy & Planning → Review and action taking → Measuring, monitoring and evaluating results
(c) Commitment, Policy & Planning - Review and action taking → Developing capabilities and support mechanism → Measuring, monitoring and evaluating results
(d) Developing capabilities and support mechanism → Commitment, Policy & Planning → Measuring, monitoring and evaluating results → Review and action taking

13. Environmental Auditing (EA) guidelines are given in ISO 14010 to 14012. Find the correct match of ISO Standards and their contents from the following:

	Standard Number	*Deals with*
(a)	ISO 14010	Qualification Criteria
(b)	ISO 14011	Audit Procedures
(c)	ISO 14012	General Principles
(d)	ISO 14010–14012	None of the above

14. ISO included Environmental Labelling (EL) Programmes in its series of environmental management standards. Which of the following is not EL Standard under ISO 14000 series?
(a) ISO 14020
(b) ISO 14021
(c) ISO 14023
(d) ISO 14031

15. ISO 14000 family of standards serve various purposes to a company. They are:
(a) Promoting a common approach to environmental management across the company
(b) Enhancing a company's ability to attain improvements in environmental performances
(c) Measuring environmental performance more rationally so as to promote continuous improvement in the system
(d) All of the above

EXERCISES

1. "Studies in cost-benefit analysis suggest that companies tend to be more competitive if they respond to environmental challenges that affect their operations." Discuss.

2. What do you understand by stakeholders' pressure on companies to improve environmental performance? Explain with the help of a diagram.
3. What are the costs of environmental management? Classify them under appropriate headings and explain what may be the possible costs of waste management.
4. The benefits of environmental management are generally classified under several groups. Enumerate the process benefits.
5. What are the fiscal benefits that may be enjoyed by the company arising out of good environmental management?
6. State the organisational barriers that are associated with environmental improvements and investment for companies. Mention the barriers that exist.
7. How would you design an environmental management system (EMS)? What attributes are essential for an EMS to be successful? Explain.
8. Many international organisations have issued guidelines and principles for environmental management to improve corporate environmental performance. Are there many common elements in those guidelines? Explain.
9. Compare in a nutshell the traditional approach of environmental management with strategic environmental management system.
10. How can you make an integrated environmental management system following Michel Porter's Value Chain approach?
11. ISO 14000 is formulated based on a set of principles. Enumerate them.
12. Examine five elements of Environmental Management System (EMS) as described in the ISO Standard.
13. Show the ISO 14001 elements corresponding with the four stages of Deming Cycle.
14. Environmental Auditing (EA) are contained in ISO 14010 to 14012. Briefly outline them.
15. State the relationship between the Environmental Management System (EMS) and its sub-systems.

REFERENCES

Ashford, N., "Understanding the Technical Responses of Industrial Firms to Environmental Problems: Implications of Government Policy", in Fischer, K. and Schot, J. (Eds.) *Environmental Strategies for Industry: International perspectives in research needs and policy implications*, Island Press, Washington DC, 1993.

Banerjee, B., "Accounting for Corporate Environmental Management in India", *The Management Accountant*, Volume 37, No. 12, December 2002.

Cascio, Joseph, Woodside, Gayle and Mitchell, Philip, *ISO 14000 Guide, The New International Environmental Management Standards*, McGraw-Hill, New York, 1996.

Chakraborty, Tanupa, *Ethical Investing—The gateway to a sustainable society*, Paper presented at the National Seminar on Corporate Social Responsibility, University of Calcutta, March 4–5, 2005.

Gouldson, A. and Murphy, J., *Regulatory Realities: The implementation and impact of industrial environmental regulation*, Earthscan, London, 1998.

Gray, R.H., "Corporate Reporting for Sustainable Development: Accounting for sustainability in AD 2000", in Welford, R. and Starkey, R. (Eds.), *Business and the Environment*, Universities Press, Hyderabad, 1996.

Hillary, Ruth (Ed.), *ISO 14001: Case studies and practical experiences*, Greenleaf Publishing, Sheffield, UK, 2000.

Jaggi, B. and Freedman, M., "An Analysis of the Information Content of Pollution Disclosures", *Financial Review*, Volume 17, No. 3, 1982, pp. 142–152.

Jaggi, Bikki, "Environmental Responsibility and Disclosures in Global Business Environment", *Proceedings of the Third International Accounting Conference*, January 4–5, 1997, Indian Accounting Association Research Foundation.

Klassen, R.D. and McLaughlin, C.P., "The Impact of Environmental Management on Firm Performance", *Management Science*, 42(8), 1996, 1199–1214.

Porter, Michael E., *Competitive Advantage: Creating and sustaining superior performance*, The Free Press, New York, 1985.

Robbins, Peter T., *Greening the Corporation–Management strategy and the environmental challenge*, Earthscan, London, 2001.

Shane, P. and Spicer, B., "Market Response to Environmental Information Produced Outside the Firm", *Accounting Review*, Volume 58, 1983, pp. 521–538.

Shrivastava, P., *Greening Business: Profiting the corporation and the environment*, Thompson Executive Press, Cincinnati, Ohio, 1996.

Stead & Stead, *Business and the Environment*, Richard Welford and Richard Starkey, 1996.

UNO, *Global Reporting Initiative—Sustainability guidelines*, New York, 2002.

Welford, Richard and Gouldson, Andrew, *Environmental Management and Business Strategy*, Pitman Publishing, London, 1993.

Welford, Richard, *Corporate Environmental Management, Systems and Strategies*, Universities Press, Hyderabad, 1996.

Welford, Richard, *Corporate Environmental Management 3: Towards sustainable development*, Earthscan, London, 2000.

Welford, Richard, *Corporate Environmental Management 2: Culture and organizations*, Earthscan, London, 1999.

Wever, Grace, *Strategic Environmental Management*, Wiley, New York, 1996.

5

Accounting and Reporting for Corporate Environmental Management

Make the Environment More Visible
—Gary Rob

5.1 INTRODUCTION

Accounting refers to measurement of economic events and summarizing and reporting them in the form of financial statements for use by the stakeholders. Reporting is thus the end function of accounting. To enhance the reliability of the accounting numbers, the financial statements need to be authenticated by an independent auditor. Without such authentication, the financial statements lose their usefulness to the stakeholders. Again, environmental accounting may be understood from two broad perspectives—one relating to national level environmental accounting and the other, corporate level environmental accounting.

Section 5.2 deals with environmental accounting, both at the national (macro) and firm (micro) levels. Section 5.3 discusses the principles of sustainability development reporting and its content, while Section 5.4 addresses issues relating to environmental auditing.

5.2 ENVIRONMENTAL ACCOUNTING

5.2.1 Macro-Perspective

Environmental accounting (EA) refers to a set of aggregate national data linking the environment to the economy. It, therefore, calls for necessary adjustments to the System of National Accounts (SNA) to incorporate the use or depletion of natural resources. SNA is a set of accounts which every national government prepares to represent the activities of the economy. Thus, SNA facilitates:

- computation of major economic indicators—GDP, GNP, saving rate, balance of trade, etc., and
- economic and environment policy making.

The United Nation's Statistical Division has suggested a standardized format for preparation of SNA and almost all the countries of the world have been following this format although the present format of SNA does not include full economic implications of environmental resources. But once SNA is computed in this format, necessary adjustments for use or depletion of environmental resources may be made to arrive at Environmentally Adjusted Economic Aggregates for Environmentally Sustainable Development[1] (EPP). This may be popularly referred to as 'Environmental Accounting' from the macro-perspective. Thus, the term 'Environmental Accounting' could be used to indicate, in a general sense, taking account of the environment and changes in it, and integrating the results with the system of national accounts (SNA) so as to provide a valuable information base for planning and laying policies for the integrated sustainable development and growth of the nation.[2] For computation of Environmentally Adjusted Net Domestic Product, see p. 134, Chapter 6.

5.2.2 Accounting for Corporate Environmental Performance

In Chapter 4, we discussed the corporate environmental management issues. Now, we have to identify the role of accounting in measuring economically environmental activities, taking decisions on environment related issues based on cost-benefit analysis, managing environmental costs, taking capital budgeting decisions based on, among others, green justification of processes and products, preparing financial statements in compliance with generally accepted accounting principles, getting the financial statements audited by an independent auditor and disclosure in financial statements to promote decision-making by the stakeholders. In short, the object is to account for economic effects of all environmental activities of the firm to improve the quality of life. We, therefore, use

1 The term is used by the UNO.

2 Dasgupta, N., *Environmental Accounting*, Wheeler Publishing, New Delhi, 1997, Chapter 4.

accounting in a broader sense to include financial, cost and management accounting issues including control functions like internal and external audits. The question then arises: What are the *relevant issues*? Some such issues are:

1. How to recognize environmental effects on conventional accounting practice and framing accounting policies accordingly?
2. Are the environment-related costs and revenues separately identified, measured and reported in the conventional accounting system?
3. What are environmental costs? Is there proper allocation of hidden environmental costs for better decision-making?
4. Is the amount incurred, if any, for taking necessary environmental measures during the period subdivided into suitable heads such as the following:
   (a) Liquids effluent treatment
   (b) Waste gas and air treatment
   (c) Solid waste treatment
   (d) Analysis, control and compliance
   (e) Remediation
   (f) Recycling
   (g) Accident and safety
   (h) Others, if any.
5. What is the financial and operational effect of environmental protection measures on the capital expenditure and earnings of the company in the current year? Do they have any specific impact on future periods also?
6. Is the capital expenditure decision-making process suitably adjusted for justifying 'green technology'?
7. What policy is followed regarding amortization of environment related capital expenditure?
8. Does the existing system of recording and reporting company's liabilities and provisions take into consideration environmental issues?
9. How does the company treat additional expenditure incurred for training of employees to enhance their environmental awareness?
10. How much is spent annually on research and development to innovate environment-friendly processes and products?
11. Is there any scope for setting up a catastrophe reserve?
12. Does the product innovation decision take care of environment friendliness? Does it involve additional cost?

13. What are environmental benefits? Can these benefits be identified, measured and disclosed under suitable classification such as the following:
    (a) Process benefits
    (b) Product benefits
    (c) Fiscal benefits
    (d) Overall other benefits?
14. What is the impact on profitability of the company for getting ISO 14000 accreditation and for following ISO 14001 standards? Can ISO 14001 increase net operating profit of the company?
15. What accounting standards do we need for measuring and reporting of economic activities that take care of environmental issues? Did the FASB or IASB issue any such standard? How can ICAI cooperate with other notable international accounting standard-setters to formulate a suitable accounting standard to capture identification, measurement and disclosure of environment costs and benefits of a firm in India?
16. Has the company introduced a separate environmental audit system? If yes, who forms part of the audit team—employees or external persons? What is the composition of the team?
17. Does the environmental audit report form part of the statutory audit report or separate environmental report?
18. What is the level of social responsibility reporting in the annual report of the company? Does the reporting of an environmental activity form part of social responsibility and shown separately? Or, is it shown only as a part of Director's Report?
19. Does the company show expenses on environmental activities in the annual report under a separate head or are they clubbed together with the items of operating expenses?

The above and many other similar issues become pertinent for discussion in the context of accounting for corporate environmental management. We now discuss some of them briefly.

Accounting policies

Accounting policies form the basis of measurement and reporting of economic activities of a firm and are critical for understanding its accounting numbers contained in the annual reports. The environmental awareness of the firm, translation of this awareness into environmental measures leading to some economic activities and treatment of environment-related expenses can be understood only when accounting policies of the firm disclose them in appropriate places of the financial statements. In India, AS 1, Disclosure of Accounting Policies, deals with the disclosure of significant accounting policies to be followed for preparation and presentation of financial statements. The purpose of this standard is to promote better understanding of financial statements by making the disclosure of significant accounting policies in the financial statements and the manner of doing so. Such disclosure facilitates a more meaningful inter-period and inter-firm comparison.[3]

What kind of disclosure should then form part of accounting policies to study the environment-related economic activities of a firm? A few of them are as follows:

1. Financial effect of environmental protection measures both in revenue and capital expenditure and the basis of such classification
2. Capitalization and accumulation of environmental costs and amortization thereof
3. Measurement and disclosure of environment-related liabilities and provisions
4. Setting up of catastrophe reserves and use of the same
5. Environment-related revenue expenses and their classification into suitable heads, viz., recycling, remediation, accident and safety, to mention a few
6. Disclosure of contingent liabilities.

The disclosure of contingent liabilities is a complex issue. The amount of contingent liabilities depends on the lack of environmental awareness of the company. The greater the measures taken by the company to promote environmental activities, the lower the amount of contingent liabilities involved and vice versa. Contingent liabilities are normally disclosed, if material, in the notes to financial statements.

---

3 There is no single list of accounting policies that are applicable in all circumstances—this depends on the circumstances an organisation operates. However, there are certain considerations in their selection: (a) **Prudence** (e.g. profits are not anticipated but recognised only when earned; similarly, all known liabilities and losses should be reasonably estimated), (b) **Substance over form** (accounting treatment and presentation of transactions and events in financial statements should be governed by their substance and not merely by the legal form), and (c) **Materiality** (all "material" items, the knowledge of which might influence the decisions of the users of financial statements, should be disclosed).

The *contingent liabilities relating to the environmental activities* of the company may include:

- Liabilities, provisions and reserves that have been set for the current period, and amounts accumulated to date;
- Contingent liabilities, with an estimate of the amount involved, if the event is likely to occur. The possible loss could be quantified to the extent reasonably practicable. A feasibility study of remediation costs may be taken to estimate the contingent liability. However, if the possible loss cannot be reasonably estimated, a description of the nature of contingent liability should be furnished and the reason why an estimate of the amount of the loss cannot be made should also appear as part of the note.

It may be mentioned that AS 4, Contingencies and Events Occurring after the Balance Sheet Date, is to be complied with both in letter and spirit. The standard requires disclosure only in respect of those contingencies and events which affect the financial position to a material extent. Simple disclosure of events occurring after the balance sheet date is not expected to be useful as it would not facilitate future projections. It is necessary to disclose anticipated effect of such events on revenues, expenses, assets and liabilities of the reporting entity.

Environmental costs management

Strategic cost management cannot ignore environment factors. Environmental costs may be hidden, contingent and those relating to image building, or such costs may be a part of allocated costs of the assets used for prevention of environmental degradation. The hidden costs are included in overhead expenses borne by all operations, rather than charged back to departments actually using the service. These items need proper analysis and allocation for decision-making and control.

Activity-based costing may be used for more accurate cost allocation. Since hidden costs occupy a significant portion of the total costs of a company, impact of more accurate allocation of indirect costs to products or services would be significant. In strategic cost management, the thrust is on prevention of misallocation of indirect costs to products and processes and ensuring more scientific allocation of the same to products and services. Thus, improved cost allocation is used as a 'superior strategy' to become, ultimately, better off in terms of decision-making compared to its competitors.

Better cost management enhances profitability and shareholder value. Some companies are able to cut costs and improve environmental performance simultaneously (*Business and the Environment*, 1991). For example, major hotel chains over the past two decades have tried to follow this approach. The strategies of these companies include reducing their solid waste generation and cutting their water and energy use. Almost all of them have replaced small bottles of shampoo and soap bar with small packs of shampoo and liquid soap saving substantial money, both in terms of consumption and waste of these articles by the customers. Many of them are also using recycled packaging for amenities.

Industrial companies may cut costs and enhance environmental performance at the same time by redesigning inflexible or wasteful routines. Take the case of Xerox Company, as an example. In the late 1980s, the Company's market share declined and its profit margin eroded substantially due to emergence of new entrants in the market. In 1990, the Company's management responded to the challenge with a new management initiative—the Environmental Leadership Programme—that eventually included waste reduction efforts, product 'take-back' schemes, and environment-friendly designs. By the mid-1990s, Xerox's large manufacturing complexes in Webster and New York were sending only 2% of its hazardous waste to landfills. The Company then labelled the programme an unqualified success (*Business and the Environment*, pp. 46–47). Thus, dramatic cost savings are possible when a company is under tremendous market pressure. Does stringent environmental regulation put the same kind of pressure on companies that competitive pressure does? It can be argued that investments in environmental improvements, like all other investments, are worthwhile if they deliver value after all the management costs have been included.

We shall devote a few lines to the *management of insurance and other costs*. For many, environmental management means 'risk management'. The primary objective is to avoid the costs that are associated with an industrial accident, a consumer boycott or an environmental law suit. Managing these areas effectively can itself be a source of competitive advantage. A company can benefit from a review of its insurance policies and risk management systems. Is the company buying the right policies? Is it retaining risk when the coverage is overpriced? Is it rewarding managers who reduce risk in their own operations or subsidizing risky behaviour by failing to control it adequately? The company can analyse the relative value of investing more in environment-friendly systems, rapid response teams, maintenance, and other systems and activities that reduce environmental risk. It can also work to change employee's attitude towards environmental and safety issues by designing suitable training programmes and frequently conducting such programmes in order to reduce the risk of accidents. Environmental risk can be managed more effectively by applying more rigorous quantitative analysis and also by increasing the company's emphasis on training and cultural change programmes. Like traditional business risks, some investment in environmental risk management is prudent.

5.3 REPORTING PRINCIPLES AND CONTENTS

Preparation and presentation of corporate financial reports are governed by Generally Accepted Accounting Principles (GAAP) that are applicable in a particular context. These are dominated by relevant Accounting Standareds. Reporting of environmental performances of the firm is generally considered to be a part of corporate social reporting and is likely to be guided by the same principles, guidelines and regulatory provisions. Earlier, in Chapter 4, we have discussed issues relating to sustainability and found that sustainable economic development encompasses economic, environmental and social performances of the company. The Royal Dutch/Shell Group of Companies considers sustainable development reporting in an interesting way as shown in Figure 5.1. In the figure, the sustainable development lens enables the management to see the world through the eyes of stakeholders.

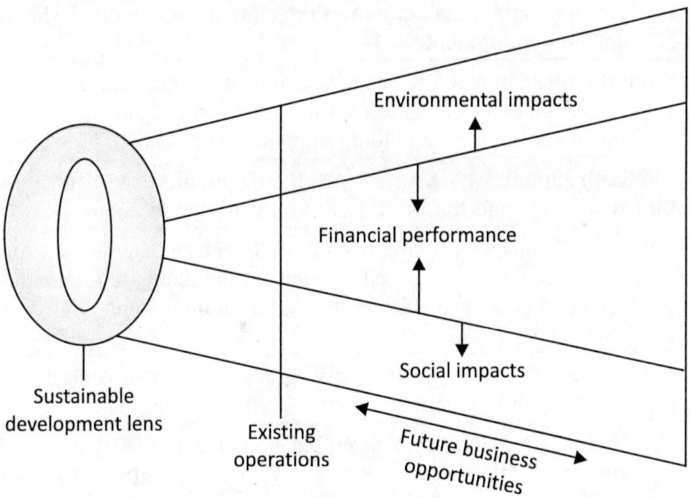

Figure 5.1 Looking through the sustainable development lens (Adapted from Cairncross, 1991.)

From the standpoint of sustainability, reporting may assume a different dimension. Accordingly, the reporting principles and contents rooted in the premise of sustainability are briefly discussed in the next Section.

5.3.1 Evolution of Sustainable Development Concept

As per the Brundtland Report, the sustainable development is defined as "the development that meets the needs of the present without compromising the ability of future generations to meet their own needs" (ICAI, 2015). The chronological evolution of the concept is provided in Table 5.1. The basic principles of Sustainable Development, however, are depicted in Figure 5.2. In the corporate world sustainable development gave rise to three important interlinked components—corporate sustainability, corporate social responsibility (CSR) and ESG reporting.

TABLE 5.1 Chronology of Sustainable Development Concept

1972	The United Nations Conference on the Human Environment at Stockholm on 16 June 1972.
1980	World Conservation Strategy at Switzerland in 1980 for defining the sustainable development.
1987	Publication of "Our Common Future" by World 16 Commission on Environment and Development that coined and defined the term sustainable development.
1991	Amnesty International, UK Business Group, a mainstream international Non-Government Organisation (NGO), established and acknowledges the role of business in upholding human rights.
1992	Rio Earth Summit where Agenda 21, the UN Framework Convention on Climate Change and the Rio Declaration was agreed upon.
2000	UN Global Compact—An initiative by UN Secretary General, Kofi Annan, to promote global corporate citizenship for upholding ten fundamental principles in the area of human rights, labour, and environment protection.
2000	UN Millennium Development Goals agreed upon to provide definitive global list of development targets by 2015.
2001	The New Partnership for Africa's Development (NEPAD) was formed to provide a common strategy for African countries to address development issues collectively.

(*Contd.*)

2001	At the Fourth World Trade Organisation (WTO) ministerial conference in Doha, Qatar, a new round of trade negotiations focused on promoting development.
2002	World Summit for Sustainable Development at Johannesburg underlines the need of working across sectors of society.
2006	Amsterdam Global Conference on Sustainability and Transparency.
2007	'Growth and Responsibility in a World Economy' G8 Summit Heiligendamm, Summit Declaration.
2009	GRI Amsterdam Declaration on Transparency and Reporting.
2011	Sustainability Accounting Standards Board (SASB) formed and developed alternative voluntary reporting approach for US publicly listed companies modeled after the financial accounting standards board.
2013	International Integrated Reporting Council released its international integrated reporting framework.
2014	The European Union Council adopted a new Directive concerning disclosure of non-financial and diversity information by large companies and groups.

Source: Compiled from Sustainability Reporting (6th ed.), ICAI, 2015.

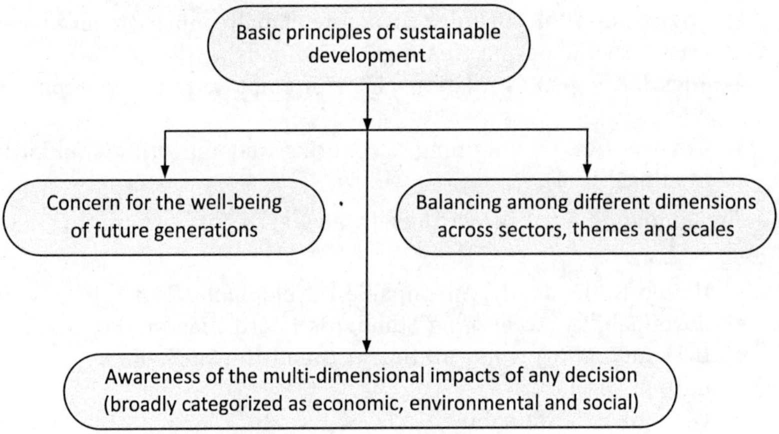

Figure 5.2 Basic Principles of Sustainability
(*Source:* Author's compilation.)

Corporate Sustainability

Sustainability in corporate sector means a balancing act which ensures systematic coordination among environment, social and financial obligations of an enterprise in a responsible, ethical and continual manner. Corporate sustainability is depended on three pillars:

- Economic obligation, that is, generation and distribution of profit.
- Social obligations, such as, maintaining social order, justice, health and hygiene, etc.
- Environmental protection or conservation of natural resources.

These three pillars are collectively referred to as *Triple Bottom Line (TBL) approach*. In 1994, John Elkington, a renowned British management consultant, coined the phrase *Triple Bottom Line* (ICAI, 2015). It advocates that a business should concentrate on its non-business obligations towards society and environment while delivering economic obligations.

Corporate Social Responsibility (CSR)[4]

Corporate social responsibility (CSR) is a qualitative assessment of initiatives taken and implemented by the corporate houses for the sake of their sustainability. The nature of CSR is qualitative and self-regulating.

Environmental Social Governance (ESG) Reporting

ESG is a quantifiable assessment of sustainability measures of business enterprises. The three main criteria covered by ESG are:

- **Environmental** (includes corporate climate policies, energy use, waste treatment and treatment of animals).
- **Social** (company's relationship with employees and community members).
- **Governance** (maintaining accounting and reporting standards in ethical way).

The following are the various frameworks for formulating ESG strategies:

- United Nations (UN) Sustainable Development Goals;
- Sustainability Accounting Standards Board's Materiality Map;
- UN Guiding Principles on Business and Human Rights;
- Carbon Disclosure Project;
- Dow Jones Sustainability Indices;
- Global Reporting Initiative, and
- Task Force on Climate-Related Financial Disclosures.

---

4 The Companies Act. 1913, made Social Responsibility Reporting obligatory in certain cases.

Relationship among ESG, CSR and Corporate Sustainability

Sustainability is the umbrella that covers both ESG reporting and CSR. ESG and CSR are instruments through which businesses can demonstrate their commitment to develop sustainable business model. CSR can be seen as the idealistic, big-picture perspective on sustainability and ESG is the practical perspective on sustainability. CSR can be seen as the precursor to ESG. The characteristics and relation between these three terms are given through Table 5.2 and Figure 5.3 respectively.

TABLE 5.2 Characteristics of ESG, CSR and Corporate Sustainability

ESG	*CSR*	*Corporate Sustainability*
Quantitative	Qualitative	Qualitative and quantitative
Externally regulated	Self-regulated	Both self and externally regulated
Directly related to business valuation	Not directly related to business valuation	Often related to business valuation
Implemented through measurable goal and audits	Implemented through corporate culture, values and brand management	Implemented through CSR and ECG.

Source: http://techtarget.com, 20/04/2023.

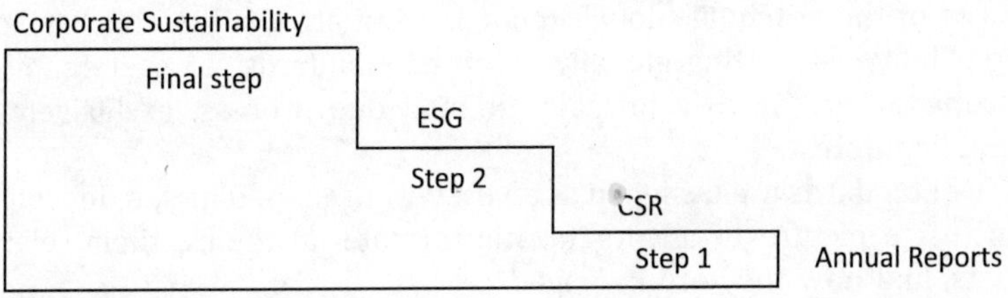

Figure 5.3 Relation between ESG, CSR and Corporate Sustainability

Sustainability Reporting

Now-a-days, 'Sustainability' forms an integral part of corporate reporting. It provides information about the organization's operations, environmental impacts, and use of resources (e.g. energy, materials, water, etc.), and outputs (in the form of waste, emissions, effluents, products) that affect the natural world (Hewitt, 2013). Experts believe that traditional financial reporting has failed to measure the social and environmental impacts that a company has on the environment, but a sustainability report can show it. Thus, simply reporting financial facts was insufficient (Yongvanich and Guthrie, 2006). Sustainability reporting is guided by three key reporting standards. These are:

- Global Reporting Initiative (GRI),
- Sustainability Accounting Standards Board (SASB), and
- Country stock exchange guidelines.

Global Reporting Initiative (GRI)

GRI is an independent international organization that helps business and other organizations take responsibility for their impacts, by providing them with the global common language to communicate those impacts. The GRI Standards help organizations understand their impacts on the economy, environment, and society—including those on human rights. This increases accountability and enhances transparency on their contribution to sustainable development. Used by more than 10,000 organizations in over 100 countries, the Standards are advancing the practice of sustainability reporting, and enabling organizations and their stakeholders to take action that creates economic, environmental and social benefits for everyone. As confirmed by 2022 research by the KPMG, the GRI Standards remain the most widely used sustainability reporting standards globally. The GRI Standards are developed and approved by the Global Sustainability Standards Board (GSSB). GSSB has been established as an independent operating entity under the auspices of the stitching Global Reporting Initiative (GRI) and has sole responsibility for setting globally accepted standards for sustainability reporting, according to a formally defined due process, exclusively in the public interest.

The Standards are designed as an easy-to-use modular set, delivering an inclusive picture of an organization's material topics, their related impacts, and how they are managed.

The Universal Standards (apply all universal standards to reporting)

- GRI 1: Foundation
- GRI 2: General Disclosures
- GRI 3: Material Topics

The Sector Standards (enable more consistent reporting on sector-specific impacts)

- GRI 11: Oil and Gas Sector
- GRI 12: Coal Sector
- GRI 13: Agriculture Aquaculture and Fishing Sectors

The Topic Standards (disclosures relevant to a particular topic)

- GRI 201: Economic Performance
- GRI 202: Market Presence
- GRI 203: Indirect Economic Impacts
- GRI 204: Procurement Practices
- GRI 205: Anti-corruption
- GRI 206: Anti-competitive Behavior
- GRI 207: Tax
- GRI 301: Materials
- GRI 302: Energy
- GRI 303: Water and Effluents
- GRI 304: Biodiversity
- GRI 305: Emissions
- GRI 306: Effluents and Waste
- GRI 306: Waste
- GRI 308: Supplier Environmental Assessment
- GRI 401: Employment
- GRI 402: Labor/Management Relations .
- GRI 403: Occupational Health and Safety
- GRI 404: Training and Education
- GRI 405: Diversity and Equal Opportunity
- GRl 406: Non-discrimination
- GR! 407: Freedom of Association and Collective Bargaining
- GRI 408: Child Labor
- GRI 409: Forced or Compulsory Labor
- GRI 410: Security Practices
- GRI 411: Rights of Indigenous Peoples
- GRI 413: Local Communities
- GRI 414: Supplier Social Assessment
- GRI 415: Public Policy
- GRI 416: Customer Health and Safety
- GRI 417: Marketing and Labeling
- GRI 418: Customer Privacy

Linking the SDGs with GRI Standards

In September 2015, the General Assembly of United Nations adopted the *2030 Agenda* for Sustainable Development that includes 17 *Sustainable Development Goals (SDGs)*. Building on the principle of "leaving no one behind", the new agenda emphasizes a holistic approach to achieve sustainable development for all. The GRI has developed tools and initiatives that help enable a strong private sector role in measuring and achieving the SDGs. The following table (Table 5.3) demonstrates how the GRI Standards are mapped with SDGs.

TABLE 5.3 Link of GRI Standards with SDGs

SDG	*GRI Standard*
Goal 1: No Poverty	207,202,203,413,411
Goal 2: Zero Hunger	411,413
Goal 3: Good Health and Well-Being	401,403,203,305,306
Goal 4: Quality Education	404
Goal 5: Gender Equality	202,203,401,405,406,414
Goal 6: Clean Water and Sanitation	303,304,306
Goal 7: Affordable and Clean Energy	302
Goal 8: Decent Work and Economic Growth	102,201,202,203,301,302,401
Goal 9: Industry Innovation and Infrastructure	201,203
Goal 10: Reduce Inequality	102,207,401,404,405
Goal 11: Sustainable Cities and Communities	203
Goal 12: Responsible Consumption and Production	301,302,303,305,306,417
Goal 13: Climate Action	201,302,305
Goal 14: Life below water	304,305,306
Goal 15: Life on Land	304,305,306
Goal 16: Peace, Justice and Strong Institution	102,206,307,403,408,410,414,416,417,418,419
Goal 17: Partnerships for the Goals	207

Source: http://www.globalreporting.org, 24/04/2023.

Sustainability Accounting Standards Board (SASB)

SASS was founded as a nonprofit organization in 2011 to help businesses and investors develop a common language about the financial impacts of sustainability. Over the years, the corporate sustainability disclosure landscape became very complex. Many global businesses and investors called for simplification and clarity in this landscape. In response, in November 2020 the International Integrated Reporting Council (IIRC) and the Sustainability Accounting Standards Board (SASB) announced their intention to merge into the Value Reporting Foundation, which was officially formed in June 2021. By integrating two entities that were focused on enterprise value creation, the merger signalled significant progress towards simplification.

The Value Reporting Foundation offered a comprehensive set of resources—including Integrated Thinking Principles, the Integrated Reporting Framework and SASB Standards—designed to help businesses and investors develop a shared understanding of enterprise value. The Value Reporting Foundation Board of Directors oversaw the strategy, finances, and operations of the entire organization, and appointed the members of the SASB Standards Board.

The SASB Standards Board was an independent board that was accountable for the due process, outcomes, and ratification of the SASB Standards.

In November 2021, the IFRS Foundation announced its plan to establish the International Sustainability Standards Board (ISSB) to develop a comprehensive global baseline of high-quality sustainability disclosure standards to meet investors' information needs. The IFRS Foundation also announced plans to consolidate with the Value Reporting Foundation and the Carbon Disclosure Standards Board (CDSB). The VRF officially consolidated into the IFRS Foundation on August 1, 2022 (https://www.sasb.org, 23/04/2023).

5.3.2 Reporting Principles of GRI

What reporting principles are essential to produce a balanced and reasonable report on an organization's economic, environmental and social performance? We give here Guidelines from *Global Reporting Initiative* (GRI) and also, in the next Section, the reporting practice of a multinational corporation, The Royal Dutch Petroleum Company. Before coming to the reporting principles, let us first give some background regarding the GRI.

GRI Guidelines

For over 25 years, GRI has developed and delivered the global best practice of sustainable reporting. It covers an organization's most significant impacts of its activities on the economy, environment, and people. The Guidelines offer Reporting Principles, Standard Disclosures and an Implementation Manual.

The GRI Secretariat is headquartered in Amstardam, Netherlands, having a network of seven regional offices worldwide (www.globalreporting.org). The GRI is an international independent standards that help businesses, governments and other organizations understand and communicate impacts of their activities.

GRI was first launched in 2000. The Guidelines were revised in 2002 based on its working experience. In 2017, 63 per cent of the largest 100 companies (N100), 75 per cent of the Global Fortune 250 (G250) prepared the Annual Reports following the GRI reporting framework. The most recent of GRI's reporting frameworks are the GRI Standards launched in October 2016. Developed by the Global Sustainability Standards Board (GSSB), the GRI standards for sustainability reporting are now a free public good.

GRI Charter Group

The Charter Group comprises organizations that publicly endorsed GRI at the time of its inauguration at the United Nations headquarters on 4th April 2002. Corporate members of the Charter Group provided financial contribution to GRI's capitalization fund. Some of the 27 participating organizations (alphabetically arranged) were:

- Accountability (Institute of Social and Ethical Accountability)
- Association of Chartered Certified Accountants
- Baxter International Inc.
- Consumers International
- Ford Motor Company
- General Motors Corporation
- Human Rights Watch
- KPMG
- Nike Inc.
- Office of the United Nations High Commissioner for Human Rights
- Price Waterhouse Coopers
- Royal Dutch/Shell
- Transparency International
- United Nations Environment Programme
- World Bank Group, and twelve other reputed organizations.

Principles of Reporting

The principles are designed with the long-term interest in mind and are expected to create an enduring foundation on which performance measurement will continue to evolve on new knowledge and learning. The questions that may be addressed in this context and the possible answers in brief are as follows:

1. What core principles form the framework of the report?
   The core principles are transparency, inclusiveness and auditability.
2. What information to report?
   It involves completeness, relevance and sustainability context.
3. What will be the criteria to check the quality or reliability of the reported information?
   The required criteria are accuracy, neutrality and comparability.
4. What will be the accessibility (how and when) of the reported information?
   It includes two important quality aspects—clarity and timeliness.
5. Is the environmental report auditable?
   The principle of auditability relates to several other principles, such as, comparability, accuracy, neutrality and completeness. Auditability signifies that the process underlying report preparation and information in the report itself meets standards for quality, reliability and other similar expectations.

The 11 principles, suggested by **GRI 2002 Guidelines**, are given in Figure 5.4. It may be mentioned that the principles of transparency and inclusiveness represent the starting point for the reporting process and are woven into the fabric of all other principles. Transparency in reporting is an exercise in accountability—the clear and open explanation of one's actions to those who have a right reason to inquire. The inclusiveness principle is rooted in the premise that stakeholder views are integral to meaningful reporting and must be incorporated during the process of designing a report.

A core principle, as shown in Figure 5.4, is auditability which refers to the extent to which information management systems and communication practices lend themselves to being examined for accuracy by both internal and external parties. In other words, reported data and information should be recorded, compiled, analysed and disclosed in a way that would enable internal or external auditors to attest to their reliability.

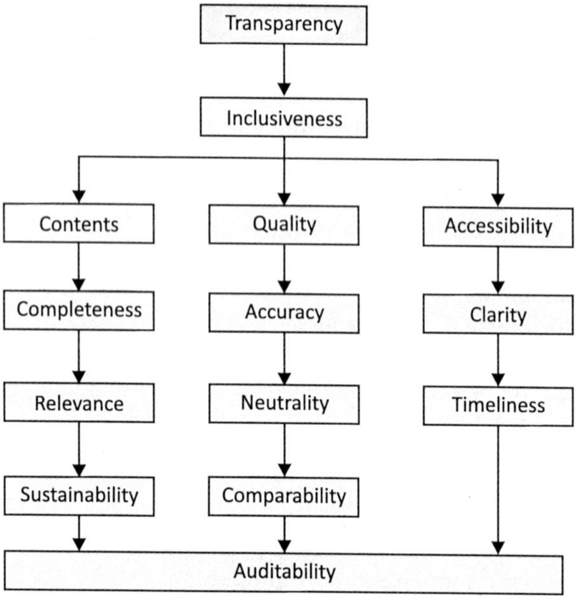

Figure 5.4 Principles of sustainable development reporting

In short, the principles outlined above should help ensure that the sustainable development report:

- presents a balanced and reasonable account of economic, environmental and social performance, and the resulting contribution of the organization to sustainable development;
- facilitates comparison over time and across organizations; and
- credibly addresses issues which are of concern to stakeholders.

5.3.3 Contents of the Reports

Part C of GRI guidelines (2002) suggests the content of the report in five sections, viz.

1. Description of vision and strategy
2. A profile of reporting organization's structure and operations and of the scope of the report
3. Governance structure and management systems
4. Content index
5. Performance indicators, namely, economic, environmental, social and integrated, if possible.

Performance indicators are grouped in terms of the three dimensions of the conventional definition of sustainability, namely, economic, environmental and social. Table 5.4 contains performance indicators according to a hierarchy of category, aspect and indicator.

TABLE 5.4 Sustainability performance indicators

	Category	*Aspect*
1.	**Economic**	
	(i) Direct economic impacts	• Customers • Suppliers • Employees • Providers of capital • Public sector (taxes, subsidies, etc.)
	(ii) Indirect economic impacts (stemming from externalities)	• Innovations (patents and partnerships) • Economic effects (positive or negative) of changes in location or operation • Contribution of a sector to GNP or national competitiveness
2.	**Environmental**	• Materials • Energy • Water • Biodiversity • Emissions, effluents and waste • Suppliers • Products and services • Compliance • Transport • Overall
3.	**Social**	
	(i) Labour practices and decent work	• Employment • Labour and management relations • Health and safety • Training and education • Diversity and opportunity
	(ii) Human rights	• Strategy and management • Non-discrimination

(*Contd.*)

TABLE 5.4 Sustainability performance indicators (*Contd.*)

	Category	*Aspect*
		• Freedom of association and collective bargaining • Child labour • Forced and compulsory labour • Disciplinary practices • Security practices • Indigenous rights
	(iii) Society	• Community • Bribery and corruption • Political contributions • Competition and pricing
	(iv) Product responsibility	• Customer health and safety • Products and services • Advertising • Respect of privacy

(Adapted from GRI, 2002, pp. 45–56.)

Performance indicators may be expressed either in qualitative or quantitative form or in both. Quantitative indicators are auditable and are more authentic information to rely upon. Qualitative indicators may be complementary to present a complete picture of an organization's economic, environmental and social performance. In a highly complex situation, where it is not possible to identify or measure quantitative indicators that capture the organization's contribution—positive or negative—to economic, environmental and social conditions, qualitative information may be the most appropriate indicator.

5.3.4 Reporting Practice of the Shell

In this section we give Shell's reporting practices for two years—2003 and 2021 to show the changes brought about by the company over time.

(i) The Shell (2003) Reporting Practice

The Royal Dutch Petroleum Company has been following the GRI Guidelines for preparation and presentation of its sustainable reporting. The Shell Report 2001 was titled as 'People, Planet and Profits'. The Company incorporated many changes in its 2001 report to improve its content and quality in succeeding years. In the Shell Report 2003, the

Company integrated the sustainable development considerations into the following (p. 8):

1. *A Social Responsibility Committee* of non-executive directors reviews the 'performance in living' by the company's Business Principles (including support for fundamental human rights and company's commitment to sustainable development).
2. *Mandatory Shell policies and standards* (business principles, health, safety and environment policies, and global environmental perfor-mance standards).
3. *Internal assurance.* Executives responsible for business segments must provide annual assurance that their operations comply with Shell policies and standards.
4. *Appraisal and reward.*
5. *Investment reviews.* All projects are required to complete integrated environmental, social and health impact assessments.
6. *Interactions with the communities.* In 2003 report, all major chemical sites introduced a social performance plan with internal reviews for high risk facilities. Major oil product sites and exploration and production companies and projects did the same in 2004.
7. *Leadership development.* The company undertakes training of employees and makes internal communication to them so that employees increasingly understand their contribution to sustainable development in respect of their jobs.

Performance data

The Shell 2003 report contains performance data (pp. 22–25) in terms of (i) economic key performance indicators, (ii) environmental key performance indicators and (iii) social key performance indicators, a few examples of each of which are given now.

Economic indicators

Total shareholder return (1994–2003) is calculated as the total of stock appreciation and yield from reinvested dividends before taxes.

Environmental indicators

1. Global warming potential (million tonnes CO_2 equivalent with target for 2010)
2. Energy efficiency (whether targets met) in respect of its
   - oil products,
   - chemicals, and
   - exploration and production.

3. Total spills (thousand tonnes) (showing target and sabotage up to 2007)
4. Flaring in exploration and production (million tonnes) (showing present position and target upto 2007)
5. External perception of environmental performance: Ranked as the 'best' or 'one of the best companies' by more than 25% of the respondents in a survey, through the Independent Reputation Tracker, conducted in 18 major Shell markets.

Social indicators

1. Diversity and inclusiveness (e.g., gender diversity in senior leadership, management and supervisory/professional staff)
2. Fatalities: fatal accident rate (among employees and contractors: per 100 million working hours)
3. Injuries—total reported case frequency (among employees and contractors; per million working hours and showing target upto 2007)
4. Reputation (Shell vs nearest competitor; survey among general public)
5. Integrity (based on survey among staff)
6. Respect for staff

The Shell Report 2003 also publishes many other milestones and data in economic, environmental and social fields (pp. 26–27).

Many of the above indicators are still relevant for companies operating in developing/emerging countries. The stakeholders will be immensely benefited to find them in financial reports of such companies.

(ii) The Shell (2021) Reporting Practice[5]

The Shell (2021) Report is divided into broad six components, viz.-

1. Core Values
2. Achieving Net-zero Emissions
3. Respecting Nature.
4. Powering Lives
5. Generating Shareholder Value, and
6. Performance Data.

Each of the above is again broken down into several sub-components and classified appropriately. We give them in some detail.

5 www.reports.shell.com/sdustainability reporti2021.

1. **Core values** comprise Business Ethics and Transparency, and Safety.
2. **Achieving net-zero emissions.** This shows working with customers and across other sectors to accelerate the *transition* to net-zero emissions.
3. **Respecting nature.** It represents protecting the environment, reducing waste and making a positive contribution to biodiversity.
4. **Powering lives.** Included in this group are information towards:
   (i) Approach to powering lives
   (ii) Providing access to energy
   (iii) Working with suppliers
   (iv) Contributing to communities
   (v) Diversity, equity and inclusion
   (vi) Worker welfare
   (vii) Respecting human rights, and
   (viii) Managing impact on people.
5. **Generating shareholder value.** The following information are included under this group of component:
   (i) Business ethics of the company
   (ii) Embedding sustainability into project
   (iii) Producing oil and natural gas
   (iv) Non-operating ventures, and
   (v) Divested ventures.
6. **Performance data.** This group includes the following:
   (i) About the data
   (ii) Standards and policies
   (iii) Powering progress targets
   (iv) Safety data
   (v) Greenhouse gas and energy data
   (vi) Other environmental data
   (vii) Social data, and
   (viii) **GRI index**. Included in the Index are:
      - Organizational profile
      - Strategy
      - Ethics and integrity
      - Governance
      - Stakeholder engagement
      - Reporting practice
      - Economic

- Environmental
- Social: labour practices and descent work
- Social: human rights
- Social: Society.

About the data of Shell it is mentioned that:

Shell began reporting voluntarily on its environmental, safety and social performance with first Shell Report in 1997. The Company supports transparency and share information and data in the current report and on www.shell.com. There are however inherent limitations to the accuracy of environmental, safety and social performance data. The Company recognizes that its data would be affected by these limitations and states that it would continue to improve data integrity by strengthening its internal controls.

Shell provides all non-financial data in this report on a 100 per cent basis for companies and joint ventures where the Company is the operator and in line with industry practice. It also believes that this boundary best reflects the regulatory requirements and internal policies for the management of potential health, safety, environmental and social impacts.

The Company included data in the report for 2021 that were confirmed by the end of March 2022. Any change will be updated in the following year's report.

Assurance[6]

Shell has clear standards and reporting requirements for its health, safety, security, environment and social performance (HSSE&SP) data. Shell companies considered and adopted these standards which define management roles and responsibilities, the scope of data facilities and how data are collected and calculated. These standards are part of HSSE&SP Control Framework. The Company cites some examples of the assurance mechanism as follows.

- Self assessment at the facility level
- Internal audits at all levels of Shell
- Quarterly reviews and assessments of the data at all levels
- An annual series of meetings between leaders at Group level and senior business managers to discuss outcomes and reporting parameters, and
- Formal sign-off by Shell's senior country leaders.

6 The most recent assurance statements are given at www.shell.com/ghg.

The Carbon Review Committee (CRC) which was formed in 2021 is tasked with ensuring that greenhouse gas (GHG) emissions measures, both absolute emissions and carbon intensity and associated metrics, comply with all regularity and legal requirements.

The Review Report Panel of independent experts helps ensure that the Company's reporting is balanced, relevant and responsive to stakeholders' interests.

Some more information about the performance data of Shell

Now let us try to measure the dimensions of the Shell Report (2021) by cursorily glancing what are included in the Performance Data of the Company. We address only four (being of non-conventional nature) of them, namely:

- Safety performance data
- Greenhouse gas and energy data
- Other environmental data, and
- Social performance data.

Safety performance data. In the (2021) Shell Report, for previous years' data (2017–2020) are given alongside the data of 2021. Under this category the following information are available:

- Personal safety
- Road Transport safety
- Process safety
- Health, and
- Security.

Greenhouse gas and energy data. All data relate to five years, 2017–2021, in respect of:

- Net carbon intensity
- Sales of gas and power produced by third parties
- Scope 1 GHG emissions (operational control)
- Scope 2 GHG emissions (operational control)
- GHG intensities (operational control):
    - Scope 1 and 2: GHG emissions (equity boundary)
    - Scope 3: GHG emissions
- Other greenhouse gas data (operational control)
- Carbon credits
- Energy use (operational control)

Other environmental data. Information for **five accounting years** are furnished in respect of:

- Air Emissions (A)
- Spills of more than 100 kg to environment
- Water use and discharge
- Waste management

Social performance data. Included in this group are the information relating to:

- Shell's People
- Training
- Diversity, equity and inclusion
- Human rights
- Contracting and procurement
- Social investment
- Tax and other payments to governments.

It is amazing to see the kind of information given in the Sustainability Report (2021) of Shell. For the sake of volume we could not give the actual data in detail under the above groups. Readers are advised to go to the Shell's website and download the required information and see for themselves why we have chosen this multinational company as a case study.

5.4 ENVIRONMENTAL AUDIT (EA)

For most environmentally conscious companies, an environmental audit is very important. In the early 1970s, the process was first developed in the United States where corporations, through EA, used to check on compliance with environmental laws (Cairncross, 1992). After the Bhopal Gas Tragedy, corporations became more anxious to ensure that their overseas subsidiaries met the same standards as their parent corporations. American multinationals started to audit abroad since then. In Europe, environmental liabilities are less severe and companies see environmental auditing as a way of discovering how they could improve their environmental performance so as to demonstrate their environmental responsibilities to the outside world. In India, the practice has not yet become popular although some companies in the private sector, viz., TISCO, ITC and a few others, have been conducting EA periodically. But from the financial year 2023–24 companies enlisted in Stock Exchanges and those under Public Sector in India will have to publish Sustainability Report.

Environmental audit refers to a systematic method of verifying that environmental regulations are complied with, the processes and products are environmentally acceptable and the business activities of the company do not affect the environment adversely. EA helps a company to identify issues before they become big problems affecting seriously the environment and the company. EA makes an objective evaluation of how well the company has been managing its environment-related activities. Environmental activists are more interested in EA. So, what are the important issues for discussion? Some of them are as follows:

1. What areas should be brought under EA in a developing country like India?
2. Who should conduct the audit and what should be the audit methodology, tools and techniques?
3. Should the EA report form part of the statutory audit report or should it become a separate report?

In the developing economies, the environmental awareness in the corporate sector is not very high, and because of less stringent legislations, environmental liabilities are also less severe. The scope of the audit may, therefore, be framed keeping in view the environmental-awareness of the company, its environment policy and commitment and, finally, the impact of its activities on the environment. The following are some of the suggested areas (Paliwal, 2001):

1. Environmental policy of the company and commitment of management
2. Resource conservation
3. Work environment, occupational health and safety
4. Compliance with regulatory requirements in terms of air and water pollution, discharge of effluents, etc.
5. Implementation of EMS if the company concerned has obtained ISO 14000 standards and following ISO 14001 standards
6. Overall impact of the company's business activities on the environment.

On the question of eligibility of an auditor, the overseas growth of EA shows that many firms without requisite expertise have entered into the business (Cairncross, p. 295). But the scenario has been changing rapidly as many multinational audit firms are joining the fray. In view of complex nature of the job that requires multidimensional approach, the work should be done by a team of experts rather than by an individual. Some companies may form the team of its own employees to start the process. For a company, which has been showing a high level of environmental performance, it may consist of external experts only. It is desirable that the team should comprise a chartered accountant (member-secretary), a chemical engineer, a mechanical engineer, a management expert, and a practising lawyer. In the absence of an acceptable standard of audit methodology, the team should define the objectives, methodology and procedures of audit, and the tools and techniques that should be applied. Companies which have obtained ISO accreditation and are following ISO 14000 standards should follow the prescribed guidelines for EA.

On the question of EA report in the developing countries, where environmental awareness is not very high even in the corporate sector, it is hard to expect that a separate report should be published along the line of statutory audit report. Rather, it should be made part of annual audit report to make the report least expensive way of bringing it to the attention of the management and the stakeholders. EA may be conducted periodically rather than making it an annual feature. Audits become far more useful when senior management backs them than when they are considered merely an obligation. Further, no company may be willing to append to its annual report the full details of its auditor's review of environmental performance on the ground of cost and public criticism. What matters, after all, is not how the report is published but what action is taken to follow up on the audit findings.

Further, Sustainability Report has been made compulsory by SEBI for listed Indian companies with effect from the financial year 2022–23. The DPE is not also falling behind. So, with improvement in corporate financial report (through publication of a Sustainability Report as a separate item, there is bound to be improvement in the practice of EA—initially through voluntary measures and later on, with intervention of regulatory bodies and influence of international practices. Then the other related issues, viz., who will conduct the EA, the composition of EA team and disclosure of EA report, etc. will be resolved.

SUMMARY

Accounting stands for measurement of economic events, preparation of financial statements through an acceptable process, getting the accounting numbers/information authenticated by an independent auditor to uphold the quality and reliability of the information disclosed.

The financial statements, popularly known as annual reports, are then placed before the shareholders at the Annual General Meeting (AGM) for approval. Apart from annual reports, there are other avenues of providing accounting information to the stakeholders (e.g., website, print and electronic media, etc.) although annual report is the most popular source of getting information on corporate performance including environmental performance. The dimension of annual report has also changed. It is now termed as Sustainability Report comprising three components—economic, environmental and social issues. The Shell Reports (both 2003 and 2021) bear testimony to the new developments in this context. So, the issues relating to financial accounting and reporting, cost and management accounting and auditing concerning management of environmental performance of the company have been raised and some of them have also been discussed in this chapter.

MULTIPLE CHOICE QUESTIONS

1. The System of National Accounts (SNA) makes some adjustments to incorporate the use or depletion of natural resources. SNA facilitates the following *except:*
   (a) Computation of GDP and GNP
   (b) Determination of saving rate
   (c) Computation of balance of trade
   (d) Computation of profit or loss of the corporate entity
2. From macro-perspective, Environment Accounting can be used for:
   (a) Taking accounting of the environment and changes in it
   (b) Integrating the results with SNA
   (c) Providing a valuable information base for planning and laying policies of the economy
   (d) All of the above
3. Environmental measures during a period may be subdivided into the following *except:*
   (a) Remediation
   (b) Treatment of process loss
   (c) Liquids effluent treatment
   (d) Accident and safety
4. Benefits of Environmental Accounting include the following:
   (a) Process benefits
   (b) Product benefits
   (c) Fiscal benefits
   (d) All of the above

5. There are certain considerations in selecting the accounting policies of a firm. They are the following *except:*
   (a) Prudence
   (b) Materiality
   (c) Accounting period
   (d) Substance over form
6. GRI Principles of Sustainable Reporting include the following:
   (a) Transparency and inclusiveness
   (b) Contents, quality and accessibility
   (c) Relevance, neutrality, timeliness and auditability
   (d) All of the above
7. Sustainability Performance Indicators under environment category include the following *except*:
   (a) Materials, energy and water
   (b) Biodiversity, emissions, effluents and waste
   (c) Strategy, management, training and education
   (d) Products, services and transport
8. Sustainability Performance Indicators under economic category does not include:
   (a) Strategy and management
   (b) Customers and suppliers
   (c) Employees and providers of capital
   (d) Public sector (taxes, subsidies, etc.)
9. Basic Principles of Sustainability include the following except:
   (a) Concern for the well-being of future generations
   (b) Defining Sustainability concept
   (c) Balancing among different dimensions across sectors, themes and scales
   (d) Awareness of the multi-dimensional impacts of any decision on economic, environmental and social
10. Corporate Sustainability does not stand on (Tick the right answer):
    (a) Economic obligation
    (b) Social obligation
    (c) International relation
    (d) Conservation of natural resources
11. The criteria covered by Environmental Social Governance (ESG) Reporting include the following:
    (a) Governance
    (b) Social Impacts
    (c) Environmental impacts
    (d) All of the above
12. The issues relating to accounting for corporate environmental performance include the following:

(a) Recognition of environmental effects on environmental accounting practice
(b) Identification of environmental costs and revenues
(c) Amortization of environment-related capital expenditure
(d) All of the above

13. GRI Principles of Sustainable reporting include the following:
(a) Transparency and inclusiveness
(b) Contents, quality and accessibility
(c) Relevance, neutrality, timeless and auditability
(d) All of the above

14. The Royal Dutch/Shell Group of Companies follows sustainable development reporting. It includes:
(a) Environmental impacts
(b) Financial performance
(c) Social impacts
(d) All of the above

15. The characteristics of Corporate Sustainability for Social Responsibility include the following *except:*
(a) Qualitative
(b) Self-regulated
(c) Quantitative
(d) Implementation through corporate culture, values, etc.

16. State the correct chronological steps/sequences of ESG, CSR, Annual Reports and Corporate Sustainability from the following:
(a) Annual Reports, ESG, CSR and Corporate Sustainability
(b) Annual Reports, CSR, ESG and Corporate Sustainability
(c) Corporate Sustainability, ESG, CSR and Annual Reports
(d) Corporate Sustainability, CSR, ESG and Annual Reports

17. GRI (Global Reporting Initiative):
(a) Is an independent international organization
(b) Provides the global common language for reporting
(c) Increases accountability and enhances transparency on their contribution to sustainable development
(d) All of the above

18. Find the correct match from the following list of Sustainable Development Goals (SDGs) and relevant GRI Standards:

Sustainable Development Goals	*GRI Standards*
(a) Goal 4: Quality Education	411
(b) Goal 6: Clean Water & Sanitation	303, 304, 306
(c) Goal 10: Reduce Inequality	201, 203
(d) Goal 13: Climate Action	207

19. Give the correct match of questions with answers regarding GRI's principles for performance measurement from the following list:

	Questions	*Answers*
(a)	What information to report?	It involves completeness, relevance & sustainability context
(b)	Criteria to check quality or reliability	Clarity and timeliness
(c)	Accessibility of the reported information (how and when)	Accuracy, neutrality and comparability
(d)	What core principles form framework of report?	It includes comparability, accuracy, Neutrality and completeness

20. The Shell (2021) Reporting Practice can be divided into several groups, viz.—
    (a) Core values and respecting nature
    (b) Achieving net-zero emissions
    (c) Powering lives and generating shareholder value
    (d) All of the above
21. GRI Index in Shell (2021) Report does not include:
    (a) Business ethics of the company
    (b) Organizational profile and strategy
    (c) Ethics, integrity and governance
    (d) Reporting practice
22. Assurance mechanism in GRI (2021) Report of Shell includes
    (a) Internal audits
    (b) Self-assessment
    (c) Quarterly review
    (d) All of the above
23. In Shell (2021) Sustainability Report, greenhouse gas and energy data include the following *except:*
    (a) Net carbon intensity
    (b) Energy use
    (c) Carbon credit
    (d) Diversity and inclusion

EXERCISES

1. Explain Environmental Accounting from macro perspective.
2. What purposes do accounting policies serve in financial reporting?
3. What considerations do influence the selection of accounting policies? Explain them briefly.
4. What kind of disclosures form part of accounting policies to study the environment-related economic activities of a firm?

5. Write a short note on disclosure of contingent liabilities relating to environmental activities of a firm.
6. 'Some companies are able to cut costs and improve environmental performance simultaneously'. Do you agree? Explain.
7. Preparation and presentation of corporate financial reports are governed by Generally Accepted Accounting Principles (GAP) that are applicable in a particular context. Elucidate the statement.
8. Sketch the sustainable development lens that may represent the sustainable development reporting adopted by Royal Dutch/Shell Group of companies.
9. Give a brief account of 11 principles suggested by GRI Guidelines. What objectives are kept in mind in these principles?
10. Sustainability Performance Indicators may be grouped under three broad indicators—economic, environmental and social. State the aspects to be covered under Environmental Indicators and explain any one of them.
11. What is Sustainable Reporting? What are its objectives and principles?
12. Give a chronology of Sustainable Development Concept.
13. What are the three pillars of corporate sustainability? Write a few words on each.
14. Explain the "Triple Bottom Line" Approach.
15. Give a few characteristics of ESG, CSR and Corporate Sustainability. Is there any relationship among them?
16. Write notes on Global Reporting Initiative (GRI).
17. Regarding GRI standards, it is said that the "standards are designed as the easy-to-use modular set, delivering an inclusive picture of an organization's material topics, their related impacts, and how they are managed." Elucidate the statement.
18. In September 2015, the General Assembly of United Nations adopted the 2030 Agenda for Sustainable Development that includes 17 sustainable development goals. Mention ten of them.
19. The Sustainability Accounting Standards Board (SASB) "develops a common language" about the financial impacts of sustainability. State a few standards and mention the sustainability goal/s served by them.
20. The Value Reporting Foundation (2021) offers a comprehensive set of resources, including Integrated Thinking Principles, the Integrated Reporting Framework and SASB standards, designed to help businesses and investors a shared understanding of enterprise value". Explain.
21. GRI issued guidelines for sustainable reporting. What purposes are served by such guidelines?
22. What are the social indicators of sustainability reports under GRI guidelines? Explain 'diversity' and 'inclusive' aspects.
23. GRI Standards can be classified into three groups: (a) Universal standards, (b) Sector standards, and (c) Topic standards. Mention two from each group.

24. GRI standards can be linked with Sustainability Development Goals (SDGs). State any five SDGs and link them with relevant GRI standards.
25. Briefly describe the role of Sustainability Accounting Standards Boards (SASB) in developing International Integrated Reporting Council (IIRC) and Value Reporting Foundation (VRF) and their functions.
26. The GRI Charter Group comprises 27 reported organizations throughout the world. Mention ten (alphabetically) of them.
27. The GRI (2002) Guidelines give 11 principles of transparency and inclusiveness for the reporting process. Enumerate them.
28. Part C of GRI (2002) Guidelines suggests the content of the report in five Sections. What are they?
29. What are six components of Shell (2021) Report? Explain any one of them.
30. Enumerate what GRI Index stands for Shell (2021) Report.
31. In preparing (2021) Report, the Shell Company follows standards and reporting requirements which are part of HSSE&SP Control Framework. Give five examples of this assurance mechanism.
32. What is Environmental Audit (EA)? State some possible areas that may be covered under EA.
33. In view of multi-dimensional nature of EA, name with justification some of the experts who may be included in a team of such audit.

REFERENCES

Cairncross, Frances, *Costing the Earth: The challenge for governments, the opportunities for business,* Harvard Business School Press, 1991.

Dasgupta, N., *Environmental Accounting,* Wheeler Publishing, New Delhi, 1997.

ICAI, *Accounting Standards (AS 1),* New Delhi, 1979.

ICAI, *Sustainability Reporting,* 6th ed., 2015.

Paliwal, Udailal, "Environmental Audit in Manufacturing Industries", *Indian Accounting Review,* Vol. 5, No. 1, June 2001.

Shell Reports, 2001, 2003 and 2021.

UN, *GRI Guidelines,* 2002 and 2021.

www.globalreporting.org

info@globalreporting.org

www.shell.com/annualreport

www.shell.com/shellreport/data

6

Corporate Environmental Accounting and Reporting in India

6.1 INTRODUCTION

Corporate environmental accounting and reporting is a part of Corporate Sustainability Report (CSR) which in turn forms part of annual accounting and reporting programme of a firm. Apart from the mandatory information, a modern company may publish a lot of other information voluntarily for the use of its stakeholders. We have discussed several issues concerning voluntary publication of environmental information in Chapters 2 and 5.

In this chapter, we give a brief account of environmental accounting and reporting practices in the corporate sector in India. Section 6.2 gives a brief description of earlier studies. Section 6.3 shows summarised results of scanning the annual reports of 14 sample companies. In Section 6.4, we also give some distinguishing features of the reporting practices of the sample companies along with comments. Section 6.5 gives new case studies in recent times.

6.2 EARLIER STUDIES

The studies published on environmental accounting are few and far between. Among them the most notable was by N. Dasgupta in 1997. The book, *Environmental Accounting*, was first of its kind in India.

Because of the close relationship between economic development issues and environmental issues, it has been felt that the Standard National Accounts (SNA) fall short of reflecting overall national well-being in its true perspective. These fail to recognize the true contribution of environment and natural resources to the economic activity and of the impact of economic activities on the environment. The neglect of environment and natural resources, and changes therein, lead to overstatement of income and growth rate. According to Dasgupta, preparation of accounts incorporating the contribution of environment and natural resources, and changes therein, in the national accounts is referred to as **Environmental Accounting**.

Based on the system of Integrated Environmental and Economic Accounting (IEEA), as suggested by the UN Statistical office (UNSTAT), the above-mentioned book describes how to prepare environmental accounts duly integrating the environment and natural resources, and changes therein, with the national accounts in a lucid and comprehensive way. According to Dasgupta (1997), when all environmental costs and other accumulations have been expressed in value terms, the deduction of environmental costs from NDP will give an Environmentally adjusted net Domestic Product (EDP).

$$\text{NDP} = C + I + (X - M)$$

where, NDP = Net domestic product
C = Final consumption excluding depreciation
I = Net capital formation after depreciation
X = Exports
M = Imports

To find EDP, all environmental costs are deducted from NDP.

The environmental costs comprise—(i) depletion in the produced economic assets, non-produced economic assets and environmental assets, and (ii) degradation of environmental assets.

Thus, EDP is divided into two parts:

(i) EDP_1: It is after depletion in the produced economic assets, non-produced economic assets and environmental assets. That is,

$\text{EDP}_1 = C + I -$ (Depletion of p_{ec} + np_{ec} + environmental assets) + $(X - M)$

or EDP_1 = NDP – Depletion of all types of assets

(ii) $\text{EDP}_2 = C + I -$ (Depletion of p_{ec} + np_{ec} + environmental assets + degradation of environmental assets) + $(X - M)$

or $EDP_2 = EDP_1$ – Degradation of environmental assets

or EDP_2 = NDP – (Depletion of all types of assets + Degradation of environmental assets).

The results that may be derived through environmental accounting would reveal, according to N. Dasgupta, useful indicators of development and sustainability. If EDP_1 and EDP_2 are decreasing, the situation is alarming and the sustainability is threatened. A number of policy questions may then be raised (Dasgupta, pp. 51–52), some of which are as follows:

1. Do royalties go for consumption, or are they channelled into productive investment?
2. Is the export of natural resources increasingly liquidating the assets?
3. Do control measures for pollution emissions roughly balance costs and benefits?
4. How do monetary and fiscal policy affect GDP and NDP?
5. What substitutes be encouraged?
6. How to protect/counteract the use or reduce the deterioration of natural resources?

Dasgupta then dealt with in detail the valuation of natural assets and changes therein (Chapter 5), merits and demerits of environmental accounting (Chapter 6), implementation of environmental accounting (Chapter 7) and, finally, environmental accounting for developing countries (Chapter 8).

To sum up, it can be said that the entire work was done from a macro-standpoint and hence environmental management and accounting for environmental management (which has been the thrust of the present book) remained outside the purview of Dasgupta's treatise.

Three other notable studies on the subject are: (i) Bhattacharyya and Banerjee, (2002); (ii) Khasnobis, (2002), and (iii) Khasnobis, (2003). While (i) and (iii) relate to important issues concerning environmental management from a macro-perspective, in (ii) we find four works that directly relate to corporate environmental management issues, viz.,

1. *Environmental Management and Sustainability: Corporate strategy for gaining competitive advantage* (M. Saha)
2. *Life Cycle Assessment: A methodology for measuring the 'triple' bottom line of 21st century business* (K. Chatterjee)
3. *Green Technology and Zero-Base Innovation for Sustainable Development* (R. Pani)
4. *Green Accounting and Reporting in India—A case study* (S. Ghosh).

While all the above articles deal with many emerging issues regarding accounting for environmental management, it is only in the 4th article that we find a case study of corporate reporting practices in India as reflected by the practices of 16 companies classified into 6 industry groups for the financial year 1999–2000. The disclosure practices with respect to key environmental issues, e.g., pollution control, green production research, energy conservation, recycling of wastes, etc., were examined. It was found that environmental information in annual accounts of the sample companies were more of qualitative type, narrative disclosure (50%), than of quantitative type (25%). According to S. Ghosh, such environmental information were provided 'casually and not systematically' mainly in the Director's Report. So, the accounting and reporting aspects of environmental management were 'weak' (p. 172).

Aloke Kumar Pramanik's volume contains 40 articles on various areas of environmental management, namely, accounting, auditing and reporting. Although it is one of the maiden treatises on the subject and it has its usefulness as a reference book, most of its articles are of general nature and do not address many of the issues under consideration in the present book.

Over the last couple of years, a number of articles appeared in professional and academic journals published in India and Bangladesh. Notable among them are the following:

1. Eresi, K., "Environment Information Disclosure in Annual Reports", *The Chartered Accountant*, Vol. 45, No. 7, January 1996.
2. Vasal, V.K., "Accounting for Sustainable Economic Development: Issues and Evidences", *Indian Journal of Accounting*, Vol. 29, No. 1, June 1998.
3. Banerjee, Ashok, "Issues in Environmental Accounting and Reporting", *Indian Journal of Accounting*, Vol. 30, No. 1, June 1999.
4. Bose, S. and De, A., "Environment—Costing and accounting", *The Management Accountant*, Vol. 34, No. 6, June 1999.
5. Mishra, K.K., "Environmental Reporting in Business", *The Management Accountant*, Vol. 34, No. 6, June 1999.
6. Banerji, U., "Environment Management System (EMS): A business tool for increased profitability", *The Management Accountant*, Vol. 35, No. 6, June 2000.
7. Bose, A., "Environment System Risk Audit and Management Control System", *The Management Accountant*, Vol. 35, No. 6, June 2000.

8. Rao, M.P., "Environmental Accounting and Auditing–A general view", *The Management Accountant*, Vol. 35, No. 6, June 2000.
9. Cheema, C.S., "Global Initiatives on Environmental Reporting", *The Management Accountant*, Vol. 35, No. 6, June 2000.
10. Sundar, Ravi, M., "Corporate Environmental Reporting: Present status and future challenges", ICFAI, Vol. 7, No. 1, January 2001.
11. Parker, L.D., "Environmental Costing: A path to implementation", *The Cost and Management*, ICMA, Bangladesh, January-February 2002.
12. Gupta, R.R., "Emerging Issues in Environmental Accounting", *The Management Accountant*, Vol. 37, No. 8, August 2002.
13. Banerjee, B., "Accounting for Corporate Environmental Management in India", *The Management Accountant*, Vol. 37, No. 12, December 2002.
14. Patra, S., "Accounting and Reporting for Environment–A case study of TISCO", *The Management Accountant*, Vol. 38, No. 6, June 2003.
15. Chattopadhyay, P., "Pollution Accounting", *The Management Accountant*, Vol. 38, No. 12, December 2003.
16. Salahuddin, A. and Salimuddin, Md., "Environmental and Natural Resource Accounting: An overview", *The Cost and Management*, ICMA, Bangladesh, May-June 2003.
17. Ghosh, A. and Chakraborty, S., "Environmental Accounting: An attempt for sustainable development with methodological approach", *The Management Accountant*, Vol. 40, No. 6, June 2005.
18. Oza, H.S., "Environmental Accounting: Linkages with management control systems", *The Management Accountant*, Vol. 40, No. 6, June 2005.

We will examine only a few articles from the above, which are relevant to our context. Eresi's study (1996) is one of the important works done on the subject. He examined, among others, whether green (environmental) awareness of many companies as expressed in different statements are translated into specific action plans. His sample comprises 68 companies for the periods 1991–92 and 1992–93. Although the samples were not drawn based on a systematic approach, Eresi's study revealed that disclosure on environmental issues was few and far between, and that such disclosure, apart from that under Section 217(1)(e), was mainly made in a narrative form in the Director's Report. Banerjee (1999), however, examined two main perspectives of environmental accounting—at the national (macro) level and at the corporate level (micro). Bose and De (1999), following

Rau and Wooten (1980), discussed Environmental Impact Assessment (EIA) which is mandatory for most of the development projects. In keeping with the growing trend of computing environmental costs of mitigating the adverse effects of developmental actions, a method of quasi-quantitative discussion making has been suggested. The cost evaluation technique takes the quantitative inputs from a traditional EIA and combines them with differential costs of project alternatives to make EIA decision making more objective. Mishra's article (1999) relates to macro aspects of environmental reporting and disclosure. He emphasizes that government can take measures through instruments like pollution tax, tradable pollution permits, surround spoiling tax, effluent charges, etc. The Institute of Chartered Accountants of India, the Institute of Cost Accountants and the Institute of Company Secretaries should be assigned to play a social role.

Rao (2000) discussed environmental accounting methods, life cycle costing, full cost accounting and benefits assessment. Environmental expenditures and normal expenditures should be separated, measured and disclosed. He suggested capitalization of environmental expenditures and setting up of catastrophe reserves. Environmental audit should cover compliance audit, EMS audit, and environmental issues management audit. Environmental audit standards are framed by individual companies. Rao also suggested disclosure of environmental policies, accounting treatment, catastrophe reserves, and contingent liabilities in the Director's Report.

Sundar (2001) addressed the information needs of various kinds of stakeholders on corporate environmental performance. While giving more emphasis to the needs of providing environmental information for investors, lenders and environmental groups, he examined the existing measurement and reporting issues in accounting in respect of environmental costs and trends in environmental reporting.

Parker (2002) classified organizations into self-regulatory, non-compliant, minimum compliant, compliant plus voluntarily more environmentally responsible, and proactive environmental leader. He then dealt with different approaches of green costing—life cycle costing, cradle-to-grave costing, full costing and activity-based costing. He classified green costs into prevention and remediation of damage costs, conservation of resources cost and environmental losses. According to him, communities and governments will ultimately press for cost estimates of the externalities of the firm's environmental impacts. These will bring more challenging measurement problems into focus.

Patra (2003) made a case study of TISCO for the financial years 1995–96 to 1999–2000 to examine environmental accounting and reporting practice and found the following.

1. The company launched environmental management programmes to protect environment from pollution.
2. As a responsible corporate citizen, it spent, on an average, an expenditure of ₹25 crore per annum towards prevention of pollution and welfare purposes.
3. Financial data have not been separately disclosed in the financial statement under the head 'Environmental cost and expenditure'. Contingent liabilities related to environmental pollution have not been disclosed.

According to the author, such initiative on the part of TISCO may encourage other companies to follow suit. He suggested that Government of India should enact a new company law to make disclosure of environmental information mandatory. Award for best presentation can also be introduced.

Oza (2005) stressed the need to be concerned for environmental imbalances by a corporate citizen, how environmental accounting can help in becoming environmentally accountable, the present status in terms of legal requirements for environment-related information and practices and what needs to be done by business firms to remain profitable for long term along with meeting the challenges of environmental accountability. He suggested a list of various environment-related information required to be generated by business firms. He quoted extensively from earlier studies to show the lack of concern of the companies to publish environment-related information in their annual reports. While enumerating the type of environmental information that may be required by internal users (management) and the external users (regulatory bodies, government, tax authorities, customers, employees, shareholders, proximate community, etc.), Oza stressed the need for developing a culture of environmental accountability within the organization—from top management to supervisory and manual staff—for progressing from legal compliances to sustainable development stage. This can be effectively achieved following an effective management control system.

All the case studies were done when the 1956 Companies Act was in vogue. Then came the new Companies Act, 2013. Section 217(1)(e) of 1956 Act was replaced by **Section 134(3)(m)** of the Act of 2013. In the new Act, there is no provision for classification of 21 industry groups for giving certain information by the Board of Directors. In the Appendix to Chapter 3 we have however provided the information for the readers.

6.3 CASE STUDY SECTION

In this Section, we provide the following information to the readers:

1. Global Trend in Sustainability Reporting
2. Emergence of Sustainability Reporting and Assurance: A Global Perspective (part of a study made by Professor Zabiholla Rezaee and two others: published in Indian Accounting Review, June 2023)
3. Evolution of Sustainability Reporting in India
4. Studies of 100 companies (in abridged form) from ET 500 top companies under the Companies Act, 1956, and
5. Case study of two companies, ITC and SAIL, for the financial year, 2021–22, to show the types of voluntary disclosures in the Corporate Annual Reports.

1. *Global Trends in Sustainability Reporting*

As per the KPMG Survey of Sustainability Reporting 2022, the N100 companies have continued to steadily increase their reporting rates with each global survey. Ten years ago, 64% of N100[1] companies reported sustainability facts. In 2022, it increased to 79%. Presently near about all top 250 companies (G250 companies) reported their sustainability measures. In 2022, the rate of reporting among the G250[2] climbed up at 96% from 93% in the year 2020 (Chart 6.1). The notable observations of the survey are as follows:

- **Regional N100 sustainable reporting rates in Asia Pacific and Europe are on the rise:** The Asia Pacific region leads in sustainability reporting among the N100, with 89 percent of its companies undertaking sustainability reporting. This is followed by Europe (82 percent), the Americas (74 percent) and the Middle East and Africa (56 percent).
- **Integrated reporting[3] culture is strong in the Middle East and Asia Pacific region:** The Middle East leads the N100 at 55 percent and with a 12 percent growth in integrated reporting since 2020. This is followed by the Asia Pacific region at 30 percent (a growth of 5 percentages from 2020) and the Latin

1 The N100 refers to a worldwide sample of 4,900 companies comprising the top 100 companies by revenue in each of the 49 countries researched in the KPMG Survey of Corporate Responsibility Reporting 2017 study.

2 The G250 refers to the world's 250 largest companies by revenue based on the Fortune 500 ranking of 2016.

3 Integrated reporting is a report that combines both financial and non-financial data in a single annual report.

America at 28 percentages (a growth rate of 12 percentages from 2022).

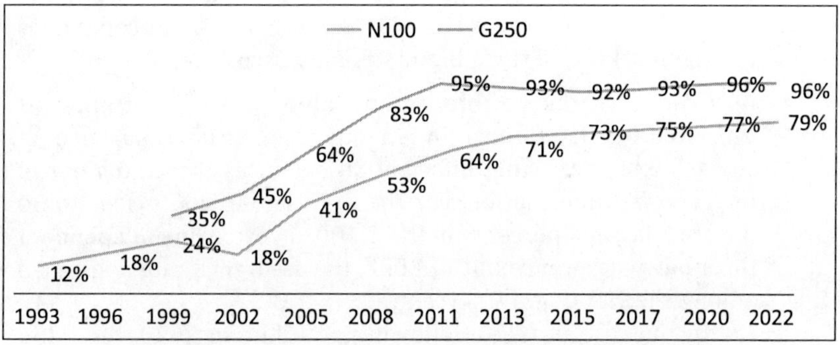

CHART 6.1 Global sustainability reporting rates (1993–2022)
(*Source:* KPMG Survey of Sustainability Reporting 2022.)

- **The GRI remains the most dominant standard used around the world:** Singapore, Taiwan and Chile lead the uptake of the GRI reporting standard and the SASB standard is the leading reporting standard among companies in the US, Canada and Brazil. But as per the survey, the leading adopters of stock exchange guidelines are South Africa, Malaysia and India.

TABLE 6.1 Top 10 countries under N100 Sustainability Reporting in 2022

As per GRI Standard	*Stock Exchange Guidelines*	*As per SASB Standard*
Singapore (100%)	South Africa (100%)	USA (75%)
Taiwan (99%)	Malaysia (95%)	Canada (72%)
Chile 96%	India (89%)	Brazil (64%)
Brazil (93%)	Singapore (85%)	Mexico (63%)
Spain (93%)	Taiwan (82%)	UK (59%)
Italy (90%)	Thailand (61%)	Chile (58%)
Austria (89%)	China (61%)	Uruguay (56%)
Finland (87%)	UAE (47%)	Hungary (56%)
Japan (87%)	Mexico (46%)	Argentina (55%)
Argentina (85%)	Kazakistan (45%)	Taiwan (52%)

Source: https://kpmg.com/xx/en/home/insights/2022/09/survey-of-sustainability-reporting-2022/global-trends, 23/04/2023.

- **Most companies are using materiality assessments[4]:** Materiality is the cornerstone of sustainability reporting. Around the world, a significant majority of sustainability reporting companies in both the N100 (71 percent) and G250 companies (77 percent) are performing materiality assessments.
- **Assurance[5] rates double among Chinese G250 companies but steady elsewhere:** Independent external assurance of sustainability reporting information enhances the credibility of the reported information. For the first time in 2020 close to 50 percent, i.e., 49 percent of the N100 invested in independent third-party assurance but in 2022, the assurance rate decreased among the N100 at 47 percent.

  In the case of G250, following a decline in 2020, the G250 assurance rate increased in 2022 from 62 percent to 63 percent. This 1 percent inclination happened only because of China. The Chinese companies in the G250 doubled its independent external assurance of sustainability reporting from 15 (in nos.) in 2020 to 30 (in nos.) in 2022.

2. *Emergence of Sustainability Reporting and Assurance: A Global Perspective*

Professor Zabiholla Rezaee and two others of Memphis University, USA, published an article[6] on Sustainable Reporting and Assurance. They examined the factors and consequences of sustainability reporting and assurance (SRA) worldwide using the Global Reporting Initiative database from 2005–2016. Sustainability factors are both quality and quantity of SRA. They constructed several variables pertaining to the consequences of SRA, such as, environmental, social and governance (ESG) sustainability performance disclosures, indices, ratings, and the use of the United Nations Sustainable Development Goals (SDGs). The sustainability factors are used as dependent variables and the

4 The materiality process assesses the impact that an ESG-related topic will have within a specific context.

5 Assurance is the process of obtaining an opinion from the third party on the reliability of information disclosed in the report or the context of information presented therein.

6 See Zabiholla, Rezaee and others, "Emergence of Sustainability Reporting and Assurance: A Global Perspective", *Indian Accounting Review,* June 2023, pp. 1–23.

sustainability consequences are explanatory variables in the regression analyses. They found a:

1. significant worldwide increase of both quantity and quality of SRA in the past decade;
2. positive association between the quality and quantity of SRA and sustainability disclosure, and the United Nations Sustainable Development Goals (SDGs);
3. significant association between the quantity, quality of sustainability reporting and the legal, social, ethical, and environmental attributes.

Their results provide an insight into both factors and consequences of SRA, which sheds light in identifying the nature and benefits of SRA in the *voluntary disclosure* literature. These findings are relevant to current debates among global policymakers, regulators, standard setters, the business community, and the accounting profession in improving the quantity and quality of SRA and the *move toward mandatory and standardized integrated sustainability reporting.*[7] The results are also relevant to the International Sustainability Standards Board in establishing sustainability guidelines in standardizing sustainability reporting and assurance.

3. *Evolution of Sustainability Reporting in India*

The journey of sustainable reporting in India started with 'Environmental Social and Governance (ESG)' reporting in 2009 when the Ministry of Corporate Affairs (MCA) issued Voluntary Guidelines on Corporate Social Responsibility which can be considered as the first step towards implementation of the business responsibility concept. Since then, the reporting landscape has come a long way with the introduction of Business Responsibility Reporting (BRR), Corporate Social Responsibility (CSR), Integrated Reporting, National Guidelines on Responsible Business Conduct (NGRBC) and now the Business Responsibility and Sustainability Report (BRSR)—introduced through a SEBI circular dated 10 May 2021. The process of evolution of Sustainable Reporting is given in Table 6.2

7 See also Sustainability Reporting Practice (2021) of Shell International Company in Chapter 5.

TABLE 6.2 Process of Evolution of Sustainable Reporting in India

Year	*Significant Development*
2009	MCA issued National Voluntary Guidelines (NVGs) on Corporate Social Responsibility.
2012	SEBI mandated that the top 100 listed companies (by market capitalisation) to file BRR based on NVGs along with their annual reports.
2014	CSR is mandated and CSR Rules come into force.
2015	Requirement for filling BRR was extended to the top 500 listed companies by market capitalisation.
2017	SEBI circular advised that Integrating Reporting may be adopted on a voluntary basis from financial year 2017–18 by the top 500 companies which are required to prepare BRR.
2018	The MCA constituted a committee on Business Responsibility Reporting to finalise business responsibility reporting formats for listed and unlisted companies, based on the framework of the NGRBC.
2019	SEBI extended the BRR requirement to the top 1000 listed companies by market capitalisation from financial year 2019–20.
2020	The ***Gyaneshwar Kumar Singh*** Committee of MCA highlighted the need to revise the existing framework and incorporate a new reporting standard called the Business Responsibility & Sustainability Reporting (BRSR).
2021	SEBI made filing of BRSR for 1000 listed entities (by market capitalization) on voluntary basis for the FY 2021–22 and on mandatory basis from the FY 2022–23.

Source: Price Water House Cooper, July 2021.

The BRSR is an initiative towards ensuring that investors have access to standardized disclosures on ESG parameters. This would enable them to identify and assess sustainability related risks and opportunities of companies and make better investment decisions. The structure of BRSR is provided in Chart 6.2 with brief description of reporting requirements. Voluntary sections are presented in Table 6.3. The nine principles of NGRBC are aligned with SDGs which help businesses to demonstrate their performance on SDG targets.

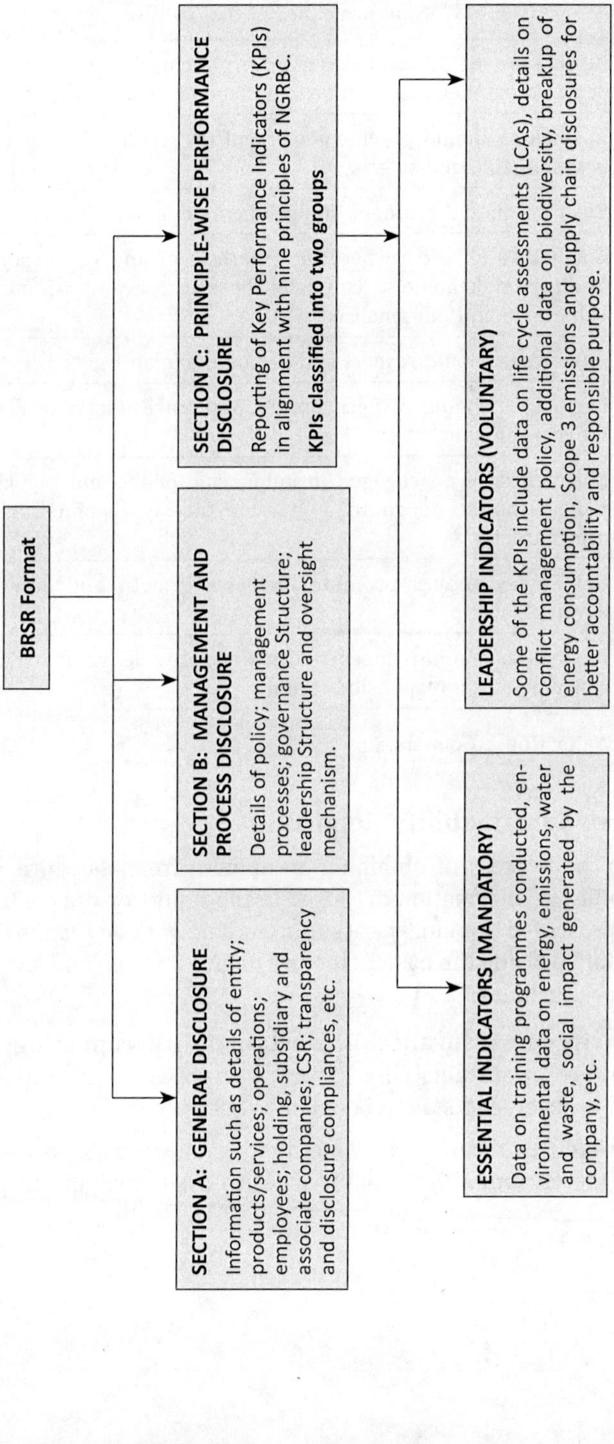

CHART 6.2

Source: Bhowmik and Dutta (2022).

TABLE 6.3 Nine principles of the NGRBC

Principle 1	Businesses should conduct and govern themselves with integrity, and in a manner that is ethical, transparent and accountable.
Principle 2	Businesses should provide goods and services in a manner that is sustainable and safe.
Principle 3	Business should promote the well-being of all employees.
Principle 4	Businesses should respect the interests of and be responsive to all its stakeholders, especially those who are disadvantaged, vulnerable and marginalised.
Principle 5	Businesses should respect and promote human rights.
Principle 6	Businesses should respect, protect and make efforts to restore the environment.
Principle 7	Businesses, when engaged in influencing public and regulatory policy, should do so in a manner that is responsible and transparent.
Principle 8	Businesses should promote inclusive growth and equitable development.
Principle 9	Businesses should engage with and provide value to their consumers in a responsible manner.

Source: Price Water House Coopers, July 2021.

Assurance of Sustainability Reporting

Assurance is the process of obtaining an opinion from the third party on the reliability of information disclosed in the report or the context of information presented therein. The assurance framework on sustainability reporting would provide the basic structure to give it shape and strength. The framework includes:

- **Maturity of assurance of sustainability reporting:** The assurance of sustainability reports has grown from responsive stage to leveraged stage via enhanced stage.
- **Approach to assurance:** Four dimensions have been used to map the current diverse approaches to assurance and to guide

possible future directions for development. They are as under: assurance, appetite assurance, methodology assurance scope, boundary and assurance providers.

- **Assurance Standards**: Currently, there are only two recognized professional standards for carrying out sustainability reporting assurance. These are:
    - AA 1000—assurance standard developed by the Institute for Social and Ethical Accountability.
    - ISAE 3000 provided by the 11 International Audit and Assurance Standard Board which is a part of the International Federation of Accountants (ICAI, 2021).

6.3.1 Case Study of Some Sample Companies under the Old Companies Act

Initial sample

The Economic Times (ET) makes every year a study of 500 companies out of the companies enlisted on the various stock exchanges in India. In 2002, it made a similar study based on the 500 companies selected on the basis of market capitalization (in March). These ET 500 companies were taken as the population for the instant study because these were the largest companies in India and together they account for a substantial portion of the total market capitalization.

From the ET 500 companies, 100 companies were randomly selected. The simple random sampling was done without replacement. This is shown in **Appendix 1**. For analyzing annual reports to find out corporate environmental accounting and reporting practices, a sample size of 100 (20% of the population) was considered. Under the Companies Act, 1956 [Sec. 217(1)(e)], companies belonging to 21 industry–groups (vide Table 6.4) are required to disclose certain information relating to conservation of energy in the Directors' Report. So, out of the sample companies of 100, those companies which fell outside the 21 industry–groups were rejected except one belonging to Banking and Finance. The reason for retaining one company belonging to Banking and Finance industry group was to examine whether service organizations care for environment. This gave us an effective number of 60 companies in the accepted sample as shown in Table 6.5.

TABLE 6.4 List of Industries Required to Disclose Particulars with respect to Conservation of Energy (Form A) as per Companies (Disclosure of Particulars in the Report of Board of Directors) Rules, 1988, Framed under Section 217(1)(e) of the Companies Act, 1956

1.	Textiles
2.	Fertilizer
3.	Aluminium
4.	Steel
5.	Refineries
6.	Petrochemicals and chemicals
7.	Cement
8.	Dairy and food processing
9.	Cold storage plant
10.	Electric arc furnaces
11.	Chlor alkali
12.	Edible oil
13.	Engineering (steel forging and re-rolling)
14.	Glass
15.	Jute
16.	Paper
17.	Refractory and pottery
18.	Tea
19.	Tyre
20.	Sugar
21.	Drugs and pharmaceuticals

TABLE 6.5 Analysis of Sample Companies

ET ranks	*No. of companies selected*	*No. of companies rejected**	*Effective number*
1–100	27	10	17
101–200	23	7	16
201–300	18	11	7
301–400	13	4	9
401–500	19	8	11
	100	**40**	**60**

[*for not falling within the 21 industy-groups under Section 217(1)(e) of the Companies Act, 1956]

These 60 companies were then approached, based on the information available from the website of the Department of Company Affairs[8], Government of India, to supply annual reports for the year ended 31st March, 2003. Out of 60, only 26 responded favourably and the remaining 34 did not respond in spite of several reminders. The analysis of corporate environmental reporting practices in India is thus based on 26 companies whose annual reports were available. This represents 5.2% of the population. An average response rate of 43.3% which, going by the general experience of data collection in India (Banerjee, 1994; Porwal, 1994; Roy, 1991), may be considered satisfactory.

Questionnaire

Fifty questions were initially framed and discussed with some academics and professional accountants, and based on the interaction some questions were reframed, some were dropped, leading to a final set of 42 questions. These were divided into five parts:

- A General (Questions 1–7)
- B Pollution related (Questions 8–16)
- C Environmental Management related (Questions 17–23)
- D Production related (having impact on environmental management) (Questions 24–29)
- E Accounting and Audit (Questions 30–42).

An administered questionnaire, as a sample, is given in **Appendix 2.**

We now present an analysis of the responses received from the respondents against specific questions.

On the location, size, etc., of the respondents

The respondent companies were classified, based on their registered offices, into Northern, Eastern, Western and Southern regions. While the Northern region includes Jammu and Kashmir, Punjab, Haryana, Delhi, Uttar Pradesh and Uttarakhand, the Eastern region comprises Bihar, Jharkhand, Chhattisgarh, Odisha, West Bengal, Sikkim, Assam, Arunachal Pradesh, Meghalaya, Nagaland, Manipur and Tripura. Rajasthan, Gujarat, Goa, Maharashtra and Madhya Pradesh were classified as falling into the Western region. The Southern region was comprised of the states of Andhra Pradesh, Karnataka, Tamil Nadu and Kerala. Table 6.6 shows the region-wise distribution of the sample companies.

8 http://www.nic.in/dca

TABLE 6.6 Location of Registered Offices of the Sample Companies

Location	*No. of companies*	*Percentage of total*
North	5	19.2
East	1	3.8
West	17	65.4
South	3	11.6
Total	**26**	**100.0**

On the size of the company, the value of total assets employed was considered and the companies were classified in four groups according to their assets value as shown in Table 6.7.

TABLE 6.7 Size of the Sample Companies

Assets value (₹/crore)	*No. of companies*	*Percentage of total*
Below 25,000	11	42.3
25,000–50,000	1	3.8
50,000–100,000	5	19.2
Above 100,000	9	34.7
Total	**26**	**100.0**

The above companies may also be classified according to different industry groups as illustrated in Table 6.8.

TABLE 6.8 Classification of Sample Companies according to Industry Groups

	No. of companies	*Percentage of total*
Aluminium	1	3.84
Automobiles	3	11.54
Banking & Finance	1	3.84
Cement	1	3.84
Chemical	3	11.54
Diversified	4	15.42
Personal Care	1	3.84
Electrical Equipment	1	3.84

TABLE 6.8 *(Contd.)*

	No. of companies	*Percentage of total*
Food Products	1	3.84
IT	2	7.68
Lubricants	1	3.84
Pharma	4	15.42
Power	1	3.84
Refineries	1	3.84
Steel	1	3.84
	26	**100.0**

Of the above sample companies, only two (7.68%) belonged to the public sector and the remaining 24 (92.32%) companies belonged to the private sector.

Major findings

On the question of release of waste by the sample companies, only a few of them filled in the required questionnaire and mentioned that the following wastes are being released by them:

- Sulphur oxides
- Alumina
- Particulate matters
- PVC sludge
- Fly ash
- Nitrogen oxides
- Fluorine compounds
- Carbon oxides.

On the treatment of wastes by the companies, i.e., disposal and recycling, the responses received from the sample companies were as shown in Table 6.9.

It is interesting to note that 50% of the sample companies did not provide information on treatment of wastes.

Measurement of the level of pollution promotes monitoring and control. On the level of pollution generated by the company and its measurement, only two companies provided relevant quantitative information while others preferred to remain silent.

TABLE 6.9 Treatment of Wastes

	No. of companies	*Percentage of total*
Disposed of	01	3.8
Recycled	09	34.6
Not mentioned	13	50.0
No waste	03	11.6
	26	**100.0**

Whether the companies are adopting suitable measures to control pollution of air, water, soil and sound, the responses are given in Table 6.10.

TABLE 6.10 Taking Suitable Pollution Control Measures

	No. of companies	*Percentage of total*
Yes	10	38.5
No	13	50.0
No pollution	3	11.5
	26	**100.0**

On the question of compliance with Section 217(1)(e) of the Companies Act, 1956, it was found that compliance was 100%. This shows that if companies are required by law to publish any vital information relating to the level of environmental management, compliance of the same becomes automatic.

In reply to Question No. 13, as to submission of return to the respective State Pollution Control Boards (SPCBs), all the companies mentioned that they complied with the provision.

In response to Question No. 14, i.e., measures taken by the respective PCBs for violation of acceptable environmental limits during the last three years, viz., 2000–01 to 2002–03, the response of one of the violating companies was as follows:

> Gujarat PCB issued notice for polluting sea in October 2003 ... The Soda Ash Plant (Gujarat) was kept closed for 4 days and appropriate remedial measures were taken.

Questions 17–23 relate to overall environmental management of the company. They comprise environmental policy, adoption of Environmental

Management System (EMS) in terms of ISO 14001, obtaining ISO 14001 certificate, formation of Environmental Action Team (EAT) to address environmental issues that affect their business, ensuring better working environment to motivate employees to contribute actively to EMS, adoption of voluntary codes of conduct as part of responsible environment care programme, etc. The responses received on the above aspects are summarized in Tables 6.11 to 6.16.

TABLE 6.11 Adopting a Specific Environmental Policy

	No. of companies	*Percentage of total*
Yes	10	38.5
No	16	61.5
	26	**100.0**

Of the companies adopting specific environmental policies, some of them coined the policy statement in an attractive and innovative way. For example, consider the following:

Reliance	'Waste to Resource'
TISCO	'Parivesh'
ITC	'Citizen First'

TABLE 6.12 Adopting EMS in Terms of ISO 14001

	No. of companies	*Percentage of total*
Yes	11	42.3
No	15	57.7
	26	**100.0**

TABLE 6.13 Obtaining ISO 14001 Certificate

	No. of companies	*Percentage of total*
Yes	09	34.6
No	15	57.7
Under consideration	02	07.7
	26	**100.0**

TABLE 6.14 Forming Separate Environmental Action Team (EAT)

	No. of companies	*Percentage of total*
Yes	02	07.7
No	24	92.3
	26	**100.0**

TABLE 6.15 Measures Aimed at Motivating Employees towards EMS

	No. of companies	*Percentage of total*
Yes	11	42.3
No	15	57.7
	26	**100.0**

TABLE 6.16 Formulating Voluntary Code of Conduct as Part of "Responsible Environment Care Programme"

	No. of companies	*Percentage of total*
Yes	02	07.7
No	24	92.3
	26	**100.0**

Questions 24–29 relate to several aspects of production processes that are environment-friendly. These include the following:

1. Implementing new, innovative and cleaner production technologies
2. Developing new product/process with environment justification
3. Implementation of ISO 14001 standards by the suppliers
4. Awareness of the employees for better housekeeping
5. Treatment of remnants of principal raw materials used in production (recycling, dumping, etc.)
6. Making capital expenditure for adopting 'Green Technology'.

Most of the companies skipped many vital issues in this section and replied to only three questions (i.e., Questions 24, 25 and 29). These responses are given in Tables 6.17 and 6.18.

TABLE 6.17 Adopting Environmental-friendly Technologies

	No. of companies	*Percentage of total*
Yes	13	50.0
No	13	50.0
	26	**100.0**

TABLE 6.18 Making Capital Expenditure for 'Green Technology'

	No. of companies	*Percentage of total*
Yes	10	38.4
No	16	61.6
	26	**100.0**

The last section of the questionnaire related to accounting and auditing matters. Although the responses here were few and far between, some of the points could, however, be scrutinized from a scanning of the Annual Reports. The responses relating to adoption of environmental audit and disclosure of environmental audit report are given in Tables 6.19 and 6.20 respectively.

TABLE 6.19 Adopting Environmental Audit

	No. of companies	*Percentage of total*
Through external agencies	05	19.2
By company staff	02	07.7
Not done	16	61.6
Not required to be done	03	11.5
	26	**100.0**

TABLE 6.20 Mode of Disclosure of Environmental Audit Report

	No. of companies	*Percentage of total*
Part of statutory audit report	06	23.1
Separate report	01	03.8
Not disclosed	16	61.6
Not required	03	11.5
	26	**100.0**

Summary of scanning

From scanning of annual reports of 14 companies out of 26 sample companies it appeared that the information disclosed varied considerably across companies. We summarize them with respect to a few common attributes as given in Table 6.21.

TABLE 6.21 Some Key Environmental Information Disclosure in the Annual Reports for the Financial Year 2002–03

Company	*Environment policy*	*Measuring & managing wastes*	*Recycle of wastes*	*Audit committee*	*Awards & penalties*
Bajaj Auto	Y	Qualitative	N	NA	NA
BHEL	Y	Qualitative	Y	External	Award
DSCL	Y	Qualitative	N	NA	Award
Gujarat Ambuja	N	Qualitative	N	NA	NA
Hero Honda	Y	Quantitative	Y	Internal	Award
Hindalco	Y	Qualitative	Y	Internal + External	Award
Indian Oil	Y	Qualitative	N	Internal	Award
ITC	Y	Quantitative	Y	Internal + External	Award
Reliance Energy	Y	Quantitative	N	External	Award
Reliance Industries	Y	Quantitative	Y	Internal	Award
SAIL	Y	Quantitative	N	Internal	Award
Tata Chem	Y	Qualitative	N	Internal	Award & Penalty
Tata Motors	N	Qualitative	N	NA	Award
Tata Steel	N	Quantitative	Y	External	Award

Abbreviations used: Y = Yes; N = No; NA = Not available.

6.4 COMMENTS ON ENVIRONMENTAL DISCLOSURES BY SAMPLE COMPANIES BASED ON EARLIER STUDIES

Some of the important features, as revealed by the Case Study, may now be stated below.

1. 38.5% of the companies took pollution control measures in addition to the requirements under the Pollution Control Act (Table 6.10).
2. About 39% companies adopted specific environment policy (Table 6.11).
3. Many companies (34.6%) obtained ISO accreditation certificate (Table 6.13) and many of them (42.3%) followed EMS (Table 6.12). It was also revealed that 42.3% of the companies

took measures aimed at motivating employees towards EMS (Tables 6.12 and 6.15).

4. In terms of formation of separate environmental action team (Table 6.14) and formulation of code of conduct voluntarily (Table 6.16), the picture is very poor—only 8% of the companies resorted to this practice.
5. It is encouraging to note that half of the companies have adopted environment-friendly technologies (Table 6.17) and a substantial number of them (38.4%, see Table 6.18) incurred capital expenditure for 'green technology'.
6. Regarding Environmental Audit (EA), it was noticed (Table 6.19) that a little over one-fourth conducted it either by their staff (8%) or by external persons (19%). But in only 4% of such cases, EA report was disclosed as a separate report and in about 23% cases (Table 6.20), it formed part of the statutory audit report.
7. Many companies adopted 'water harvesting' scheme. Quite a large number of them (12 out of 14, i.e., 86%, see Table 6.21) got award from different bodies for showing environmental awareness and adopting measures that became environment-friendly.

6.5 CASE STUDY OF ITC AND SAIL IN RECENT TIMES

We have earlier mentioned that the Companies Act was completely revised and a new Act came into being in 2013. SEBI (Securities and Exchange Board of India) and DPE (Department of Public Enterprises) have been changing their guidelines from time to time keeping in view changing requirements of the economy and also international developments. Accordingly, the reporting environment also changed over time.

Earlier, the annual reports were consolidated one and even information on environmental and social performance was part of annual reports of companies as a voluntary disclosure. Now also the annual reports show the economic performance of the company and environmental and social performance in a consolidated manner. But companies are attaching more importance to sustainability issues because of host of domestic factors and international developments. Companies started disclosing sustainability report on voluntary basis much before it has been prescribed by the regulatory authorities. In some cases, companies even attached integrated reports in their websites. SEBI, however, made publication of Sustainability Report (Business Responsibility and Sustainability Report) compulsory for listed Indian companies with effect from the financial year 2022–23. The DPE is not also falling behind.

In the above background, we will now examine the Sustainability Report of only one company in the private sector, namely, the ITC Ltd., and one company in the Public Sector, namely, the Steel Authority of India (SAIL). Both the companies' earlier record for disclosure of information in their respective annual reports was excellent. Being a public limited company, ITC has to follow provisions of the Companies Act, 1913 and the SEBI Guidelines. On the other hand, for SAIL it is the DPE Guidelines which need to be complied with in addition the provisions of the Companies Act, 2013.

1. ITC Limited

ITC Ltd. (formally known as Indian Tobacco Company[9]) is a conglomerate company headquartered in Kolkata. It is a diversified company having its presence across industries, such as, FMCG, hotel, software, packing paperboards, specially papers and agro businesses. In 2022 Annual Report, the share of business in terms of segments are given below:

Segment	*% of turnover of 2022*
♦ FMCG	66.69
♦ Agri-business	20.52
♦ Paperboards, Paper & Packaging	10.63
♦ Hotels	2.16
Total	**100.00**

9 Let us first give the historical background (www.Googles: Wikipedia). ITC was originally named "Imperial Tobacco Company of India Ltd., succeeding W.D. & H.O. Wills on 24th August, 1910 as a British owned company registered in Kolkata. Since the Company was primarily based on agricultural resources, it went into partnership in 1911 with farmers from the Southern Part of India for getting tobacco leaves. The Indian Leaf Tobacco Development Company Ltd. was founded in Guntur in 1912. In 1913, the first Cigarette factory of the Company was set up in Bangalore. In 1935, ITC acquired Carreras Tobacco Company in 1935 and also an indigenous cigarette tissue paper making plant in 1946 to reduce import costs significantly. Then in 1949 a factory for printing and packaging was set up in Madras in 1949. In 1953, the Company acquired the manufacturing business of Tobacco Manufacturing (India) Ltd. Then the Company was converted into a Public Ltd. Company on October 27, 1954.

The company has 13 businesses in 5 segments exporting its products to 90 countries and its products are available in 6 million retail outlets. In December 2022, ITC's market cap stood at ₹4,22,447.30 crore. Its rank is 12th among the top 500 companies. The company employs 36,500 people at more than 60 locations across India. Its turnover for the year 2022 stood at ₹59,101 crore. Keeping the above profile in mind, we will now examine its annual accounts for the year 2022, particularly those portions that deal with sustainability, environmental and social performance.

ITC Ltd. presented its Annual Report 2022 with the slogan—Consumer Centricity, Innovation, Digital Transformation and Sustainability. It then outlined the 'Triple Bottom-line' contributions categorized under Economic, Social and Environmental parameters along with recognitions that it received for Sustainability measures (Annexure-1). The Annual Report is divided into the following broad components:

- ITC Wining the Future (Board of Directors & Committees; Corporate Governance Report; Management Discussion & Analysis; Auditor's Report and CEO & CFO Compliance Certificates)
- Financial Statement (Stand alone and consolidated Financial Statements, Ten Years at a Glance, etc.)
- Financial Highlights (BRSR, Awards & Accolades, Business Friendly Solutions and Creating Enduring Institutions)

Besides, the company also provided Sustainability and Integrated Report 2022. It disclosed Business Responsibility and Sustainability Report (BRSR) under three sections—General Disclosures, Management and Process Disclosures and Principle-wise Performance Disclosures (wherein the performance of the company under the nine principles of National Guidelines for Responsible Business Conduct is noted). The company has been investing in renewable energy driven operations and 42% of its energy consumption was met up from renewable sources. Its corporate sustainability measures as disclosed in the report can be better summarized under the following heads:

ITC Social Investment Initiatives

- e-Choupal Ecosystem
- Afforestation Programme
- Watershed Development Programme
- Sustainable Agriculture
- Livestock Development
- Women Empowerment
- Primary Education

- Skilling and Vocational Training
- Health and Sanitation
- Solid Waste Management

Framework of capitals and their objectives

Nature of Capitals	*Objectives*
Financial Capital	*Responsible Capitalism* through *Triple Bottom Line Approach.*
Manufactured Capital	Investing in renewable energy and green infrastructure.
Intellectual Capital	Leveraging the innovation platforms of science.
Human Capital	Talent development practices within ITC Ltd.
Natural Capital	Conservation and restoration of natural resources.
Social and Relationship Capital	Creates larger societal value.

Source: Sustainability and Integrated Report, 2022, pp. 10–11.

We now give some information about the Company in respect of (i) Governance Structure, (ii) Programme of Sustainability and Inclusive Growth and (iii) Achievements in 2021–22 keeping Sustainability Goals 2:00 of 2030 in the following tables (Table 6.22 and Table 6.23).

Involvement in Governance structure: *CSR and Sustainability Committee* is the part of the Board of Directors. (Sustainability and Integrated Report, 2022, p. 24)

TABLE 6.22 Mission Sunehra Kal: Flagship Programme of Sustainability and Inclusive Growth

Priority Area	*Linkage with Govt. Scheme*	*SDG Alignment (Page 133)*
Social Forestry	♦ National Agro-forestry Policy, 2014	13,15,16
Water Stewardship and Biodiversity Conservation	♦ Jal Shakti Avijan ♦ PM Krishi Sinchai Yojana ♦ National Biodiversity Action Plan, 2008	6,13,15,16,17

Priority Area	*Linkage with Govt. Scheme*	*SDG Alignment (Page 133)*
Climate Smart Agriculture	National Mission for Sustainable Agriculture	1,2,9,13,15,16,17
Integrated animal Husbandry	National Livestock Mission	1,2,3
Women Empowerment	Support to Training and Employment Programme for Women	1,2,5,8,9,10,16,17
Primary Education	♦ Sarva Shiksha Avijan ♦ National Education Policy, 2020	4,6,9,10,16,17
Vocational Training	♦ PM Kaushal Vikas Yojana	4,8,10
Sanitation and Solid Waste Management	♦ Swachh Bharat Mission	3,6,9,11,17
Mother and Child Health	♦ Integrated Child development Services ♦ POSHAN Abhijan	3,16,17

Source: Sustainability and Integrated Report, 2022, pp. 133–135.

TABLE 6.23 Adopting Sustainability 2.0 Goals in 2030 and Achievements in 2021–22

Key Performance Indicators	*Targets, 2030*	*Achievements, 2021–22*	*Level of Achievements*	*Remarks, if any*
Total Energy Consumed from Renewable Sources	50%	42%	84%	
Total Electrical Energy (Grid Purchased) from Renewable Sources	100%	50%	50%	
Reduction in GHG Emissions (Scope 1, 2) per Unit of Production	50%	45%	90%	Agri Business Division:7% increase FMCG Cigarettes: 9% increase

(*Contd.*)

TABLE 6.23 Adopting Sustainability 2.0 Goals in 2030 and Achievements in 2021–22 (*Contd.*)

Key Performance Indicators	*Targets, 2030*	*Achievements, 2021–22*	*Level of Achievements*	*Remarks, if any*
Reduction in Energy Consumed per Unit of Production	30%	65%	216%	
Area under Social and Farm Forestry (Acres)	15,00,000	9,53,000	64%	
Reduction in Water Consumed per Unit of Production	40%	76%	190%	
Ratio of Rainwater Harvesting Potential created and Net Water Consumed in Operations	5X	4X	80%	
No. of AWS Certified Sites	8 sites by 2023 All high-risk sites by 2035	1 Site AWS certified	NA	
Watershed Area (Acres)	22,00,000	13,30,000 (cumulative)	60%	
Water Harvesting Structures (Nos)	50,000	25,000+ (cumulative)	50%	
Storage Potential (Million KL)	60	45.27	75.45%	
Million KLs of Potential Water Saved	2000	496.5	24.825%	
Plastic Packaging Utilized that is Recyclable, Reusable or Compostable/Bio-degradable	100%	99.9%	99.9%	Less than 0.1% of Packaging Portfolio is Non-Recyclable or Hard to Recycle—Phase out plans in place
Plastic Neutrality	>100%	>100%	100%	

Key Performance Indicators	*Targets, 2030*	*Achievements, 2021–22*	*Level of Achievements*	*Remarks, if any*
Promote climate smart village approach in core agribusiness catchments	30,00,000 Acres	8,20,000 Acres	**27.33%**	
Revive and Sustain Ecosystem Services Provided by Nature and Provisioning of Products through Adoption of Nature-based Solutions and Biodiversity Conservation.	10,00,000 Acres	1,33,000 Acres	**1.33%**	
Revive and Sustain Ecosystem Services Provided by Nature and Provisioning of Products through Adoption of Nature-based Solutions and Biodiversity Conservation	10,00,000 Acres	6,00,000 Acres	**60%**	
Supporting sustainable livelihoods for 10 million people by 2030	1,00,00,000 nos.	60,00,000 nos.	60%	

Sources: (i) Sustainability and Integrated Report, 2022, pp. 45–47.
(ii) Author's Compilation.

[*Note:* Level of achievements:
- Very High (above 100%)
- High (80% to 100%)
- Medium (50% to less than 80%)
- Low (less than 50%)]

Some comments

From the above statistics, it can be concluded that both the performance and its disclosure of relevant information especially with regard to corporate sustainability measures, ITC has done an excellent job. The

Company has therefore maintained its reputation as a good corporate citizen trying hard to maintain balance between economic, social and environmental responsibility.

Some specific information on ITC's performance during recent years are given below:

- ITC has been publishing 'Sustainability Report' since 2004, much before the sustainability drive.
- ITC is the only company of the world of comparable dimensions to be carbon, water and solid waste recycling positive.
- About 42% of total energy consumption of ITC is coming from renewable sources.
- All ITC's premier luxury hotels are LEED Platinum certified.
- ITC has been rated AA every year since 2018 under MSCI ESG Ratings.
- ITC has been a member of Dow Jones Sustainability Indices.
- Regarding climate change and water security, ITC is ahead of Asia and Global average 'B'.

Sustainability Awards

2022:

- ITC Wins First Prize At National Water Awards by the Ministry of Jal Shakti, 2022.

2021:

- ITC PSPD's Unit Bhadrachalam was declared as "The Winner" in "Within the Fence" category under CII-National Awards for Excellence in Water Management, 2021.
- ITC PSPD's Unit Bhadrachalam was declared as "The Winner" in "Excellent Energy Efficient Unit" award category under CII-National Awards for Excellence in Energy Management 2021.

2020:

- ITC has received ratings from Sustainalytics, a leading independent ESG and corporate governance research, ratings and analytics firm.
- ITC Limited has been adjudged 'Best Governed Company' at the 20th ICSI National Awards for Excellence in Corporate Governance in the Listed Segment: Large Category, 2020.
- ITC PSPD's FiloPack, FiloServe & FiloBev brands and Green Stiffener technology have been Awarded as 'Most Innovative

Environmental Project' at 7th Edition of CII Environmental Best Practices Awards, 2020.

- ITC PSPD's Bhadrachalam unit received prizes for 'Excellent Energy Efficient Unit' and 'Best Innovative Project' Awards at the 21st National Awards for Excellence in Energy Management by CII, 2020.

2019:

- The Bhadrachalam and Kovai units won awards for Excellence in Energy Management at 20th National Award for Excellence in Energy Management in the Pulp & Paper sector category, 2019.
- The Tiruvottiyur unit ranked no. 1 in the CII-Southern Region EHS Excellence Awards for FMCG packaging, 2019.
- The Bhadrachalam and Kovai units won awards for Excellence in Energy Management at 20th National Award for Excellence in Energy Management in the Pulp & Paper sector category, 2019.

Some References for ITC Only

1. ITC Annual Report 2022 (https://www.itcportal.com/about-itc/shareholder-value/annual-reports/itc-annual-report-2022/pdf/ITC-Report-and-Accounts-2022.pdf)
2. ITC Sustainability & Integrated Report 2022 (https://www.itcportal.com/sustainability/sustainability-integrated-report-2022/ITC-Sustainability-Integrated-Report-2022.pdf)

Annexure 1

ITC REPORT

ITC Limited
REPORT AND ACCOUNTS 2022

ITC's Triple Bottom Line Contribution

Economic

₹59,101 cr
Gross Revenue*

Amongst Top 3
Corporates in the Private Sector in terms of Contribution to Exchequer over the years

75%
of Value-added Accrues to the Exchequer

Free Cash Flow Generation of
₹13,000 cr

12
Future-ready Businesses spanning all 3 Sectors of the Economy-
Agriculture, Manufacturing, Services

200+
Manufacturing Units

113
Hotel Properties

25+
World-class Indian Brands

Over 900
Patents Filed

Nearly
7 Million
Retail Outlets Serviced

*for the year ended 31st March, 2022

ITC Limited
REPORT AND ACCOUNTS 2022
Social
6 Million
Sustainable
Livelihoods Supported
e-Choupal:
4 Million
Farmers Empowered
Livestock Development:
Over 20,00,000
Milch Animals Covered
Women Empowerment:
Over 86,000
Poor Women Benefitted
Primary Education:
Over 8,64,000
Children Benefitted
Skilling and Vocational Training:
Over 1,00,000
Youth Enrolled
Environmental
Watershed Development:
Over 13,30,000
Acres Covered
Afforestation:
Over 9,50,000
Acres Greened
Biodiversity Conservation:
Over 1,30,000
Acres Covered
Climate Smart Agriculture:
4,50,000
Farmers Benefitted
Collecting and
Sustainably Managing
54,000 tonnes
of Plastic Waste
Well Being Out of Waste
Covers Over
1.8 Crore
Citizens
38
Platinum-rated
Green Buildings
Around 42%
of ITC's Energy from
Renewable Sources

ITC Limited
REPORT AND ACCOUNTS 2022

Recognition for ITC's Sustainability Initiatives

First Prize in 'Best Industry for CSR Activities' category by the **Ministry of Jal Shakti,** Government of India

CSR Excellence Award in the 'Large' category by the Institute of Company Secretaries of India (ICSI)

Achieved goal of becoming plastic neutral, collecting and sustainably managing 54000+ MT **of plastic waste**

Sustained **'AA' rating by MSCI** for the 4th consecutive year

Achieved **'A-' Leadership score under CDP ratings - ahead of Asia & Global average** in Climate Change (B-) & Water Security (B)

ITC included in the **Dow Jones Sustainability Emerging Markets Index**

2. ESG Reporting of Steel Authority of India Limited (2021–2022)[10]

Steel Authority of India Limited (SAIL), a Government of India Undertaking and a Maharatna Central Public Sector Enterprise, is the premier steel-making organization of India. It is a fully integrated iron and steel maker, producing both basic and special steels for domestic construction, engineering, power, railway, automotive & defence industries and for sale in export markets. (https://sail.co.in/en/company/about-us). Apart from Annual Report, SAIL disclosed Sustainability Report under Corporate Citizenship menu since 2010–11 (Around 12 years before SEBI made it mandatory in the form of BRSR). Annual Report of SAIL for the year ended 2021–22 presents all the items as annual report of other listed companies disclosed. But it is unique in the sense that the report contained two separate sections—'Particulars on Energy Conservation & Technology Absorption' and 'Annual Report of Corporate Social Responsibility Activities'. This is perhaps because of the fact that steel manufacturing is one of the polluting industries and as such it has to walk ahead of other companies so far as managing environmental and social impact of its operations are concerned.

Moreover, its voluminous Sustainability Report (104 pages) provided detailed information about its commitment and measures to carry out operations at all Plants, Mines and Units in socially, ethically and environment friendly manner. By having a Sustainable Development Policy, it highlights it's responsibility towards business integrity, governance, product, social, and environmental issues. The major points covering sustainability issues are presented under the following headings:

Sustainable Priorities

- To conduct business with high ethical standards;
- To excel in the area of environmental management by adopting 'state-of-the-art' technologies;
- To track and incorporate functional upgrades into company's comprehensive business model;
- To fulfil social commitments by being a socially responsible entity;

---

10 Annual Report of SAIL 2021–2022 (Link: https://sail.co.in/en/investors-relation/annual-reports)
Annual Sustainability Report of SAIL 2021–2022 (Link: https://sail.co.in/en/sustainability-report)

- To form a participative mechanisms for all the stakeholders such as employees, customers, suppliers and community so that "development with sustainability" remains its focus area;
- To keep the business sustainable by adopting multidimensional approaches in the areas of cost and financial management, technology up-gradation, value addition on products along with addition of new products that align with the future demands.

Board Level Committees

The company keeps a continuous monitoring of achieving the above priorities with the help of different committees, such as, Audit Committee, Nomination & Remuneration Committee, Stakeholders' Relationship Committee, Risk Management Committee, Corporate Social Responsibility Committee, Health, Safety & Environment Committee, etc.

CSR Committee is entrusted to look after whether the company is conducting its business operation in an economically, socially, and environmentally sustainable manner and to serve the interests of the society, by taking responsibility for the impact of their activities. Health, Safety & Environment Committee, on the other hand, reviews the policy, procedures and systems on Health, Safety and Environmental matters in respect of Plants & Mines.

Sustainability Framework of SAIL

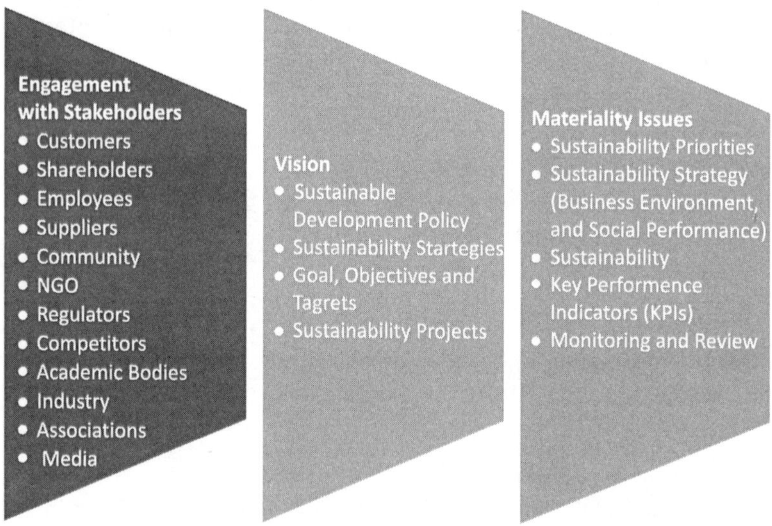

Environmental Management System (EMS)

- EMS linked with ISO: 14001 is a voluntary approach to manage the immediate and long-term environmental impacts of products, services and processes.
- SAIL has been a fore bearer in the establishment of the EMS in the steel industry in the Country.
- All the Integrated Steel Plants, major Units and Warehouses of SAIL are compliant with EMS ISO: 14001 Standard.

Environmental Sustainability SAIL

The main focus of Environmental sustainability of the company is to "protect the environment by integrating sound environmental practices for control and prevention of pollution from all its activities" and "contribute towards mitigation of climate change through the adoption of measures to reduce emission of greenhouse gases, enhancing green coverage, adopting energy efficient technologies, enhancing use of green energy".

Environmental Risks and Risk Mitigation Strategy

Environmental Risks	*Risk Mitigation Strategies*
♦ Increased global concern for climate change prompting adoption of challenging targets by the Regulators. ♦ Operational and Financial risk to the industry in the form of carbon taxes, emission caps, etc. ♦ Increasing quantity of waste requiring proper management and disposal. ♦ Deteriorating air and water quality as a result of increasing concentration of industries in the vicinity.	♦ Regular adoption of clean technologies to reduce CO_2 emissions. ♦ Venturing in environmental protection measures and in the process of fixing up internal carbon price to offset this risk. ♦ Developing strategies for proper handling, recycling and reuse of waste. ♦ Preparing for beyond compliance scenario, greenery development and interaction with statutory bodies.

Highlights of Environmental Performance

- SAIL Plants and Units have the robust environment management systems with latest technologies for conservation of energy and prevention of environmental pollution.
- Energy conservation, resource optimization, biodiversity protection and eco-restoration measures taken by it on continual basis.

- Clean environment practice as mandatory for its every industrial activity.
- Conducting operations in an environmentally responsible manner to comply with applicable regulations and striving to go beyond.
- Strict surveillance of the key environmental parameters as per the statutes is carried out through NABET (National Accreditation Board for Education and Training) accredited environmental laboratories as well as through real time monitoring of environmental parameters with the help of online monitoring systems and same is linked-up with the servers catering to the State Pollution Control Boards as well as the Central Pollution Control Board.
- Various management practices like ISO 9001, ISO 14001, ISO 45001 and SA 8000 have also been introduced in most of the SAIL Steel Plants, Mines and Units.
- Integration of business values and operations in an ethical and transparent manner to demonstrate its commitment towards sustainable development.
- Curtailing the stack emissions from chimneys.
- New pollution control equipment of higher capacity is being installed in place of older and obsolete equipment to meet the stricter statutory norms.
- Particulate Matter Emission reduced in the year 2021–22 as compared to previous years as shown in the chart below:

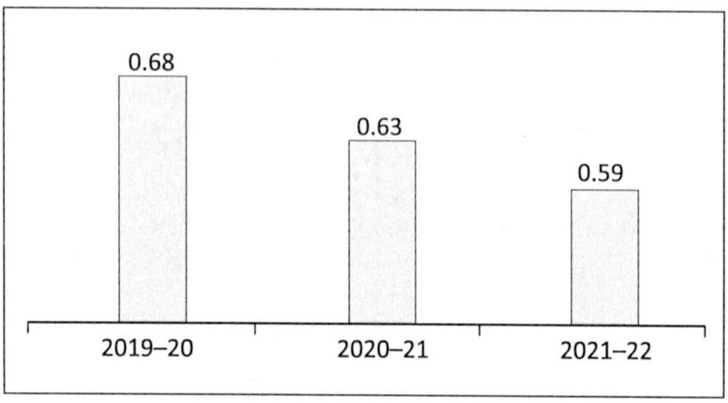

The Specific Particulate Matter Emission Load (kg/tcs)

- Emission of SO_2 is curbed through use of low sulphur coal and desulphurized coke oven gas.
- Specially designed burners for controlling NO_x emission.

- Measures taken to control the emission within the applicable environmental norms.

Initiatives towards Carbon Neutrality

- SAIL has fixed up a target of 2.30 T of CO_2 emissions per ton of crude steel production by 2030.
- Commitment to substantially reduce CO_2 emission and increase share of renewable/non-conventional energy by 2030 as well as to achieve net zero emission by 2070.
- Decisive actions to minimise impact of its operations on global climate change.
- By introducing energy saving clean technologies in process resulted in achieving 19% CO_2 emission reduction during 2021–22 from 2005 level.
- Aim to achieve carbon neutrality by 2070, through gradual shift to alternate steel-making, adoption and propagation of Hydrogen Steel making, availing full renewable energy generation potential and wide coverage of Carbon Capture Utilisation and Storage.

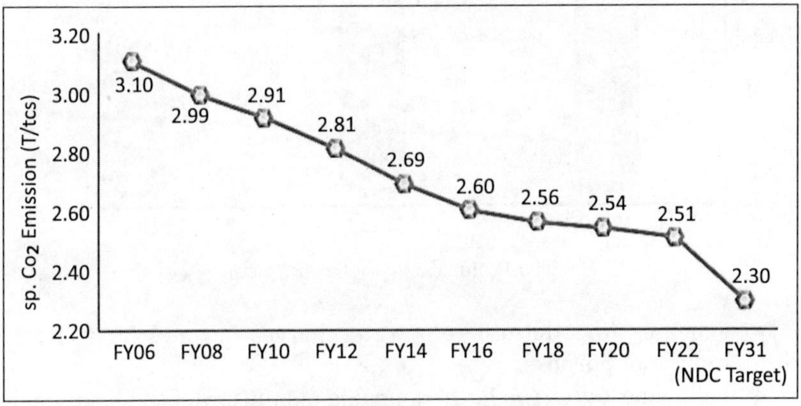

Specific CO_2 Emission (T/TCS)

Initiatives towards Conserving Water

- "Management of Water Resource" is identified as one of the important sustainability challenges.
- Adoption of principle "reduce, recover, recycle and reuse" in its operations for conservation of natural resources, including water.
- Target for water consumption is part of the Company's Annual Business Plan.

- It avoids withdrawing of water from water stress areas.
- Following are some initiatives taken by the company for water:
  - Awareness campaigning
  - Revamping of localized recirculation systems
  - Water auditing by third party
  - Online monitoring of quality and quantity of effluent discharged from shops as well as outfalls
  - Rain water harvesting schemes
  - State-of-the-art effluent treatment plants in upcoming units
- Specific water consumption has been reduced by around 14% in last five years.

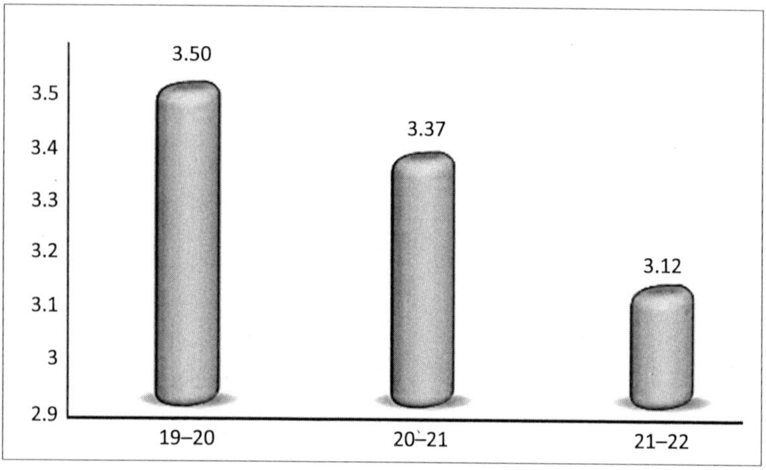

Specific Water Consumption (m^3/tcs)

- Schemes for roof-top rain water harvesting and its use for industrial purpose.
- Following '***Catch the Rain***' campaign of Ministry of Jal Shakti, rain water harvesting facility is envisaged during conceptualization of any upcoming project.
- To preserve water quality of natural water bodies, the quality of effluent discharged from company's Plants and Mines is maintained through meticulous operation of effluent treatment plants.
- Environment Impact Assessment (EIA) studies have been carried out for production facilities to identify its impact on the environment and society.

- No adverse impact was observed on the water sources or the nearby water bodies.
- "Zero Liquid Discharge" through adequate treatment and recycling of effluent being discharged through the outfalls at the Plant boundary.
- Specific Effluent Discharge and Specific Effluent Load of SAIL are shown below:

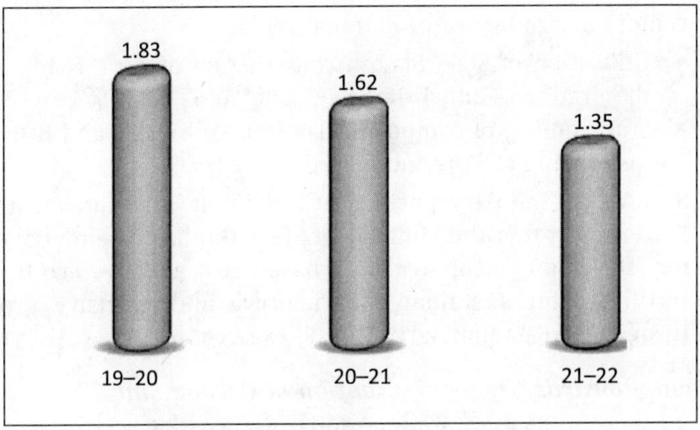

Specific Effluents Discharged (m^3/tss)

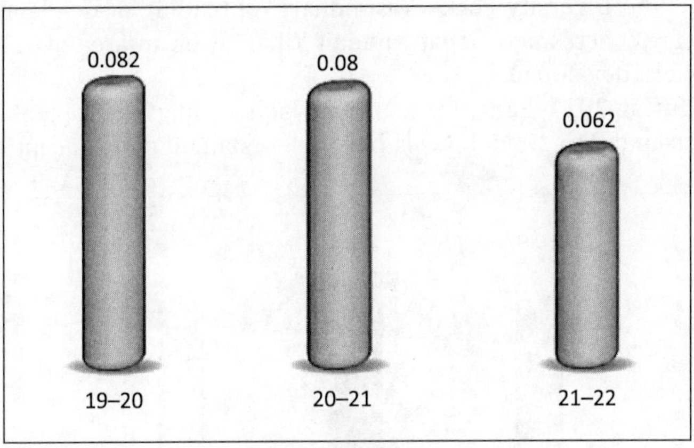

Specific Effluents Load (m^3/tcs)

Initiatives towards Managing Wastes

- SAIL has adopted the "4R's Policy" (Reduce, Recover, Recycle and Reuse) across all its processes related to steel-making in order to improve sustainability of the industry.

- Management of solid wastes in our Company is aimed to extract maximum practical benefits from waste products and to generate minimum amount of waste to comply with the environmental legislation & regulations and economics of disposal in the present scenario.
- With an objective to enhance the utilisation of waste, following R&D based initiatives are being undertaken either through in-house research wing or in association with other research centers or academies of national repute.
  - Utilisation of Steel Slag in construction of rural roads under the Pradhan Mantri Gramin Sadak Yojna (PMGSY)
  - Study on use of composite slag (mix of BF slag and BOF slag) for making of Portland Slag Cement (PSC)
- SAIL as an industry partner is intimately associated with the R&D project that the Ministry of Steel, GoI has recently taken up for "Development of steel slag based cost effective eco-friendly fertilizers for sustainable agriculture and inclusive growth" through ICAR-Indian Agricultural Research Institute (IARI), Delhi.

Movements towards Greenery–Creation of Carbon Sink

- Structured plantation programmes are carried out every year in all the Plants and Mines.
- A "Bio Diversity Park—Vasundhara" spreading over a landscape of 409 acres and "Ispat Nandan Vihar" over an area of 1.5 acres were developed.
- During 2021–22, more than 3.28 lakh saplings were planted and around 215.42 lakh trees have been planted since inception.

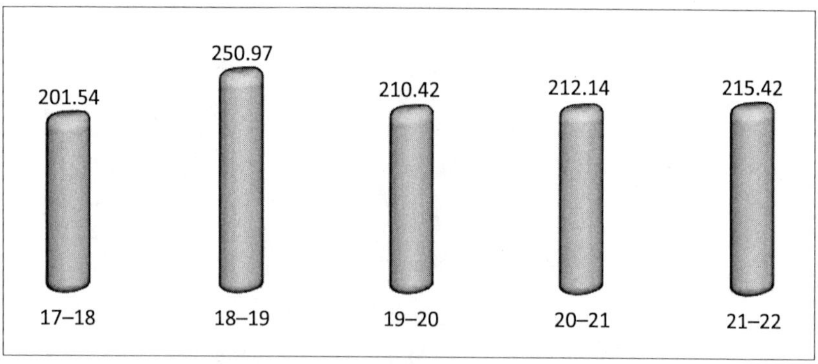

Cummulative Plantation (No. in Lakhs)

Energy Conservation Initiatives

- Promotion of energy conservation, CO_2 emission reduction and improvement in resource efficiency throughout the entire Iron & Steel making process.
- Research & Development Centre for Iron & Steel (RDCIS) of the company is continually exploring different avenues for energy efficiency.
- Every Plant has dedicated "Energy Management Department" to minutely monitor, analyze the energy consumption of sub-process/operations and to envisage Plant specific energy conservation measures for implementation.
- SAIL recorded the best ever specific energy consumption for the period 2021–22 owing to continual concerted efforts during the reporting period.

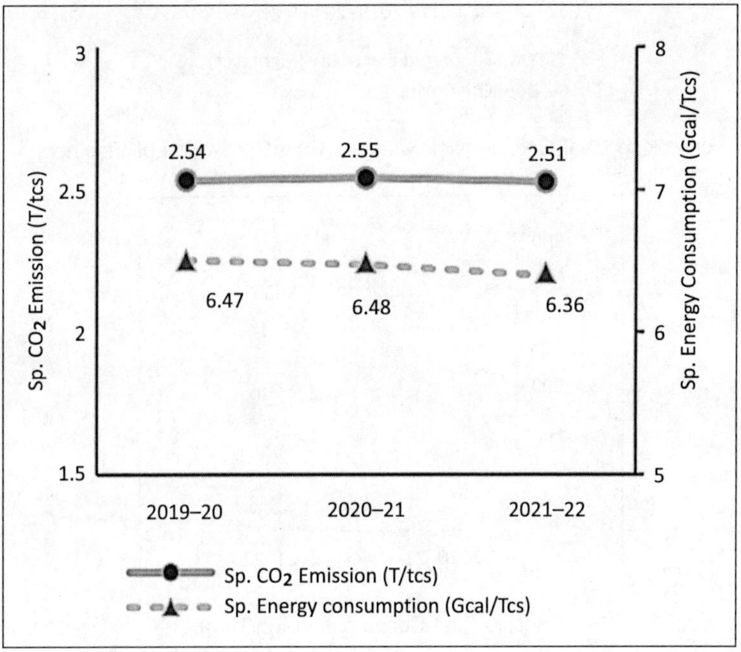

Specific Energy Consumption vis-à-vis Specific CO_2 Emission

- Emphasis has been given on maximizing recovery of by-product gaseous fuel and their uses for Power Generation and supply of heat for internal use.

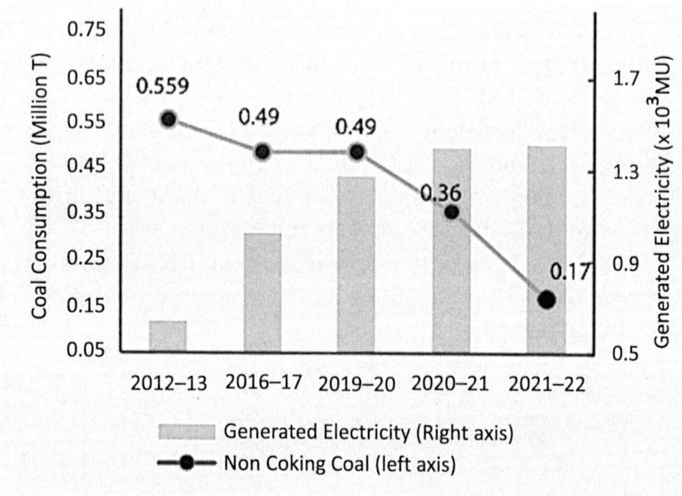

Non-coking Coal Consumption vis-à-vis Own Generation of Electricity

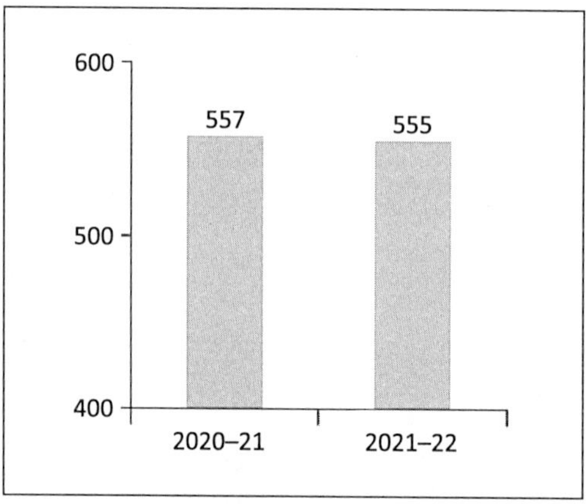

Specific Fuel Consumption (kg/Thm)

- It has laid adequate emphasis on development and usage of renewable power sources.
- It has implemented many schemes for promotion of renewable energy in its Plants, Mines and Peripheral villages/areas.

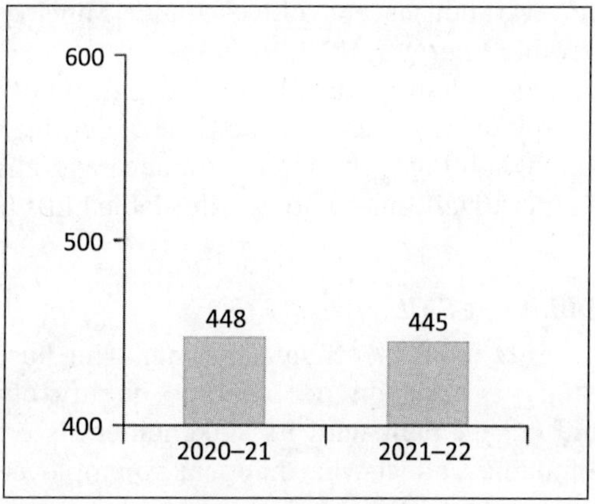

Coke Rate (kg/Thm)

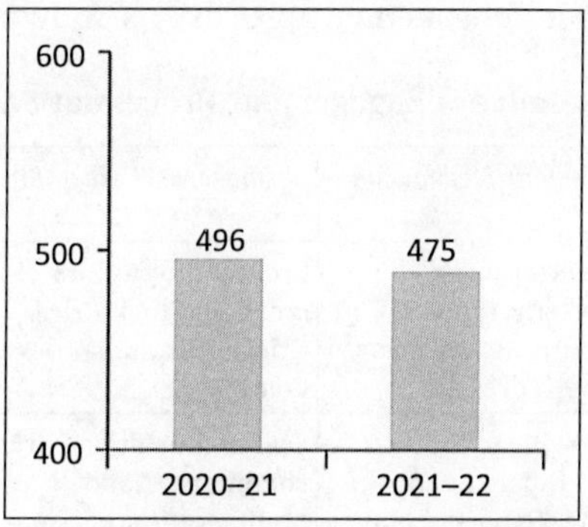

Specific Power Consumption (kWh/TSS)

- Following solar power projects have already been implemented in recent years:
  - 1 MW ground mounted Solar Power Plant connected with electrical grid system of the State Electricity Board
  - Grid connected 2 MW roof-top solar units have also been set-up
  - 0.360 MW Roof top solar power units on Guest house and Hospital building
- In addition, following renewable energy projects/schemes are presently under progress:
  - 10 MW Hydel Power Plant
  - 6.195 MW roof-top solar units on different buildings of SAIL

plants, warehouses and offices under Ministry of New and Renewable Energy (MNRE) scheme

- The company Plants and Units are gradually shifting to more energy-efficient and durable LED lighting system from conventional lighting system in consonance with the Government of India's initiative "UnnatJyoti by Affordable LEDs for All (UJALA) Scheme".

Social Sustainability at SAIL

Social sustainability is about identifying and managing business impacts, both positive and negative, on people. The quality of a company's relationships and engagement with its stakeholders is critical. Directly or indirectly, companies' affect what happens to employees, workers in the value chain, customers and local communities, and it is important to manage impacts proactively. Therefore, the company established a dedicated stakeholders engagement process as shown below:

Stakeholders Engagement Process at SAIL

Stakeholder Groups	*Engagement Mechanism*	*Concerns/Perceptions*	*Accrued Benefits*
Shareholders	AGM, Quarterly and half-quarterly reports, investors meets, investor grievance redressal, etc.	Profitability wealth creation, Stock Price, Grievances and Complaints.	Creation of wealth for Shareholders.
Employees	Meeting with Labor Unions—Bipartite and Tripartite, Departmental and Zonal Committee, Employee Satisfaction Surveys, Annual Appraisals, Internal newsletters, etc.	Safe and healthy working conditions, Good remuneration package, Professional growth, Quality of life, Welfare measures, Training and Career Development.	Inspired, encouraged, satisfied and enthused workforce.
Suppliers	Vendor meetings, Meetings with suppliers, Ancillary Association Meetings, Supplier Relationship Management	Partnership with value creation, Timely payment, Engaging more local suppliers, Supplier satisfaction, etc.	Contented suppliers.
Customers	Customer meets, Plant visits, Director's conference with customer groups, visits to customers and customer satisfaction surveys.	Partnership with value creation, Product quality, Delivery compliance, Customer satisfaction, Resolution of complaints, etc.	Long-lasting association, contented customer.

Stakeholder Groups	*Engagement Mechanism*	*Concerns/Perceptions*	*Accrued Benefits*
NGO's	Visit to Plants, Seminars, Conferences, Interactions, etc.	Environment quality, Human rights, Freedom of association, Compliance to regulations.	Safe and healthy labour force, Environment friendly operations, Ethical operations, Compliance to Standards.
Regulators	Meetings with Central and State Govt./Steel Ministry/ Trade Bodies, Industry Associations, Ministry of Environment, Forests & Climate Change, Other Statutory bodies, etc.	Economic, Environmental and Social Compliance, Human Rights, Safety, Compliance to ILO Conventions.	Legal Compliance, Beyond Compliance.
Competitors	Knowledge sharing, Partnership with value creation, Anti-competitive behaviour, Consumer privacy.	Fair business, Partnership, Public policy advocacy.	Knowledge sharing, Best practices, Ethical Business.
Academic Bodies	Conferences, Workshops, Seminars	Knowledge Management, R&D activities, Partnership for value creation.	Knowledge sharing, New Technology.
Professionals/ Consultants	Visit to Plants, Seminars, Conferences, Interactions.	Partnership with value creation, Training and development	Knowledge building, Value creation, Collaboration
Media	Press Meets, Interactions with Plants & Corporate Communications	Economic, Environmental and Social performance Achievements	Transparency and communication

- The Research and Development Centre for Iron & Steel (RDCIS) at Ranchi is India's premier research organization in the field of ferrous metallurgy.
- Well-equipped R&D Centre facilitates development and assimilation of new technologies & process innovations are basic tenets for sustainable growth.
- Number of innovations in steel processing technology have been introduced which significantly lower carbon footprint.
- During the year 2021–22, eleven products have been developed and some of the noteworthy products include high strength high

GSM galvanized steel, low carbon (Si killed) formable quality electrical stamping steel; API X 70 line pipe hot rolled steel coils etc.

- SAIL is the only domestic producer catering to the forged steel wheel requirements of Indian Railways.
- The company manufactures steel products, the design of which incorporates social, environmental concerns, risks and opportunities.
- There was no incidence of non-compliance with respect to regulations and voluntary codes concerning product and service information and labeling.
- Dealer distributor meet has been organized extensively throughout the Country, mason meet and "Gaon ki ore" programs are conducted for rural connect by retail group, ASD (Architect, Structural and Designers) meets are conducted in Tier 1 and 2 cities.
- All products conform to the applicable regulations and standards as prescribed by the Bureau of Indian Standards.
- Hazardous waste handling is done as per the Hazardous Waste Management Rules, 2016.
- During 2021–22, no incident has been reported on non-compliance with regulations and voluntary codes concerning marketing communications, including advertising, promotion and sponsorship. No complaint has been received regarding any breach of customer privacy and loss of customer data during the year.
- In general, this has not only improved the operational efficiency but also the environment in and around the Plants and Mines.
- In order to ensure a healthy and safe environment within warehouses, the Company has in place procedures and manuals pertaining to health and safety. A total 13 no. of SAIL warehouses are accredited with ISO 14001.
- No significant negative environmental impact (s) is/are noticeable in supply chain as vehicles (trucks and trailers) complying with statutory pollution norms are engaged in transport of material at the warehouses.

Major Actions on Safety and Health

- It has been continually and consistently improving its safety and health management systems and practices with the ultimate aim to have safe and healthy workplace.

- Safety and Health issues are monitored and guided from the apex level of management as well as Board Sub-committee on Health, Safety and Environment.
- Internationally established standards—OHSAS 18001/ISO 45001, ISO 9001 and ISO 14001 are followed religiously for Safety, Occupational Health and Environment protection.
- In each department/shop, Departmental Safety Officer (DSO) and Safety Steward/Captain/Warrior ensures adherence to laid down standards and safe working procedures.
- Systematic approach is adopted by following 3 E's of Safety Management, i.e. Engineering, Enforcement and Education in all spheres of working.
- Adequate emphasis is given towards safety during execution and commissioning of new projects/facilities by adhering to Safe Commissioning Procedures and Protocols.
- 'Permit to Work' and 'Protocol' Systems, having necessary safeguards, are religiously followed during execution of hazardous and critical jobs involving multiple agencies.
- All work related incidents are investigated to find out the root cause and appropriate actions are taken to prevent its recurrence.
- A compulsory safety and work environment related training is duly provided to every contractual worker before deployment on any job.
- Salient activities undertaken by OHS centres are as follows:
  - Periodical Medical Examination of employees carried out.
  - OHS OPD services provided to 56,832 employees.
  - Many training programmes conducted by OHSC.
  - Special Days like World Day for Safety and Health at Work, International Yoga Day, World Malaria Day, International Women's Day, National Occupational Health Day, World No Tobacco Day, World Diabetes Day and World AIDS Day celebrated.

Corporate Social Responsibility at SAIL

The objective of the Company is not only to manufacture steel, but also to conduct business in ways that result in social, environmental and economic benefits to the communities in which it operates. So, it has been structuring and implementing CSR initiatives right from the inception. These efforts have seen the erstwhile obscure villages located around SAIL plants, turn into large industrial hubs today.

- SAIL CSR initiatives are undertaken in conformity with the prevalent statutes like 'The Companies Act, 2013', its Schedule-VII, CSR Rules, 2014 and Companies (CSR Policy) Amendment Rules, 2021.
- SAIL carries out CSR projects in and around steel townships, mines and far flung location across the Country in following areas like:
    - Maintenance of Model Steel Villages (MSVs)
    - Providing Health Care
    - Immunization,
    - Ante/post natal care
    - Education,*
    - Access to water facilities
    - Roadside tree plantation,
    - Environment sustenance
    - Women empowerment,
    - Sustainable Income generation through Self Help Groups
    - Assistance to Sr. Citizens, Divyangs,
    - Trainings to promote Sports
    - Promotion of traditional Art and Culture, etc.
- During FY 2021–22, SAIL has incurred an expenditure of ₹13.77 crore in excess of the mandatory CSR budget of ₹80.47 crore.
- SAIL activated a scaled response towards management of the Covid-19 pandemic at its Plants, Units, Mines and Townships.
- In addition, SAIL Hospitals manned by more than 900 qualified doctors and 1,500 para-medical staff to extend round the clock Healthcare, have earmarked 1,000 dedicated Covid-19 beds with oxygen support and 129 ICU beds with ventilator support in view of surge in cases, created 600 beds Quarantine Facilities and developed Covid-19 testing facilities like RAT, RTPCR, TRU-NAT in coordination with respective State Governments.
- In order to support the vulnerable sections of society, daily-wage earners/labourers, poor peasants and their families, SAIL Plants and Units distributed dry ration packets, Milk packets, Milk powder, Khichdi, routine medicines, daily cooked meals to patients and healthcare workers, sanitary napkins for women, facilitated stitching/distribution of Face Masks, Aprons, and Gloves, etc.
- It is supporting about 77 schools providing modern education to more than 40,000 children in the steel townships.

- It is assisting over 600 Govt. schools in Bhilai and Rourkela with about 63,000 students by providing mid-day meals and dry ration kits in association with Akshya Patra Foundation.
- Nineteen Special Schools (Kalyan and Mukul Vidyalayas) benefitting around 4865 BPL category students at Integrated Steel Plant locations with facilities like free education, mid-day meals, uniform including shoes, textbooks, stationary items, school bags and water bottles, etc. are running under CSR.

Some Comments on Performance of SAIL

The Economic, Social and Governance (ESG) Reports of SAIL for 2021–22 can be claimed as one of the best among PEs in India. In particular, the Social Responsibility Report gives all expected directions of SAIL's activities in Indian economy. The multi-dimensional aspects of reporting speak volume in favour of SAIL's performance. However, the economic performance of SAIL cannot be compared with ITC Ltd. or other enlisted companies because SAIL has to meet a host of social obligations being part of the Public Enterprises. In the matter of pricing of its products, it has to comply with Government policy.

Even before globalization and change in some government policies, SAIL used to maintain a good tradition of making innovation in its annual reports. For example, in 1980s both SAIL and BHE (Bharat Heavy Electricals Ltd.), were the pioneers in the field of corporate financial reporting. SAIL published Social Income Report[11] apart from traditional financial statements under the supervision of erstwhile Bureau of Public Enterprises. During that time BHEL was also known for giving separately Human Resources Accounts apart from its traditional financial reports.

Some specific information on SAIL's performance are given below:

1. SAIL started disclosing Sustainability Report from the year 2010–11 in addition to Annual Report. Its website contents

11 In August 26–27, 1988, the present author gave his first international seminar, after attending the American Accounting Association's International Conference in New York, on *Corporate Financial Reporting in Public Enterprises in India with special reference to Steel Authority of India,* in the Accounting Department of the University of Tuscaloosa, USA. When the presentation of SAIL's Social Income Report was made, the accounting and management faculty was fascinated by the innovative idea of SAIL and Dr. Cathleen Bindon preferred to keep the hard copy of the Annual Report of SAIL for the Faculty Library (Ref. Banerjee, Bhabatosh, *My Journey—Down the Memory Lane,* IAA Research Foundation, 2021, pp. 250 and 256–257).

under 'Climate Change & SAIL' and 'Corporate Citizenship' provide ample information about its plan, policies and initiatives towards the development of nearby society.

2. Much before 'Corporate Social Responsibility' became a buzzword, SAIL put in place systems for socio-economic development of the neighbourhoods and communities amidst which its plants and units operate. The objective was to plough prosperity back into the environment from which its strengths emanate, to minimise inequalities by providing quality education, healthcare, infrastructure and employment avenues to all, to ensure that man and nature live in harmony, to preserve the originality and beauty of Indian culture while simultaneously promoting scientific temperament and modern technology. SAIL's role as a responsible corporate citizen in nation building has not gone unrecognised. The company has won prestigious awards, honours and accolades in this sphere such as:
    - SAIL bagged the Top Rankers Excellence Award 2020 for best corporate communication.
    - In 2019, Rourkela Steel Plant awarded with Golden Peacock Award 2018 for the effectiveness of its CSR initiatives. In the same year, it also received CII HR Excellence Award for strong commitment towards HR.
    - In 2018, the company was awarded with 15th National Award for Excellence in Cost Management.
    - SCOPE Meritorious Award for Corporate Social Responsibility and Responsiveness for the year 2008–09.
    - Annual FICCI Awards 2008–09 in the category of "The Vision Corporate Triple Impact-Business Performance: Social and Environmental Action and Globalisation Award".
    - Businessworld—FICCI-SEDF CSR Award for the year 2006.
    - FICCI Award for Rural and Community Development (2006–07).
    - CSR Award of the Ministry of Rural Development, Government of India.
    - Golden Peacock Award—for CSR to Bhilai Steel Plant of SAIL for three consecutive years.
    - CSR Award of Tamil Nadu Government for the year 2007–08 and 2008–09 to Salem Steel Plant.
    - SAIL was also a finalist of the Stevie Award for Best CSR Programme in Asia (Subcontinent, Australia and New Zealand).

SUMMARY

What conclusion can we draw from the results of the Case Studies? Has the environmental awareness gone up in the corporate sector? Is the level of disclosure of environmental information satisfactory? If not, how can this be improved? Has the position improved over time? Are we lagging behind as compared to the scenario in the developed countries in this respect? Is there any necessity to take some measures by the regulatory bodies to enhance the environmental awareness in the corporate sector?

We find that the disclosure of environmental information by the sample companies in their annual reports is not significant in the earlier (2002–2003) case study. Very few companies are disclosing quantitative environmental information voluntarily. Many of the sample companies are publishing some general information, viz., policy, awareness, measures taken, and the commitment of the company in this context, in a descriptive way, generally in the Director's Report. Of course, there are some good examples too, e.g., Indian Oil Co., ITC and Tata Motors.

In general, publication of quantitative information was few and far between. Although time-series analysis shows an improvement in the disclosure of environmental information by the sample companies (Eresi, 1996; Banerjee, 2002; Pramanik, 2002; Khasnobis, 2002), there was hardly any publication of financial information relating to accounting and auditing. One positive feature was that many companies were getting ISO accreditation and adopting ISO 14000 series of standards. Getting environmental audit by a few is another good feature. These are indeed a remarkable improvement of the situation over time. If the results of the sample companies show any indication, then it can be said that things will tend to improve in the future.

The above conclusion, however, is subject to one caveat regarding methodology. The sample size is too small and in most cases annual reports of one accounting year, 2002–03, could only be considered. This naturally hindered comparison over time in this study. The observations of the respondents could not be cross-checked through published secondary data. No statistical technique could be used to arrive at the conclusion for obvious reason. In spite of these, the results of the 26 sample companies bear a testimony of how the big public limited companies were managing environment-related activities and disclosing them in the annual reports. These practices stand as a pointer to the environmental responsibilities of the corporate sector in India.

The two case studies (ITC and SAIL) for 2021–2022, show very remarkable disclosure of environmental management related information as a voluntary measure. There is significant improvement in the scenario over time. From 2022–23 financial year Sustainability Reporting and many other disclosure of information relating to governance, assurance, etc. will be mandatory. India's corporate sector will then be able to complete with its counterparts internationally.

MULTIPLE CHOICE QUESTIONS

1. The KPMG Survey (2022) of Sustainability Reporting gives some notable observations, such as:
   (a) GRI remains the most dominant standard used around the world
   (b) Regional N100 (World-wide top 100 companies) sustainability reporting rates in Asia Pacific and Europe are on the rise
   (c) Integrated Reporting Culture is strong in the Middle East and Asia Pacific
   (d) All of the above
2. Professor Zabiholla Rezaee and two others of Memphis University, USA in their study (2023) found a:
   (a) Significant worldwide increase of both quantity and quality of SRA (Sustainable Reporting and Assurance)
   (b) Positive association between the quantity and quality of SRA and sustainability disclosure, and United Nations Development Goals (SDGs)
   (c) Significant association between the quantity, quality of sustainability reporting and the legal, social, ethical and environmental attributes
   (d) All of the above
3. The Business Responsibility and Sustainability Report (2021) of SEBI includes the following format:
   (a) General Disclosure
   (b) Management and Process Disclosure
   (c) Principle-based Performance Disclosure
   (d) All of the above
4. The Key Performance Indicators of NGRBC (National Guidelines on Responsible Business Conduct) include the following *except:*
   (a) Essential Indicators (Mandatory)
   (b) Leadership Indicators (Voluntary)
   (c) Three dimensions of Assurance Approaches
   (d) Nine principles

5. The Assurance of Sustainable Reforming framework does not include:
   (a) IASB Standard No. I
   (b) Approach to Assurance
   (c) AA 1000 Assurance Standards
   (d) ISAE 3000 Standards
6. The Environmental Management System (EMS) includes:
   (a) EMS linked with ISO: 14001
   (b) SAIL has been fore-bearer in establishment of EMS
   (c) All the Integrated Steel Plants, major Units and Warehouses of SAIL are compliant with EMS ISO: 14001 Standard
   (d) All of the above
7. Sustainability Framework of SAIL does not include:
   (a) Engagement with Stakeholders
   (b) Mission
   (c) Vision
   (d) Materiality Issues
8. Risk Mitigation Strategies with respect to Environmental Risks in SAIL does not include:
   (a) Waste management and disposal
   (b) Regular adoption of clean technologies to reduce GHG emissions
   (c) Venturing in environmental protection measures
   (d) Preparing for beyond compliance scenario, greenery development and interaction with statutory bodies
9. The waste management in SAIL is guided by policies relating to:
   (a) Recover the waste
   (b) Reduce the waste
   (c) Recycle and reuse
   (d) All of the above
10. Select the correct sequence of Waste Management Policies (Four R's) adopted by SAIL:
    (a) Reduce, recover, recycle and reuse
    (b) Recover, reduce, recycle and reuse
    (c) Recycle, reduce, reuse and recover
    (d) Recover, reuse, recycle and recover

EXERCISES

1. "Based on the system of Integrated Environmental and Economic Accounting (IEEA), as per UN Statistical Office (UNSTAT), environmental accounts duly integrating the environment and natural resources, and changes therein, with the national accounts can be prepared." Elucidate the statement.

2. Mention a few earlier studies (2002, 2003) relating to important issues concerning environmental management from a macro-perspective. Mention three of them and their contributions.
3. What are the important findings of Patra's study (2003), *Accounting and Reporting for Environment—A Case study of TISCO* (1995–96—1999–2000)?
4. State in brief global trends in Sustainability Reporting.
5. Give a brief description of sustainability reporting in India.
6. Enumerate the process of evolution of sustainability reporting in India.
7. What are nine principles of NGRBC (National Guidelines on Responsible Business Conduct)?
8. Section 217(1)(e) of the Companies Act, 1956 gives a list of 21 Companies those were required to disclose "conservation of energy" information in the Report of the Board of Directors. Enumerate 15 such companies.
9. Prepare a Questionnaire for administering among the 20 sample companies belonging to hazardous group to study the information relating to environment management in their annual reports.
10. What was the mode of disclosure of environment management information in the annual reports of 60 surveyed companies (2002–2003)? Write short notes on any four key information.
11. Give a brief history of ITC Ltd.
12. What are the framework of capitals and their objectives in ITC Ltd.?
13. What are the achievements of ITC in 2021–22 having regard to adopting 2.0 Goals in relation to the target of 2030?
14. Based upon the data relating to 2021–22 of ITC Annual Report, comment upon its performance.
15. What are 'sustainable priorities' as mentioned by SAIL in its ESG Reporting (2021–22)?
16. State the Sustainability Framework of SAIL.
17. Briefly highlight the environmental performance of SAIL.
18. Summarise the initiatives taken by SAIL towards Carbon Neutrality.
19. SAIL has taken a number of initiatives towards Conserving Water. Enumerate any ten out of them.
20. SAIL has adopted four R's Policy across all its processes relating to Waste Management. List them and comment.
21. What do you understand by Energy Conservation Initiatives? Explain in brief.

22. "Social sustainability is about identifying and managing business impacts, both positive and negative on people". Elucidate the statement.
23. What is Corporate Social Responsibility? How SAIL has been managing corporate social responsibility. Give a few important examples.
24. Examine SAIL's Engagement Mechanism with respect to Regulators and Competitors?
25. Employees have a key role in the performance of any company. Comment upon the Engagement Process at SAIL with respect to employees.

REFERENCES

Banerjee, Ashok, "Issues in Environmental Accounting and Reporting", *Indian Journal of Accounting*, Vol. 30, No. 1, June 1999.

Banerjee, B., "Accounting for Corporate Environmental Management in India", *The Management Accountant*, Vol. 37, No. 12, December 2002.

Banerji, U., "Environment Management System (EMS): A business tool for increased profitability", *The Management Accountant*, Vol. 35, No. 6, June 2000.

Bhattacharyya, R. and Banerjee, S. (Eds.), *Air Pollution in Developing Countries and the Victim's Willingness to Pay for it: A ready reckoner*, DRS Programme, Department of Commerce and Business Management, University of Calcutta, 2002.

Bhowmik, G. and Dutta, S., Sustainable Water Management Reporting Practice, *Indian Accounting Review*, 26(1): 20–23, 2022.

Bose, A., "Environment System Risk Audit and Management Control System", *The Management Accountant*, Vol. 35, No. 6, June, 2000.

Bose, S. and De, A., "Environment—Costing and accounting", *The Management Accountant*, Vol. 34, No. 6, June 1999.

Chattopadhyay, P., "Pollution Accounting", *The Management Accountant*, Vol. 38, No. 12, December 2003.

Cheema, C.S., "Global Initiatives on Environmental Reporting", *The Management Accountant*, Vol. 35, No. 6, June 2000.

Companies Act, 2013, with Rules.

Dasgupta, N., *Environmental Accounting*, Wheeler Publishing, New Delhi, 1997.

Eresi, K., "Information Disclosure in Annual Reports", *The Chartered Accountant*, Vol. 44, No. 7, January 1996.

Ghosh, A. and Chakraborty, S., "Environmental Accounting: An attempt for sustainable development with methodological approach", *The Management Accountant*, Vol. 40, No. 6, June 2005.

Gupta, R.R., "Emerging Issues in Environmental Accounting", *The Management Accountant*, August 2002.

Hewitt, G., *Improving Natural Capital Reporting and Finding the Tools to Help*, 2013, 12.

ICAI, *Sustainability Reporting* (6th ed.), 2015.

Khasnobis, R. (Ed.), *Ecology, Economy and Society: A collection of essays*, Departmental Research Support (DRS) Programme, University of Calcutta, 2003.

KPMG Survey of Sustainable Reporting, 2022.

Khasnobis, R. (Ed.), *Issues in Sustainable Development*, DRS Programme, Department of Business Management, University of Calcutta, 2002.

Mishra, K.K., "Environmental Reporting in Business", *The Management Accountant*, Vol. 34, No. 6, June 1999.

Oza, H.S., "Environmental Accounting: Linkages with management control systems", *The Management Accountant*, Vol. 40, No. 6, June 2005.

Parker, L.D., "Environmental Costing: A path to implementation", *The Cost and Management*, ICMA, Bangladesh, January–February 2002.

Patra, S., "Accounting and Reporting for Environment—A case study of TISCO", *The Management Accountant*, Vol. 38, No. 6, June 2003.

Pramanik, Alok (Ed.), *Environmental Accounting and Reporting*, Deep and Deep Publications, New Delhi, 2002.

Price Water House Copper, July 2021.

Rao, M.P., "Environmental Accounting and Auditing—A general view", *The Management Accountant*, Vol. 35, No. 6, June 2000.

Rau, John G. and Wooten, David, C., *Environmental Impact Assessment Handbook*, McGraw-Hill, New York, 1980.

Roy, G.D., "Indian Accounting and its Comparative Strive after Research Developments", in Banerjee, B. (Ed.), *Contemporary Issues in Accounting Research*, IAA Research Foundation, 1991.

Salahuddin, A. and Salimuddin, Md., "Environmental and Natural Resource Accounting: An overview", *The Cost and Management*, ICMA of Bangladesh, May–June 2003.

Sundar, Ravi, M., "Corporate Environmental Reporting: Present status and future challenges", ICFAI, Vol. 7, No. 1, January 2001.

Vasal, V.K., "Accounting for Sustainable Economic Development: Issues and evidences", *Indian Journal of Accounting*, Vol. 29, No. 1, June 1998.

APPENDIX 1

List of Sample Companies Selected from the ET 500: Ranking based on Market Capitalization in March, 2002

Sl. No.	*Rank*	*Company's name*	*Status*
1.	6	ITC Ltd.	
2.	14	Housing Development Finance Co.	Rejected
3.	15	Hindustan Petroleum Co.	
4.	16	HCL Technologies	Rejected
5.	20	HDFC Bank	Rejected
6.	23	Hindalco Industries	
7.	24	Larsen & Toubro	
8.	29	Bharat Heavy Electricals Ltd.	
9.	36	Associated Cement Co.	
10.	42	ICICI Bank	Rejected
11.	49	Indian Petrochemicals Corporation	
12.	55	Container Corpn. of India	Rejected
13.	61	Bank of Baroda	Rejected
14.	63	Gillette India	
15.	64	Hindustan Zinc	
16.	66	Cummins India	
17.	67	Pfizer	
18.	71	Bharat Electronics	
19.	72	Indo-Gulf Corporation	
20.	73	Procter & Gamble India	
21.	75	Polaris Software Lab	Rejected
22.	76	Hughes Telecom (I)	Rejected
23.	84	Siemens	
24.	93	Reliance Capital	Rejected
25.	94	Sterlite Industries (India)	
26.	96	TVS Motor Co.	
27.	100	UTI Bank (now Axis Bank)	Rejected

Sl. No.	*Rank*	*Company's name*	*Status*
28.	102	Mascot Systems	Rejected
29.	107	CMC	Rejected
30.	109	Morepen Laboratories	
31.	116	E Merck (India)	
32.	118	Jaiprakash Industries	
33.	119	Silverline Technologies	Rejected
34.	126	Finolex Cables	
35.	127	Ingersoll-Rand (India)	
36.	130	Philips India	
37.	131	Balaji Telefilms	Rejected
38.	133	Finolex Industries	
39.	135	Hindustan Inks & Resins	
40.	142	Knoll Pharmaceuticals	
41.	144	Ahmedabad Electricity	
42.	153	ITC Bhadrachalam Paperboards	
43.	168	Jagatjit Industries	
44.	171	Birla 3M	
45.	179	Bajaj Tempo	
46.	180	IDBI Bank	Rejected
47.	185	Mcdowell & Co.	
48.	187	Global Trust Bank (now Oriental Bank of Commerce)	Rejected
49.	190	Tata Infotech	Rejected
50.	192	Glenmark Pharmaceuticals	
51.	203	Aftek Infosys	Rejected
52.	209	Mirc Electronics	
53.	213	German Remedies	
54.	215	JB Chemicals & Pharma	
55.	226	Berger Paints (India)	
56.	229	Tata Telecom	Rejected
57.	231	Geometric Software Soln.	Rejected

Sl. No.	Rank	Company's name	Status
58.	237	Blue Dart Express	Rejected
59.	245	Burroughs Wellcome (India)	
60.	248	Rashel Agrotech	Rejected
61.	249	Shree Rama Multitech	Rejected
62.	259	State Bank of Bikaner & Jaipur	Rejected
63.	271	Agee Gold Refiners	Rejected
64.	274	Voltas	
65.	279	State Bank of Travancore	Rejected
66.	296	Centurion Bank (now HDFC)	Rejected
67.	297	Max India	Rejected
68.	299	Madura Coats	
69.	306	Bank of Punjab	Rejected
70.	310	Dalmia Cement (Bharat)	
71.	314	Coromandel Fertilisers	
72.	319	Trigyn Technologies	Rejected
73.	321	Crompton Greaves	
74.	330	Maharashtra Seamless	
75.	334	Patel Engineering	
76.	338	Gujarat Heavy Chemicals	
77.	350	Ambica Agar	
78.	374	National Organic Chemical Industry	
79.	376	Mid-Day Multimedia	Rejected
80.	380	Hotel Leela Venture	Rejected
81.	392	DCM Shriram Consolidated	
82.	409	Megasoft	Rejected
83.	413	Carborundum Universal	
84.	416	Zandu Pharmaceutical Works	
85.	426	Tata Finance	Rejected
86.	432	Gesco Corporation	Rejected
87.	434	Rama Newsprint & Paper	Rejected

Sl. No.	*Rank*	*Company's name*	*Status*
88.	436	Timex Watches	Rejected
89.	440	Creative Eye	Rejected
90.	445	Wheels India	
91.	446	Rallis India	
92.	450	Hi-Tech Gears	
93.	453	Nahar Spinning Mills	
94.	458	Ashima	
95.	462	Alstom	
96.	464	Birla Ericsson Optical	Rejected
97.	468	Albright & Weilson Chemicals	
98.	469	Ajanta Pharma	
99.	478	Southern Petrochem Industrial Corp.	
100.	497	Moschip Semiconductor Tech.	Rejected

Initial size of the sample 100
Number of companies rejected 40
Effective size of the sample 60

APPENDIX 2

Questionnaire

Accounting for Corporate Environmental Management

[*Kindly tick the appropriate answer. Where no answer is given, use your wisdom in providing the appropriate answer.*]

A. GENERAL

1. Name of the Company:
2. Address of Registered Office:
3. Location of Factories

(1)

(2)

(3)

4. Total assets employed by the company during (₹ lakh)

1999–2000:

2000–2001:

2001–2002:

5. Net turnover of the company during

    1999–2000:

    2000–2001:

    2001–2002:

6. Industry Group to which the company belongs:
   (e.g., Steel, Chemical, etc.)
7. No. of products manufactured by the company:

B. POLLUTION

8. (a) What are the wastes your company releases?
   (b) How do you dispose of such wastes?
   (i)
   (ii)
9. What is the level of pollution generated by the company:
   (a) Air (ppm) (b) Water (BOD)
   (c) Soil (TT pa) (d) Sound (Decibel)
10. What measures do you adopt to control pollution of the following?
   (a) Air (b) Water
   (c) Soil (d) Sound
11. Do you recycle scrap, waste, etc.? Yes/No
12. Which of the products pollutes most the environment? Yes/No
13. Are you submitting return to the State Pollution Control Board (SPCB) regularly? Yes/No
14. Have you been fined by the PCB for violation of acceptable environmental limits during: Yes/No
    1999–2000 Yes/No
    2000–2001 Yes/No
    2001–2002 Yes/No
15. Have you been complying with Section 217(1)(e) of the Companies Act, 1956? Yes/No
16. (a) Have you received any complaints from local community regarding damages caused due to operations of your business? Yes/No
    (b) If yes, what corrective or preventive measures have you taken?

C. MANAGEMENT

17. (a) Have you adopted any environmental policy? Yes/No
    (b) If yes, mention the policy statement. ____________

18. (a) Does your company follow Environmental Management System (EMS) in terms of ISO 14001? Yes/No
    (b) If yes, when did you implement it?
    (c) If yes, did you receive ISO 14001 Certificate from International Standards Organization (ISO)? Yes/No
    (d) If no, is it under consideration for implementation? Yes/No
19. (a) Do you have Environmental Action Team (EAT) to address environmental issues that affect the business? Yes/No
    (b) If yes, what is the size and composition of the team?

    Size (No.):

    Composition (Designations only):
20. (a) Do you have an Environmental Manager for effective management of environmental issues? Yes/No
    (b) If no, do you feel its desirability for better environmental management? Yes/No
21. Have you created a better working environment (health and safety aspects) to motivate employees to contribute actively to EMS? Yes/No
22. (a) Do you have a formal system for managing environmental risks? Yes/No
    (b) If yes, what measures do you take for environmental risk management?
23. Do you have voluntary codes of conduct as part of 'Responsible Environment Care Programme'? Yes/No

D. PRODUCTION

24. Do you implement new, innovative and clearer production technologies? Yes/No
25. Do you develop new product/process with 'environmental justification'? Yes/No
26. Do your suppliers implement ISO 14001? Yes/No
27. Are your employees conscious about better housekeeping? Yes/No

28. (a) How do you treat remnants of the principal raw materials used in production?
    - Recycled to produce by-product
    - Dumped at the factory site for ultimate transfer
      to Municipal/Corporation's dumping ground
    - Others (specify):

    (b) If not recycled presently, is there any economic use of such waste? ______________________

29. Have you spent money to adopt 'green-technology' during

    1999–2000: Yes/No

    2000–2001: Yes/No

    2001–2002: Yes/No

E. ACCOUNTING AND AUDIT

30. Do your accounting policies specify anything about measurement and reporting of environment related costs, provisions and contingencies? Yes/No
31. Do you show separately the amount charged to Profit and Loss Account during the current accounting period in respect of expenditure to protect employees and society in general from the consequences of damage to the environment caused by the operations of your company? Yes/No
32. Do you mention separately expensing and capitalization of environmental expenditure? Yes/No
33. How do you allocate hidden costs (costs of waste treatment, compliance management, training, legal support, etc.) of environmental management?
34. Do you show separately provisions or contingent liabilities for managing environmental risks? Yes/No
35. How do you make capitalization of environmental expenditure and its amortization?
36. How do you treat government grants received, if any, for expenditure that protects the environment?
37. How do you measure and disclose environment-related liabilities?

38. (a) Do you take preventive financial measures, such as making catastrophe reserves? Yes/No

(b) If yes, how much reserve was made during

₹ lakh

1999–2000: (% of Net Profit)

2000–2001: (% of Net Profit)

2001–2002: (% of Net Profit)

39. (a) What was the amount of capital expenditure, if any, for environmental management during the last three years?

₹ lakh

1999–2000:

2000–2001:

2001–2002:

(b) If yes, did the above investment result in any betterment in EMS? Yes/No

40. In taking capital expenditure decisions, do you evaluate the alternatives with environmental justification? Yes/No

41. (a) Is there any system of environmental audit? Yes/No

(b) If yes, how do you disclose such report?

(i) as part of statutory audit report Yes/No

(ii) as a separate audit report Yes/No

(c) If yes, who is conducting the environment audit? (mention size and composition)

42. (a) Do you recommend the formulation of accounting and auditing standards by the relevant authorities for better EMS? Yes/No

(b) If yes, who should perform the task?

- ICAI
- Government
- Central Pollution Control Board
- Others (specify):

Dated:

Signature : ____________

Name : ____________

Designation : ____________

Company : ____________

7

Some Emerging Topics

7.1 INTRODUCTION

We have covered various matters relating to corporate environmental management in the earlier chapters including case studies on financial reporting. Since the matter is very complex in nature, it is difficult to cover every aspect of environment and its management. Accordingly, we propose to discuss the following important items relating to accounting for environmental management in this chapter.

- Green Economy and Green Accounting
- Carbon Accounting or Greenhouse Gas (GHG) Accounting
- Carbon Credit
- Climate Change vs. Global Warming, etc.

At the end, we would give, as annexures, copy of one revised published paper, *Green Economy*, and one of my presentation on *Climate Change* at an international conference in Dhaka (January 29, 2023) with a view to increasing the horizon of knowledge of the readers on the subject and its allied areas.

7.2 GREEN ECONOMY AND GREEN ACCOUNTING

Green economy is the economy where every stakeholder is aware of environmental issues and adopts measures that contribute to the better "lifestyle". It aims to transition of economy into a low carbon economy through facilitating green business and green jobs. Who are the stakeholders? At least the following groups can be identified among them:

1. The public in general.
2. The transport system, both public and the private.
3. The corporate sector, and
4. Others (those not included among the above groups).

Each of the above groups has a role, minor or major, to play in contributing either positively or negatively to the green economy. Thus, it is a wholesome concept. For example, the job-seekers in the economy should have the desirable background. If not, an in-house training should be imparted to them. In the education system of the country, green education and green training should also be part of the system. Among all the stockholders, the impact of activities of the corporate sector may be devastating (for lack of proper management of their activities keeping in view the environmental issues) or may be a very strong driver of contributing to environment management issues.[1]

Green accounting[2] follows from the concept of green economy. It may be thought of from macro level and also micro level. Green accounting is a popular term for combined environmental and economic accounting at national and corporate levels. It is comparable with traditional commercial accounting in the sense that natural resources are a form of capital because they produce value for society over time. So, green accounting is a type of accounting that attempts to include environmental costs in business results. The main purpose of green accounting is to help companies understand and manage potential trade-offs between traditional economic and environmental goals. The term was first brought into common usage by economist Professor Peter Wood in the 1980s.[3]

Green accounting is also termed as Environmental Accounting because it is associated with environmental services and goods. It considers the costs and benefits which arise through environmental protection and depletion of the existing capital. It integrates the economy, society and the environment which is the main approach to sustainability or sustainable accounting.

Green accounting requires not only focuses on Profit but also on People and the Planet—also called as Triple Bottom Line approach. This approach came about because of the world's concern for environment that is continuously damaged. The corporate sector is the main polluter

1 For further details see Annexure 1.
2 https//www.sciencedirect.com
3 Schalteggar, S. and Burrit, R. *Contemporary Environmental Accounting Issues, Concept and Practice,* Sheffield Greenleaf, 2000 ISBN.

of the environment in spite of its contribution to the economy. Important laws having direct influence on green accounting in India include the following:

- Prevention and Control of Pollution Act, 1974
- Water (Prevention and Control of Pollution) Act, 1974
- Water (Prevention and Control of Pollution) Cess Act, 1977
- Water Biomedical Waste (Management and Handling) Rules, 1996
- The Air (Prevention and Control of Pollution) Act, 1981
- The Environment Protection Act, 1986.

Many of the above-mentioned environmental legislations were enacted prior to Stockholm Conference.

The System of National Accounts (SNA) defines net domestic product (NDP) as:

$$\text{NDP} = \text{Net exports} + \text{Final consumption (C)} + \text{Net investment (I)}$$

But Green Accounting uses the System of Environmental Economic Accounting (SEEA) which focuses on the depletion of scarce natural resources and measures the costs of environmental degradation along with its prevention. Accordingly, NDP is newly defined as Green NDP, or also as EDP. Thus, the Green Accounting formula[4] is:

$$\text{EDP} = \text{Net exports} + \text{C} + \text{NAp.ec} + (\text{NAnp.ec} - \text{NAnp.n})$$

where

EDP = Environmental domestic product
C = Final consumption
Nap.ec = Net accumulation of produced economic assets
NAnp.ec = Net accumulation of non-produced economic assets
NAnp.n = Net accumulation of non-produced natural assets

7.3 CARBON ACCOUNTING

Carbon accounting is a framework of methods to measure and track how much Greenhouse Gas (GHG) an organization emits. It is also known as Greenhouse Gas accounting (Google Wikipedia)[5]. Carbon accounting can also be used to track projects or actions to reduce emissions in sectors such as forestry and renewable energy. Companies, cities and

4 Green Accounting: Need, Objectives, Problems and other Details, Your Article Library, Retrieved 2015.12.07.

5 Carbon Accounting, Corporate Finance Institute, Retrieved 6 January, 2023.

other groups use these techniques to help limit climate change. These techniques can help understand the impact of specific products and services by quantifying their GHG emissions throughout their lifecycles.

Carbon accounting represents a wide range of practices—physical carbon accounting and financial carbon accounting. The first category quantifies the physical amount of GHG emitted while the financial carbon accounting attempts to give carbon a financial market value. The advantage of the physical carbon accounting is that the company can fix a target for reduction of GHG emissions over time once the total quantity of GHG emissions are known. On the other hand, the financial carbon accounting gives the measure in financial term in respect of GHG emitted. So, both the types have their own usefulness.

Drivers of carbon accounting. The drivers of carbon accounting include the following:

1. **Internal company drivers:** A variety of business considerations drive carbon accounting. These include rankings alongside other companies.
2. **Government requirements (*External*):** Legal requirements provide another type of driver. The EU's Corporate Sustainable Reporting is part of the Green Deal. It is intended to make EU countries carbon neutral by 2050. As per this Directive, many large companies and companies enlisted on stock exchanges in EU-Regulated Markets are required to disclose a broader array of ESG information including GHG emissions. In the US, the GHG Reporting Program covers 41 industrial categories.
3. **Non-governmental organization programs:** Many NGOs have developed programs that both promote GHG accounting and reporting.

Frameworks and standards. Many of today's carbon accounting standards have incorporated principles from the IPCC (Intergovernmental Panel on Climate Change) Principle of Comparability which is less widely applied. These standards typically cover the greenhouse gases first regulated under the Kyoto Protocol.

1. *Corporate/local government standards:* Companies and facilities use a variety of methods to track and report GHG emissions. These include those from GHG Protocol, the Task-force on Climate-related Financial Disclosure, the Sustainability Accounting Standards Board, the Global Reporting Initiative, the Climate Disclosure Standards Board, etc.

2. *GHG protocol:* It refers to a group of standards that are most common in GHG accounting. These standards reflect a number of accounting principles including relevance, completeness, consistency, transparency and accuracy. The standards divide emissions into three scopes.

   Scope 1: Covers all *direct* emissions within a corporate boundary.

   Scope 2: Covers *indirect* GHG emissions from consumption of purchased electricity, heat, cooling or steam. At least one third of GHG emissions come from this scope. If there is an internal plant for generation of electricity, then the company has to report carbon intensity in connection with generation of electricity. Carbon intensity refers to how many grams of carbon dioxide (CO_2) are released to produce one kilowatt hour (kWh) of electricity. Thus, electricity generation process is more carbon intensive as the process by which it is generated creates more CO_2 emissions.

   Scope 3: Emissions from suppliers and product users.
3. *ISO 14064*: ISO published the standard 14064 in 2006 for GHG accounting and verification. Part I of the standard specifies principles and requirements for estimating and reporting GHG emissions and removals. Part III provides guidance for conducting and managing the verification of GHG reporting.
4. *EPA GHG program:* The United States Environmental Protection Agency (EPA) requires facility and supplier's based reporting for many categories of emission sources. The program includes guidelines about how emissions are to be estimated and reported.
5. *Task force on climate-related financial disclosures*: The TCFD disclosure standard for companies covers four thematic areas—governance, strategy, risk management, and metrics and targets.

7.4 CARBON CREDIT AND CARBON CREDIT TRADING IN INDIA

Carbon Credit is a permit or certificate that allows a country or an organization to produce a certain amount of carbon emissions which can be traded if the full allowance is not used. The holder of the permit enjoys a right to emit one ton of carbon dioxide or an equivalent of another GHG. Most prices of carbon credits are below $40–$80 per metric ton of CO_2 emitted to keep the global warming within 2 degree Celsius as per Paris Agreement.

The need for **carbon trading** was terribly felt when industrial emissions of CHG resulted in global warming. It was therefore realized that the only way to get attention of the world towards these problems was by attaching some financial incentive to it. Accordingly, Article 21 of the Kyoto Protocol allows a country with an emission-reduction or emission-limitation commitment to implement emission-reduction project in developing countries.

India's **carbon market** is huge and is one of the fastest growing markets in the world. She has already generated 30 million carbon credits which is the second highest transacted volumes in the world. The growth of carbon trading market in India is faster than many other booming sectors, such as, information technology, biotechnology and BPO sectors (Woogle.com). In India, green energy companies, such as, Adani Greens, and Carbon Off-setters like EKI Energy Services, have come together to develop a carbon credit market to help achieve energy transition goals[6]. A few examples of carbon trading in India may be given below:

1. **Jindal Vijaynagar Steel:** $225 million worth of saved carbon because the steel plant uses the Corex Furnace technology which prevents 15 million tons of carbon from being discharged into the atmosphere.
2. **Powerguda in Andhra Pradesh:** Saved about 147 million tons of CO_2 by extracting bio-diesel from 4,500 Pongania trees in their village.
3. **Handia Forest in Madhya Pradesh:** 95 very poor villages would jointly earn at least US $300 every year from carbon payments by restoring 10,000 hectares of degraded community forests.

So carbon trading is becoming popular with its consequential advantage of reducing GHG emissions.

On August 8, 2022 India made revisions to its carbon credit policies to ban export. This was done with a view to meeting the Nation's climate goals of reducing 1 billion tons of carbon by 2030 and achieving net-zero emissions by 2070. The Government is planning to increase its

6 https//www.legalservicesindia.com. See an overview of Carbon Trading in India.

share of green energy up to 50% from the current 42% by the end of the decade and become a net exporter of energy in the coming years (www.investindia.gov.in/team-india-blogs/indias-evolving-carbon-credit-market).

7.5 GLOBAL WARMING AND CLIMATE CHANGE

Global warming refers to rise in global temperatures due mainly to concentration of greenhouse gases in the atmosphere. It is also called Earth's rising surface temperature.

Climate change refers to the increasing changes in the measures of climate over a long period of time. It includes precipitation, temperature and wind pattern.

Sometimes, these two terms are used interchangeably. But since the 20th century, human activity is mainly responsible for the increase of greenhouse gas emissions. These gases trap the sun's rays and heat up our planet. The scientists call it *global warming*.

In 1992, the UNO in its Earth Summit produced the United Nations Framework Convention on Climate Change (UNFCCC).[7] Since then it got the official recognition. The UNO defined it as "long-term shifts in temperatures and weather patterns. These shifts may be natural, but since the 1800s human activities have been the main driver of climate change, primarily due to the burning of fossil fuels (like coal, oil and gas), which produces heat-trapping gases." Thus, the main cause of climate change is burning fossil fuels, such as oil, gas and coal. When burnt, fossil fuels release carbon dioxide into the air, causing the planet to heat up. There are many devastating impacts of climate change. We have briefly mentioned them in Chapter 3.

7 https:www.un.org>global-issues>climatechange

Annexure 1

GREEN ECONOMY*

Green economy represents the economy where every stakeholder becomes aware of environmental issues and adopts measures that contribute to the better quality of life. It aims to transition the economy into a low carbon economy through facilitating green business and hence green jobs. The job-seekers should have the desirable background. So, among other things, green education and green training should also be part of the education system. The World Bank reports/surveys[8] give some background for seriously examining the issues relating to green economy. They can be summarised below:

- India's remarkable growth record has been clouded by a degrading environment and growing scarcity of natural resources. The economy is also likely to be affected by growth in population because India now occupies number one position followed by China in population.
- In a study of 178 countries whose environments were surveyed, India ranked 155th overall and almost last in air pollution exposure. The survey also concluded that India's environmental quality is even far below all BRICK countries [South Africa (72), Russia (73), Brazil (77) and China (118)].
- According to another recent WHO survey, across the G-20 economies, 13 of the 20 most polluted cities are in India.
- Poverty remains both a cause and a consequence of resource degradation: agricultural yields are lower on degraded lands, and forests and grasslands are depleted as livelihood resources decline.
- Environmental degradation costs India $80 billion per year or 5.7% of its economy.

What may be the possible solutions to the environmental problems? The survey reports also made a few important points:

* Banerjee, Bhabatosh, Revised version of "Towards a Green Economy", *The Management Accountant*, ICAI, July, 2017.

8 www.worldbank.org/en/news/features/2014

- Environmental sustainability could become the next major challenge as India surges along its projected growth trajectory. It is important to note that India is the fastest growing economy in the world. Her GDP growth rate in 2022–23[9] is 7.2% as against 9.1% in 2021–22, as per data released by National Statistical Office (NSC), surpassing all other countries including China.
- A low-emission, resource-efficient greening of the economy should be possible at a very low cost in terms of GDP growth.
- Lastly, for an environmentally sustainable future, India needs to value its natural resources and ecosystem services to better informed policy and decision making.

In view of the above, we delve on some of the important polluting activities of the stakeholders and suggest measures which can bring about some improvement in the situation with a view to improving the quality of life.

IDENTIFYING THE STAKEHOLDERS AND THEIR ACTIVITIES

The important question is: who are the stakeholders and how do they pollute environment?

Among a large number of the stakeholders, we identify the following three groups:

1. The public in general
2. The transport system (both public and private)
3. The corporate sector.

The impact of various activities of the corporate sector is huge. There are many dimensions also, e.g. green growth, green economy and sustainable development, impact, if any, on poverty eradication in a developing country like India, etc. Therefore, in view of its nature, importance and volume, we deal with the corporate sector separately elsewhere. After addressing the first two, we also touch upon global warming, some of its impact and the Paris Accord as a possible remedy.

1. The Public in General

General public in every country can contribute significantly towards the quality of life by self-regulating their behaviour. Even in a developing country an overwhelming majority of the people has concern about the

9 Google.com/search?q=what+is+the+GDP+Growth+rate+in 2022-23.

environment and it is the minority who vitiates it. Such activities are committing nuisance in the public place or road, using and throwing plastic-carry bags below the standard specified by local authorities, cutting off trees, etc. But good sense and awareness can cure these evils. The first photo taken in front of a co-operative building in a good locality in Kolkata shows that local citizens have come forward to stop the practice of committing nuisance on the road or on the wall by the side of a main road by adopting a unique method, i.e. implanting photo of mighty Hanumanji on the wall. Photos of many other Gods and Goddesses implanted on the wall in many other areas in the City can also be seen. This is in spite of the fact there is no dearth of public toilets usable on a nominal charge in each area. The use of sub-standard plastic-carry bags is another menace not only to the environment but also to the drainage system which gets chocked very often due to heavy rain when plastic bags are found lying all around. This is a common scenario in many cities in spite of some measures taken by the municipalities. Can local municipalities impose fine on selling of goods along with sub-standard plastic carry bags? Of course, the awareness of the people concerned is more important.

Source: Author's own collection.

Another important issue is preventing cutting of trees and planting new trees in each area. Happily, there are many environmental-activists who very often fight it out. There are Green Benches in High Courts and Supreme Court of India to take action on the erring public. Most importantly, the awareness of the public has to be enhanced. It is generally said that one tree can give oxygen to 30 persons in that locality. The Hyderabad Urban Development Authority (HUDA) planting many trees around Hussain Sagar has come out with a slogan for public awareness: "Plant a Tree and Get Oxygen Free." The Japanese citizens are very environment friendly. When a person dies, members of the deceased family plant a tree as a ritual. So, it has become part of their culture.

Plantation in any city can be enforced by the local authority which sanctions plan for housing construction. It should be incumbent on the part of the builder to plant trees systematically in compliance with rules, if any. An example can be drawn from a small newly built beautiful township, namely, Bethlehem in Pennsylvania in the USA, wherein a builder is required to plant trees whenever a new house is built. Zoning laws here mandate the builder to plant a tree every 50 ft with at least 10 ft from the road. Photo below shows the present scenario of a part of this locality which is 20+ years old and shows matured trees and some newly planted small trees. Can we not build up such practices in India whenever new areas are developed or new townships are built?

Source: Author's own collection.

2. The Transport System

Vehicles run by petrol and diesel are one of the major contributing agents to pollute the level of air quality. An example of environmental friendly transport system is the tram or bus run by overhead electrical lines to operate in specified routes within the city. The City of Kolkata is one of the oldest examples when in British India Calcutta Tramways Company used to operate its fleet of trams in the corporation area as the main public transport system. There are some other good examples in this regard, viz. Melbourne City (Australia), Hong Kong (having double-decker trams). Even after nationalisation of tram services, over time, Kolkata has been witnessing gradual withdrawal of tram services from many routes in the name of town-planning and faster transport service. But was environmental issue given any serious consideration by the decision making authorities?[10] Interestingly, we find a reverse trend elsewhere. For example, in Paris, the city municipal authorities are experimenting running of trucks within the city by electrical overhead lines. In Nepal, we also find that buses do run by the same system. Although the initial cost of arranging the overhead wiring is high, its operating costs is low because of consumption of low-cost electricity instead of using high-cost petrol or diesel. On the top of everything, it is tremendously environment-friendly. Thus, while considering planning of new towns in the country, should we not seriously give consideration to operation of environmental friendly public transport system? Let us now come to the issue of operation of transport system by mini-bus, bus, private and public cars which normally run using petrol or diesel, a non-renewable resource.

India is now the world's third largest producer of motor cars. Major cities are showing signs of increasing number of use of motor cars, thanks to the changing pattern of life styles among the upper and middle class families. This is contributing significantly to not only "air pollution" but also "noise pollution" which are addressed below.

(i) Air Quality Index (AQI): The Pollution Board in India notifies AQI for the public about the declining air quality level and the possible associated health hazards. AQI is the only tool that provides the correct information about air quality to people. An expert group comprising medical professionals, air quality experts, academics, advocacy groups, and State Pollution Control Boards has been constituted and the authority of technical study is awarded to IIT Kanpur.

---

10 In a welcome move, a Division Bench of Calcutta High Court, led by the Hon'ble Chief Justice, in a recent order "set up panel to restore, preserve, run trams". It commented "Kolkatans should be proud of 150-year-old Heritage Transport Mode" (*The Times of India,* Kolkata, June 22, 2023, p. 4).

The AQI considers eight pollutants (PM10, PM2.5, NO_2, SO_2, CO, O_3, NH_3 and Pb) for which short-term (up to 24-hourly averaging period) national ambient air quality standards are prescribed. The AQI has six sub-categories of AQI values, namely, good (0–50), satisfactory (51–100), moderately polluted (101–200), poor (201–300), very poor (301–400) and severe (401–500). Based on the particulate matter count in the air, side effects of air pollution are also suggested. For example, while good represents minimum impact on health, severe stands for respiratory impact even on healthy people, serious health impacts on people with lung/heart disease, might feel exhausted even during light physical activity.

According to World Health Organization study, as stated earlier, 13 Indian cities are among the top 20 in the world as far as fine particulate matter (PM2.5) is considered. The position in four metropolitan cities[11] is given below:

AQI (PM2.5) as on December 23, 2015

Delhi	442	severe
Kolkata	264	poor
Mumbai	245	poor
Chennai	50	good

The position is very alarming and local governments need to introduce measures that will bring down pollution in air quality. There is no doubt that change in technology is the best option although it will require huge investment and time by the automobile industries around the world. Accordingly, some countries are taking ad hoc shortcut conservative method to fight the pollution in air quality.

China declared war against pollution by introducing "odd-even" traffic curbs along with closing down of pollution factors in the Beijing city for three days from 8th to 10th December 2015. This was followed by Government of Delhi in 2016. The details of the latter are given here.

Odd-even traffic curbs introduced in Delhi: The Government of Delhi introduced the "odd-even" traffic scheme from New Year's

11 See Chapter 2, Table 2.1, for a recent study of five metropolitan cities.

Day January 1, 2016) from 8.00 a.m. to 8 p.m. as a trial for 15 days[12]. It was reviewed after 15 days' experience.

- To start with two-wheelers (over 50 lakh of 92 lakh vehicles registered in Delhi) and woman drivers were excluded. Although, the scheme is on a trial basis, a fine of ₹2,000 was payable by a violator.
- On the first day of trial, about 1 lakh less vehicle was on the road. To ease the pressure on public transport, the Government introduced 3,000 additional buses.

The then Chief Justice of India and a few top political leaders supported the scheme. The scheme will lead to behavioural change of people because there will be more car pooling, more travel by metro, walking short-distance for marketing, etc.

To sum up, the operation of the "odd-even" scheme for a period of 15 days in Delhi led to some good result in improving the level of air quality. May be in future, some other cities in India will follow this ad hoc measure from time to time at least to give some temporary respite to the public in general

(ii) **Sound pollution: blowing horns while driving vehicles:** Like varieties of cars, there are many varieties of motor horns—some loud and clear, some sounding anguished or in deep pain. Many mini and private buses use loud electrical horns. So, we have to live to hear a continuous honking of horns and, thanks to God, we have learnt to live with it.

One professor from the Massey University (New Zealand) came to attend an international conference in Kolkata a few years ago. She was amused to know that nothing happens if someone blows horns unnecessarily and continuously. With laughter she gave the name of the City as the "City of Horns". Such behaviour on the part of driving community is hard to be found in many advanced countries like Singapore, Australia, EU countries, England, Canada and North America, to mention a few. There are other good examples also. In Aizawl, capital of Mizoram, drivers do not blow horns while driving their vehicles no matter how much time it takes for a journey. Police does not

12 In a Public Interest Litigation, the Delhi High Court refused to grant a stay order with the observations "the scheme may have caused hardship to a section of society but courts were not experts in deciding if a policy decision was correct or the best available option."

have to intervene because hardly there will be any offender. The system operates very well because it has become part of the culture of the drivers in Mizoram.[13]

What are then the possible remedies? First, stringent law is to be enacted and implemented efficiently and objectively. In Singapore, for offence beyond certain points, even license of an offending driver is cancelled and he or she has to undergo training afresh for getting a new licence[14]. It involves additional cost and also loss of earnings. Similarly, laws in many other countries are stringent and there is proper implementation of the laws. What is our experience in India?

We inherited many things from the British including many laws—so there may not be dearth of laws but our experience shows that implementation is weak or very poor. This is one area where we need improvement. Second, there should be orientation course for the drivers periodically given the average background of them so that compliance of traffic rules and regulations becomes part of their normal behaviour and, over time, a part of their culture as we find in Aizawl. It is no doubt a huge task. The Traffic Police Department on behalf of the Government may also introduce scheme for giving award (both cash and certificate) which will act as further motivating factor to comply with traffic rules.

3. Global Warming and Historic Paris Accord

Global warming occurs when carbon dioxide (CO_2) and other air pollutants and greenhouse gasses collect in the atmosphere and absorb sunlight and solar radiation that have bounced off the earth's surface. Normally, this radiation would escape into space—but these pollutants, which can last for years to centuries in the atmosphere, trap the heat and cause the planet to get hotter. That's what's known as the greenhouse

13 The Kolkata Traffic Police Department has recently started cautioning the city drivers "not honk unnecessarily" though no penal measure is reported to have been introduced.

14 The Kolkata Traffic Police Department introduced a 3-month license ban for flouting road rules. License may be cancelled for repeat offence. This action follows the Supreme Court order. According to rules laid down by the Supreme Court, driving licence to be suspended for flouting road rules (for details *see* TOI, Kolkata, March 8, 2017, p. 2).

effect.[15] The burning of fossil fuels to make electricity is the largest source of heat-trapping pollution, producing huge quantity of CO_2 every year. Coal-burning power plants are by far the biggest polluters. The other source of carbon pollution is the transportation sector which generates tons of CO_2 emissions a year in a country. Curbing dangerous climate requires very deep cuts in emissions as well as the use of alternatives to fossil fuels worldwide.

What are the likely effects of global warming? Global warming has many effects in the physical world, such as:

(a) More heat waves[16]
(b) Heavier rainstorms,
(c) High sea level, etc.

Thus, the important question is: what will climate change mean for human welfare? Scientific papers have predicted effects as varied as a greater spread of tropical diseases, more death from hot weather than on cold weather, bumpier rides in the flights. Interestingly, another prediction enters in the literature, i.e., people will get lesser sleep in the night because of hotter world. In a paper published recently by the *Journal Science Advances*, Dr. Nick Obradovich[17] predicted more restless nights especially in the summer, as global temperature rises. Poor people, not having air-condition systems, and elderly ones will be hit hard as they will face more difficulty in regulating their body temperature. "As world warms up, people will stay awake six nights a month by 2050", claims the Scientist. In view of the devastating impact of global warming, both developed and developing countries had been negotiating to find out workable solutions to the problem. This at last resulted in historic global climate deal mentioned below.

On 12th December 2015, a historic climate deal with 198 countries approving the Paris Agreement text that aims to transform fossil fuel-driven economies within decades and slow global warming. The deal was signed by 195 countries (including China and North Korea) on April 22, 2016, at UNO office in New York.

According to Paris Agreement[18] the global warming is to be kept

15 www.nrdc.org/stories/globalwarming-101
16 *The Times of India*, Kolkata, May 28, 2017, p. 15.
17 Dr. Obradovich is a political Scientist researching both on the politics of climate change and its likely human impacts, having link with Harvard and MIT in the States (for further details *see* TOI, *ibid.*).
18 TOI, Kolkata, December 13, 2015, pp. 1 and 13. (for full report log on to www.timesofindia.com).

well below 2°C, 1.5°C if possible. India's key concerns, viz. developed countries will take 'enhanced action' on mitigation, adaptation, climate finance, tech transfer, capacity building and transparency, have been met. The deal was expected to take place in 2020. Developed countries will review actions in 2023 and then every 5 years. Developing countries will do so voluntarily.

India has already submitted her action targets till 2030 and all listed companies and public enterprises are to mention from 2022–23 in the Sustainability Report their achievements for the year having regard to the target of 2030.[19] Regarding "climate finance" the developed countries were expected to provide $100 billion by 2020 and potentially scale it up later but this point is not legally binding. "India has always espoused the case of sustainable development and climate justice—both these have been found mentioned in the text. That is an important achievement for India"—says the environment scientists.

But on June 1, 2017, by a Presidential Order, the US pulled out of the Paris Accord on the premise that "climate change goals by reducing its carbon foot-print is detrimental to the US economy and will affect job creation." But, happily, the US Government reconsidered the issue and rejoined the other member countries within a year. Experts feel that now onus will be on the USA, China, EU and India to carry the accord forward. Growth of renewal energy in India and China will drive the deal. India may not cut raise her emission-cut targets keeping development goals in mind.

CONCLUDING OBSERVATIONS

We have already suggested remedies to the problems in different sections. Some of the measures can be taken immediately to fight against pollution, while others need a time frame for implementation. All said and done, changing our behaviour and building awareness among us is the key. Both State and Central Governments have been relentlessly campaigning in favour of many schemes introduced to fight against pollution to enhance the quality of life. Happily, at the school and college levels, short courses on environment have been reported to be introduced and this makes the younger generation more conscious about protection of environment. The present author has also recommended outlines for two Courses—one at the undergraduate level, and the other at the post-graduate level (see Appendix). So, we can dream for a better future.

19 See ITC Sustainability Report.

Annexure 2

CLIMATE CHANGE—SAVING THE HUMANITY FROM ITS IMPACT: SOME THOUGHTS*

WHY TALKING ABOUT CLIMATE CHANGE?

- To get an idea about the negative impact of climate change which is of great concern to the living beings.
- To promote awareness of all concerned because collectively we have to face the problem as otherwise, as the Secretary General of United Nations puts it very realistically during the Opening Convention of COP27, "either co-operate or perish".
- To ascertain as to what extent member-countries of UNO have been adopting measures to mitigate the adverse impact of Climate Change so as to make this planet worthy of living.

CONCEPTS

- In ordinary parlance, it is the shift of weather from one season to the other.
- Generally, changes take place in four seasons of the year: Summer, Autumn, Winter and Spring. In Bengal and Bangladesh, it is generally referred to *Grishma, Barsa, Sarat, Hemanta, Shit and Basanta.* Whatever may be the duration of the season, 4 months or 2 months, the change is likely to take place from one season to the other, in that order.
- But now it has wider connotations embracing all nations and all areas of the world.
- It refers to "long-term shifts in temperatures and weather patterns. These shifts are natural. But since 1860s human activities have been the main drivers of climate change primarily due to burning

* It is based on the Valedictory Address given by the author at the First International Conference organized by the Bangladesh Accounting Association in association with Indian Accounting Association Research Foundation at Merriot Hotel, Dhaka, on January 29, 2023.

of fossil fuels like coal, oil and gas which produce heat trapping gases" (UNO, 1992).

GENERAL IMPACT OF CLIMATE CHANGE

Adverse impact of climate change is multidimensional. They include:

- Devastating cyclones, floods, earthquakes and draughts.
- A fair proportion of global land being affected by draught.
- Heat-linked deaths particularly among 65+ age-group people.
- Loss of labour hour due to heat exposure.
- Rise in diseases like malaria, dengue, etc.

IMPACT IN BANGLADESH AND INDIA

- Severe damage caused to ecologically crucial but fragile Sunderbans, spread across West Bengal (India) and Bangladesh.
- Temperature increased 1°C in past century and may increase by up to 3.7°C by 2100.
- From 2000 to 2020, 110 sq km of mangroves disappeared. The loss of mangroves has made embankments weaker.
- In the last 23 years, the area has witnessed 13 super-cyclones. The occurrence has increased by 26% between 1881 and 2001.

Source: https://mumbaigloss.in/trip-to-sunderbans-from-kolkata-for-bengal-tiger/

- Sunderbans have suffered losses of more than 2 lakh crore ($25 billion in current exchange rate) in life, property and livelihood in the last four decades (IPCC).[20]

EVIDENCE FROM EUROPE

- Europe experienced its second warmest year in 2022 and world's 5th warmest year since 1850 (European Scientists).
- Severe heat wave caused over 20,000 "excess" deaths in countries including France, Spain and Britain.
- Lack of rain hit hydropower generation and slashed maize and soybean crop yields.
- The hot, dry spell fuelled intense wildfires (Spain, Slovenia) unleashing more emissions across EU and Britain.

EARTH SUMMIT (1992)

The thrust of the Summit, held in Rio de Janeiro (Brazil), was to:

- provide an understanding of development that would support socio-economic development;
- prevent continued deterioration of environment, and
- build a foundation for a global partnership between the developing and more industrialized countries for serving mutual needs and interests towards a healthy future for the planet.

108 member-countries attended the Summit. Replacement of the traditional goal of economic development by sustainable development comprising three components—economic, environmental and social developments.

KYOTO PROTOCOL (1997)

- Adopted regulated Greenhouse Gas reductions for a few countries within 2008 to 2012.
- However, the protocol was not ratified.
- It was ratified in Paris in 2015.

20 World Bank has approved a loan of ₹1,050 crore to West Bengal Government for the second phase of six years for accelerated development of minor irrigation project (State's share being ₹450 crore). The project will augment water availability and improve irrigated agriculture in the coastal saline belt, and hilly and mono-crop areas and increase food security for close to 9.6 lakh people (*The Times of India*, Kolkata, June 22, 2023, p. 4).

PARIS AGREEMENT (COP26)

- Legally binding Treaty on Climate Change.
- Adopted by 195 member-countries and the EU.
- It was signed by the parties in 2016 at UN headquarters.
- It is a long-term agreement, the goal of which is to reduce global temperature well blow 2°C.
- Reduce greenhouse gas emissions as soon as possible to achieve a climate neutral world by 2050.
- Landmark in the multilateral Climate Change process.
- Countries come to common cause to undertake very ambitious efforts to combat Climate Change and adapt to it's effects.
- It requires economic and social transformation on the part of member-countries.
- Methods were suggested to track the progress.
- The Agreement also requires a few other steps for implementation:
  - (i) Technology Development and Transfer,
  - (ii) Capacity Building, and
  - (iii) Climate Finance.

WARNING OF WMO REGARDING HEAT-WAVES DUE TO CLIMATE CHANGE

The World Meterological Organisation (WMO)[21] warned the global community to get ready for the "upcoming challenges of warming" in the coming months because of the developments combining with human induced climate change to push global temperature into "unchartered territory".

Before we go through the WMO findings and recommendations let us first address a few fundamental questions[22], viz.;

- What causes heat-waves,
- What is heat-wave warning, and
- What risks are involved because of heat-waves?

Heat-waves are the results of trapped air. Normally, air circulates the globe in large prevailing winds. But if it is trapped over one region it is allowed to warm uncharacteristic temperatures due to sunlight. The air is often trapped due to high pressure systems. So far as heat-

21 *The Times of India*, Kolkata, May 18, 2023, p. 14.

22 www.google.com/search?=who+warning+on...

wave is concerned, it is done by the local weather office. A heat-wave is declared when maximum temperature reaches 45 degree C (in India and Bangladesh) or more for two consecutive days.

Coming to the last issue, that is risks of heat-waves, the risks can be divided into two groups, physical and economical. People with chronic diseases (who take daily medicines) have a greater risk of complications and death during a heat-wave. Older people and children have also greater health risk. Heat can cause severe dehydration, acute cerebrovascular accidents contributing to thrombogenesis (blood clots).

The other risks relate to downturn of the economy due to lower GDP growth rate and higher inflation rate if the climate change persists for a considerable period of time.[23]

Let us now come back to WMO report. According to Petteri Taalas, Secretary General of WMO, "this will have far-reaching repercussions for health, food security, water management and environment. We need to be prepared." The report of WMO underlined that the annual mean global near-surface temperature for each year between 2023 and 2027 will be between 1.1 degree C and 1.8 degree C higher than the 1850–1900 average.

It may be recalled here that the Paris Agreement sets long-term goals to guide all nations to substantially reduce GHG emissions to limit the global temperature (the goal being 1.5 degree C by 2050). The rapid attribution analysis by a global team of climate scientists as part of the World Weather Attribution (WWA) initiative focused on four countries—India, Bangladesh, Thailand and Laos PDR—that reported record temperatures and heat-wave triggered casualties in April, 2023.

Because of the above, what will be the impact on India and Bangladesh? According to WMO parlance, heat index is a measure that combines temperature and humidity and reflects more accurately the impacts of heat-waves on the human body. The findings are that, in both the regions, climate change would make these parts at least 2 degrees celius hotter. Until overall GHG emissions are halted, global temperatures will continue to increase. In Bangladesh and India, heat-wave events used to occur less than once a century on an average. It is also said that "record heat-waves are likely once in five years."

---

23 See, for example, Misra, Udit, "Economics of Climate Change", *The Indian Express*, Kolkata, May 23, 2023, p. 12.

CLIMATE SUMMIT (COP 2022)

- Secretary-General (UNO): "Humanity has a choice: co-operate or perish. It is either a Climate Solidarity Pact or a Collective Suicide Pact."
- Major decisions taken:
    - Setting up a "loss and damage" fund
    - Institutional arrangements for averting, minimizing and addressing 'loss and damage'
    - Integrate water into adaptation efforts
    - Inclusion of "sustainable life style"
    - Commitments of Paris Agreement reaffirmed

CONCLUDING OBSERVATIONS

- The three-dimensional approach to address the problem requires huge investments. But who will make such investments? What about technology transfer in a competitive market environment?
- Energy is going to be the biggest challenge in 21st century and beyond. Added to this, the present energy crisis due to Pandemic and Russia-Ukraine war has broken supply chain resulting in high inflation in almost all countries of the world.
- According to one estimate, the energy requirement will increase by four fold by the end of this century. Does it not mean further damage to the climate?
- The contribution to "Loss and Damage Fund" (COP27) is voluntary. India and Bangladesh account for a maximum of 0.50% of the world's pollution. Who will compensate for the damage caused to these and many other Asian countries due to adverse impact of Climate Change?
- Nevertheless, one silver line is that many advanced countries are aggressively investing fund in R&D to innovate new Energy Systems. Green Hydrogen Gas is an example.
- Indo-Bangla Trans-boundary 'Peace Park' tag for Sundarbans in offing. Both India and Bangladesh will jointly manage the unique eco-system which is vulnerable to accelerated climate change.[24]

The Sundarbans delta is a single eco-system, which is cleaved by the man-made national boundaries of India and Bangladesh. Happily, both the Indian Sundarbans and the Bangladeshi Sundarbans are **World Heritage Sites**.

---

24 *Times of India,* Kolkata, July 1, 2023, p. 1 and p. 6.

EXERCISES

1. Explain the concept of Green Economy.
2. What do you understand by Green Accounting?
3. "The main purpose of green accounting is to help companies understand and manage potential trade-offs between traditional economic and environmental goals." Do you agree? Explain.
4. What are the Green Accounting Laws in India? What purposes do they serve?
5. What do you understand by Environmental Domestic Product (EDP)? How can it be measured?
6. What is Carbon Accounting? State the functions of two types of Carbon Accounting.
7. State the Drivers of Carbon Accounting and explain one of them.
8. What is Carbon Intensity and how do you measure it?
9. Write in brief the Frameworks and Standards of Carbon Accounting.
10. Define Carbon Credit.
11. What is the value of 1 Carbon Credit in the Carbon Market?
12. What is the approximate value of India's carbon market?
13. State in brief the carbon trading market in India with suitable examples.
14. Define global warming and climate change and distinguish between the two.
15. What causes climate change? Elucidate your answer.
16. State the warnings of WMO (World Metereological Organisation) in respect of heat-waves in the coming years.
17. Write short notes on "Indo-Bangla Trans-boundary Peace Park" for Sundarbans. What will be the possible benefits to both the countries?

Appendix

Suggested Course Outlines

ENVIRONMENTAL MANAGEMENT (100 MARKS)
(Suggested Outlines for an Undergraduate Course)

Module 1 (25 marks)

- Green Economy and Green Accounting
- Sustainable Development Concept
- Greenhouse Gas (GHG) Accounting or Carbon Accounting
- Carbon Credit and Carbon Credit Market
- Global Warming
- Climate Change
- Impact of Climate Change

Module 2 (25 marks)

- Cost-benefit analysis of environmental management system
- Environmental Challenges
- Managing Environment—the role of general public, household sector, transport sector and corporate organisations
- Environmental Management Systems (including a brief outline of accounting and audit)

Module 3 (25 marks)
International Developments

- The Earth Summit (1992)

- The Climate Summit (2022)
- Change in the pattern of Reporting by corporate organisations—Sustainability Reporting
- Responses to Climate Summits (country specific and for one country)
- Green Hydrogen Technology

Module 4 (25 marks)

Case Study on Air Pollution by Motor Transport System in a City (Suggested outlines)

The usefulness of the public transport system—Air quality measurement, good quality required for better public health—Examples of some good international transport systems to avoid air pollution, such as, Tram Services in Hong Kong, Melbourne, Old Calcutta; operation of public buses through electrical ropes, e.g. Nepal, Paris, etc. Some ad hoc measures to control pollution pending the replacement of the traditional transport system, such as Odd-even traffic curbs introduced in Beijing in December 2015, Delhi in 2016—Sound pollution: curbing frequent honking while driving, the culture of Aizwal not to honk while driving, move introduced by the Kolkata Police for the City—Case study of a Motor Transport System in a City—Conclusions and recommendations.

REFERENCES

1. Banerjee, Bhabatosh, "Towards a Green Economy", *The Management Accountant*, ICAI, pp. 74–78, July 2017.
2. *Corporate Environmental Management*, 2nd ed., PHI Learning, 2023, Chapters 2 and 7 by the same author.

CORPORATE ENVIRONMENTAL MANAGEMENT (100 MARKS)
(Suggested Outlines for a Postgraduate Course)

Module 1 (25 marks)

Conceptual Aspects: Green Economy and Green Accounting, Greenhouse Gas (GHG) Accounting, Global Warming, Carbon Credit and Caron Market, Social Responsibility Reporting (CSR), Sustainable Development Goals (SDGs), Sustainable Development Governance (SDG), Sustainability Reporting (SR).

Environmental Regulations (country specific)—some important legislations.

Module 2 (25 marks)
Environmental Challenges and Corporate Responses

Challenges: Atmosphere, Air Pollution. Toxic chemicals and hazardous waste, fresh water, land, oceans, biotechnology and biodiversity.

Corporate Responses to the Challenges: Social contract argument and quality of life argument.

Why Environmental Information is Required? Investors' needs, needs of regulatory authorities, Society's needs, international dimension, stock market considerations, political costs considerations, Ideological goal consideration.

Module 3 (25 marks)
Management of Environment

- Cost-benefit analysis of environmental management system
- Managing environmental aspects of corporate activities
- Designing an environmental management system
- Sustainable economic development and strategic environmental management system
- Standardisation in environmental management systems
- Accounting and reporting for environmental management system

Module 4 (25 marks)
International Developments and Country-responses

- The Earth Summit (1992) and The Climate Summit (2022)
- Impact of Climate Changes—An Overview

- Evolution of Sustainable Development Concept: Basic principles and chronology of the development system
- Corporate Social Responsibility and Corporate Social Governance (CSG)
- Global Reporting Initiative
- Sustainability Accounting Standards Board
- A Case Study of a Sustainability Reporting of a global company operating in India

REFERENCES

Books:

- Banerjee, Bhabatosh, *Corporate Environmental Management,* PHI Learning, 2nd ed., 2023.
- Krishnamoorthy, Bala, *Environmental Management—Text and Cases,* PHI Learning, 3rd ed., 2022.

Articles:

- Banerjee, Bhabatosh, "Towards a Green Economy", *The Management Accountant,* ICAI, July 2017, pp. 74–78.
- Ray, Srirupa and Dandapat, Dhrubaranjan, "Corporate Social Responsibility—A Study on Indian Maharatna Companies", *Indian Accounting Review,* June 2021, pp. 20–42.

Answers to Multiple Choice Questions

CHAPTER 3

1. (d) 2. (b) 3. (a) 4. (d)
5. (d) 6. (b) 7. (c) 8. (d)
9. (a) 10. (d) 11. (b) 12. (d)

CHAPTER 4

1. (a) 2. (b) 3. (d) 4. (d)
5. (a) 6. (b) 7. (d) 8. (a)
9. (c) 10. (b) 11. (d) 12. (a)
13. (b) 14. (d) 15. (d)

CHAPTER 5

1. (d) 2. (d) 3. (b) 4. (d)
5. (c) 6. (d) 7. (c) 8. (a)
9. (b) 10. (c) 11. (d) 12. (d)
13. (d) 14. (d) 15. (c) 16. (b)
17. (d) 18. (b) 19. (a) 20. (d)
21. (a) 22. (d) 23. (d)

CHAPTER 6

1. (d) 2. (d) 3. (d) 4. (c)
5. (a) 6. (d) 7. (b) 8. (a)
9. (d) 10. (a)

Index